NIKOS A. SALINGAROS

A THEORY OF ARCHITECTURE

Quote on front cover by Kenneth G. Masden II

Nikos A. Salingaros
A THEORY OF ARCHITECTURE
ISBN 978-3-937954-07-4
© 2006, 2008 Nikos A. Salingaros & UMBAU-VERLAG

www.umbau-verlag.com

NIKOS A. SALINGAROS

A THEORY OF ARCHITECTURE

**With contributions by Michael W. Mehaffy, Terry M. Mikiten,
Débora M. Tejada, and Hing-Sing Yu.**

More than a decade in the making, this is a textbook of architecture, useful for every architect: from first-year students, to those taking senior design studio, to graduate students writing a Ph.D. dissertation in architectural theory, to experienced practicing architects. It is very carefully written so that it can be read even by the beginning architecture student. The information contained here is a veritable gold mine of design techniques. This book teaches the reader how to design by adapting to human needs and sensibilities, yet independently of any particular style. Here is a unification of genuine architectural knowledge that brings a new clarity to the discipline. It explains much of what people instinctively know about architecture, and puts that knowledge for the first time in a concise, understandable form. Dr. Salingaros has already published a widely-used book on urbanism, "Principles of Urban Structure" (2005), which is being praised as a fundamental synthesis and understanding of urban processes. He has experience in the organization of the built environment that few practicing architects have. The later chapters of this new book touch on very sensitive topics: what drives architects to produce the forms they build; and why architects use only a very restricted visual vocabulary. Is it personal inventiveness, or is it something more, which perhaps they are not even aware of? There has not been such a book treating the very essence of architecture. The only other author who is capable of raising a similar degree of passion (and controversy) is Christopher Alexander, who happens to be Dr. Salingaros's friend and architectural mentor.

PREFACE

by His Royal Highness
The Prince Of Wales

CLARENCE HOUSE

For some time now I have been fascinated by the work of the mathematician Professor Nikos Salingaros. His provocative new scientific perspective on architecture gives much food for thought, whatever one's views on the state of the modern built environment or the response of contemporary avant-garde architects might be.

Perhaps uncomfortably, Professor Salingaros challenges us to reconsider the relation between science and architecture. For him, the role of science is not merely to spin a dazzling, but ultimately meaningless, web of ever more technology. Rather, it is to better the human condition by putting the human being at the centre of our thinking and our building process. In so doing, he seeks to balance the daring sculptural conception of architecture that has become so extreme and, if I may say, so desperate in recent years.

A debate about these issues is critical and one which we should welcome in the interest of creating a better built environment. In some ways it is an intriguing return to the old humane ideals of the very early Modernists, adding some new tools to the rich "collective intelligence".

As a growing number of stakeholders seek today to identify common ground to improve the built environment, my view is that we must consider provocative new voices, arguing for fresh new thinking. Surely no voice is more thought-provoking than that of this intriguing, perhaps historically important, new thinker?

FOREWORD

By Kenneth G. Masden II

At a time when contemporary architectural discourse appears to be losing its theoretical footing, the shifting ground on which it stands seems to be convulsing with new-found speculations of every type. Architectural theorists from all over the world, wishing to take part in this re-stratification, seem to be desperate in their attempts to advance their ideas beyond the idiosyncratic ponderings of the dominant architectural elite. Looking outside architecture as a means to garner greater validity, their speculations have run the full gamut from mathematical theorems, to the postulates of French philosophers, to the loosely construed intimation of chaos theory and fractal logic into the domain of architectural design, to the near coercion of quantum mechanics and field theory as a means to extend their rhetoric. Each new theory offers but yet another invented way to conceptualize architecture.

The connection between architecture and the physical logic of our world is unquestionable. The recognition of this relationship is in-and-of-itself a step forward and backward at the same time. Back to a time when architecture was conceived and built within the limits of its materiality; and forward to the re-appropriation of ideas that were once nothing more than trial and error, but which can now be fully prescribed by modern science. The difficulty with such modern theories is in the translation or transference of ideas and information. Excluding any truly cross-disciplinary dialogue, these theories might well present little more than a glimpse into the unsettled realm that constitutes architectural theory today. In the midst of the clamor, it is becoming increasingly difficult to discern what are valid theories and what are not, or what is even useful information.

If we are to fully understand the architectural implication of advanced mathematics and science it seems only logical to engage authorities outside our own discipline, i.e. to seek real scientific knowledge from real scientists. As chance would have it, four years ago my path crossed that of Dr. Salingaros, a professionally trained Mathematical Physicist whose career had led him to discover a direct relationship between physical structures and processes, found throughout the material world, and that of man-made architectural and urban entities.

Having just taken my position in the School of Architecture at the University of Texas at San Antonio, Léon Krier asked if I had yet to meet his friend Nikos. What began as a tenuous, but interesting, first meeting has lead to a collegial relationship which is now going on five years. Over the course of this time Nikos has given me access to a way of thinking about the built environment which is more appositely grounded in the physicality of the real world, surprisingly not unlike pre-modern architecture.

Presented in this theory of architecture we see a series of principles for making a more livable world at every level, i.e. domestic, civic, urban, regional and global. To imagine what Dr. Salingaros envisions for the world around us, however, you must be prepared to leave the comfort of what you have come to believe to be architectural theory. You must be willing to look beyond the limits of ideology, to connect with a body of knowledge outside your own, one which has profound implications in the way we make buildings and find ourselves in relationship to the built environment.

Utilizing recently developed mathematics of fractals, information theory, and complexity, Dr. Salingaros reveals how advanced physics can have clear applications in the design and construction of human structures. In this book, he attempts nothing less than to reconstruct the relationship between man and the built environment: between life and matter, as it were. Architecture, for too long, has been left to a succession of aesthetic solutions through which entire civilizations expressed their indomitable "will to form". Architecture, as proffered by Dr. Salingaros, is seen more clearly in an intimate and inextricable relationship with the system of forces that give shape and rhythm to the physical world in which we live. Architecture at any scale, be it building or entire urban matrix, should no longer be defined by how it appears, but rather by how it relates to humans in their everyday existence. It must begin to assume a much greater role in the making of place, and today's architects must come to this realization quickly if we are to sustain any sense of humanity.

Taking as a point of departure the mind's compulsion to establish a connection with our environment, Dr. Salingaros shows how natural and man-made patterns serve as the principal conveyance of meaning about the world around us. He presents a theory of how these ideas and information are nested within a fractal scheme, putting forward a fractal theory of the human mind which helps to explain aspects of how we transfer meaning from our surroundings to our awareness. Through what is described as a symbiotic relationship between ideas, images, texts, and biological forms, Dr. Salingaros further explains how human culture consists of created objects as information that form an integral part of what we are, essentially extending our biological bodies into our environment. "A more human architecture", as Charles the Prince of Wales has called it, is shown here by Dr. Salingaros to carry with it the same intrinsic structural order that underlies all physical and biological entities.

Natural laws for generating buildings with intensely human qualities are found throughout the text, and are exampled in architecture from all parts of the world: for example Classical, Byzantine, Gothic, Renaissance, Baroque, Islamic, Near Eastern, and Far Eastern. Given the breath of theory, and the ideologically unbounded nature of the text, it is no wonder that at the time of this writing, "A Theory of Architecture" has already been translated into Farsi. It will be utilized in the service of non-western students who seek an alternative way in which to conceive of architecture, one which resides in a more authentic sense of existence outside the dominance of western architectural ideologies.

In this era of globalization, cultural entities too often succumb to the paradigm of perceived progress, one assumptive of change as presented by contemporary western models. Developing countries, in an effort to maintain their place in the world, will find the source of their new architecture within arm's reach; i.e. in the materials and practices of their region. Through this text they will understand the underlying principles that govern the manner in which the physical world reveals itself, recognizing at once its uncanny similarity to the rich vernaculars of their local traditions.

To fully appreciate Dr. Salingaros' vision, we must give credit to both Nikos and his long-time colleague Christopher Alexander, for whom he edited the recently published series of four books on the Nature of Order. It is through just such relationships that Dr. Salingaros has been able to ascertain and extend his theories and principles throughout the domain of theoretical physics and biology.

Driven by his passion and compelled by his knowledge, it is sometimes difficult for Nikos to contain his enthusiasm. In his zeal for what he sees as the unrealized potential of this work, he is quick to take aim at the architectural establishment, holding both architects and architectural academic institutions accountable for the dismal state of the built environment and education of design students. Understandably, this position has ruffled a few feathers along the way, but the integrity of the theories and principles he presents should not be underestimated or summarily dismissed due to the sometimes jarring nature of his critique. At the end of the day, both practicing architects and students, those who are seeking a greater clarity of how the physical world operates, will find this book instrumental in understanding how to operate within this new-found dimension. To date, my students have taken great interest in Dr. Salingaros' work, finding ever greater possibilities in their design and a much greater appreciation for the real architecture of the real world.

CONTENTS

Chapter 1.

THE LAWS OF ARCHITECTURE FROM A PHYSICIST'S PERSPECTIVE

There are three laws of architectural order, which are obtained through analogy from basic physical principles. They apply to both natural and man-made structures. These laws may be used to create buildings that match the emotional comfort and beauty of the world's great historical buildings. The laws are consistent with architecture from all parts of the world: for example Classical, Byzantine, Gothic, Renaissance, Baroque, Islamic, Near Eastern, Far Eastern, and Art Nouveau architectures; but not with many of the architectural forms of the past seventy years. It seems that twentieth-century architecture contradicts all other architectures in actually preventing certain components of structural order.

Chapter 2.

A SCIENTIFIC BASIS FOR CREATING ARCHITECTURAL FORMS

A scaling rule helps to achieve visual coherence by linking the small scale to the large scale. This work develops results of Christopher Alexander derived from theoretical physics and biology. I propose a scaling hierarchy and scaling rule based on natural objects having scale differentiations of a ratio of about 2.7 from the largest down to the very small. Buildings satisfying this scaling rule are subconsciously perceived as sharing essential qualities with natural and biological forms. As a consequence, they appear more comfortable psychologically. Scaling coherence is a feature of traditional and vernacular architectures, but is largely absent from contemporary architecture.

Chapter 3.

HIERARCHICAL COOPERATION IN ARCHITECTURE: THE MATHEMATICAL NECESSITY FOR ORNAMENT

The case is made that architectural design needs to be organized hierarchically. A method and formula for doing so are derived based on biology and computer science. Fractal simplicity, in which there is self-similar scaling, replaces the outdated notion of rectangular simplicity. Architectural units on different scales are able to cooperate in an intrinsic manner to achieve an emergent property, which is not present in the individual components. The theory of hierarchical systems from Engineering Science explains how to relate different scales to each other. In buildings, the correlation between architectural scales determines whether a structure is perceived as coherent or incoherent, independently of its actual design, form, and composition. This Chapter presents a scientific proof of why organized detail (i.e. small-scale ornament) is essential to the overall coherence of architectural forms.   P 63

Chapter 4.

THE SENSORY VALUE OF ORNAMENT

Ornament is a valuable component in any architecture of buildings and cities that aims to connect to human beings. The suppression of ornament, on the other hand, results in alien forms that generate physiological and psychological distress. Early twentieth-century architects proposed major stylistic changes — now universally adopted — without having a full understanding of how the human eye/brain system works.   P 84

Chapter 5.

LIFE AND COMPLEXITY IN ARCHITECTURE FROM A THERMODYNAMIC ANALOGY

Using an analogy with thermodynamics, a simple mathematical model can be constructed following ideas of Christopher Alexander, which estimates certain intrinsic qualities of a building. This model predicts a building's emotional impact. The architectural temperature T is defined as the degree of detail, curvature, and color in architectural forms; whereas the architectural harmony H measures the degree of visual coherence and internal symmetry in the visual structure. The impression of how much "life" a building has is measured by the quantity $L = TH$, and the perceived complexity of a design is measured by the quantity $C = T(10 - H)$, where $10 - H$ corresponds to an architectural entropy (disorder). With the help of this model, new structures can be designed that have a dramatically increased feeling of life, yet do not copy existing buildings.   P 105

Chapter 6.

ARCHITECTURE, PATTERNS, AND MATHEMATICS

This Chapter posits the importance of architectural patterns in every human being's intellectual development, examining how twentieth century architectural attitudes towards decoration and pattern have impoverished our experience of both mathematics and the built environment. P 129

Chapter 7.

PAVEMENTS AS EMBODIMENTS OF MEANING FOR A FRACTAL MIND
(WITH TERRY M. MIKITEN AND HING-SING YU)

This Chapter examines the role of pavement design as a vehicle for conveying meaning, taking as a point of departure how the mind establishes a connection with our environment. A theory is developed for how ideas and information may be stored within a fractal scheme. By putting forward a fractal theory of the human mind, we can explain some aspects of how we transfer meaning from our surroundings to our awareness. Interacting with our environment is an important theme seen during the evolution of the brain. P 144

Chapter 8.

MODULARITY AND THE NUMBER OF DESIGN CHOICES
(WITH DÉBORA M. TEJADA)

This Chapter analyzes one aspect of what is commonly understood as "modularity" in the architectural literature. There are arguments to be made in favor of modularity, but we argue against empty modularity, using mathematics to prove our point. Empty modules eliminate internal information, and their repetition eliminates information from the entire region that they cover. Modularity works in a positive sense only when there is substructure to organize. If we have a large quantity of structural information, then modular design can organize this information to prevent randomness and sensory overload. In that case, the module is not an empty module, but a rich, complex module containing a considerable amount of substructure. P 159

Chapter 9.

GEOMETRICAL FUNDAMENTALISM
(WITH MICHAEL W. MEHAFFY)

"Geometrical fundamentalism" aims to impose simple geometrical solids such as cubes, pyramids, and rectangular slabs on the built environment. This defines a characteristic of twentieth-century architecture and planning. The more complex connective geometry found in pre-twentieth-century architecture and in the architecture of traditional cultures is replaced. Geometrical fundamentalism may be in part responsible for the resentment the rest of the world feels against the industrialized western nations, because it replaces traditional buildings and cities with structures that are perceived as inhuman. A philosophy about geometrical shapes thus has an enormous socio-economic impact, by generating forces against globalization. The modernist movement promised a radical new utopian society based on a fundamentalist belief in pure abstractions. The extremely influential twentieth-century architect and urbanist Le Corbusier was entranced by the reductionist machine geometry of his time, and imposed it upon buildings and cities around the world. This misapplication of elementary abstractions constitutes a gross cognitive error, and fails to create satisfying human environments — the core purpose of architecture and the building arts. It parallels other totalitarian abstractions of the twentieth century, and this point will be discussed here. P 172

Chapter 10.

DARWINIAN PROCESSES AND MEMES IN ARCHITECTURE: A MEMETIC THEORY OF MODERNISM (WITH TERRY M. MIKITEN)

The process of design in architecture parallels generative processes in biology and the natural sciences. This Chapter examines how the ideas of Darwinian selection might apply to architecture. Design selects from among randomly-generated options in the mind of the architect. Multiple stages of selection generate a design that reflects the set of selection criteria used. The goal of traditional architecture is to adapt a design to human physical and psychological needs. At the same time, however, any particular style of architecture (adaptive or not) constitutes a group of visual memes that are copied for as long as that style remains in favor. Darwinian selection also explains why non-adaptive minimalist forms have been so successful at proliferating. The reason is because they act like simple biological entities such as viruses, which replicate much faster than do more complex life forms. Simple visual memes thus parasitize the ordered complexity of the built environment. P 195

Chapter 11.

TWO LANGUAGES FOR ARCHITECTURE

Design in architecture and urbanism is guided by two distinct complementary languages: a pattern language, and a form language. The pattern language contains rules for how human beings interact with built forms — a pattern language codifies practical solutions developed over millennia, which are appropriate to local customs, society, and climate. A form language, on the other hand, consists of geometrical rules for putting matter together. It is visual and tectonic, traditionally arising from available materials and their human uses rather than from images. Different form languages correspond to different architectural traditions, or styles. The problem is that not all form languages are adaptive to human sensibilities. Those that are not adaptive can never connect to a pattern language. Every adaptive design method combines a pattern language with a viable form language, otherwise it inevitably creates alien environments.   P 220

Chapter 12.

ARCHITECTURAL MEMES IN
A UNIVERSE OF INFORMATION

I describe here a symbiosis between ideas, images, texts, and biological forms. Human culture consists of created objects as information, which form an integral part of what we are — i.e., an essential extension of our biological bodies into our environment. This sensory, informational extension and mechanism for interaction defines a universe of information. With the advent of electronic communications, a relatively autonomous virtual world has been created. The space of information has proved a fertile breeding ground for the same informational entities — called "memes" — that formerly inhabited only human minds and artifacts. Architectural memes that took generations to diffuse through a restricted society can now spread around the world almost instantly, and will eventually alter its physical appearance. This Chapter aims to understand this process.   P 242

INTRODUCTION

In a short period of time, contemporary architecture has captured the imagination of millions of people the world over. Thick, glossy, and expensive books and magazines featuring photos of the world's premier architects along with their buildings adorn the living-room tables and libraries of those who can afford them. Millions of dollars are spent on flashy new buildings, when something much more reasonable could do. Developing countries with severely limited budgets frantically compete to engage the most fashionable of our "star" architects to build something for them, too. Architecture is thus highly visible in our media. It is clearly "in" with the times, thus providing a magnet for young persons wishing to make an exciting and challenging career choice.

What is it that a young student actually studies to become an architect, however? Is there a body of information to be mastered, such as for example the foundations of biology or medicine? There is a practical side requiring training and an apprenticeship of several years, but where are the thick books containing all of accumulated architectural knowledge, labeled "Principles of Architecture" (analogous to, say, "Principles of Physics") and running into one thousand pages? Surprisingly, thick architecture books are either full of pictures of contemporary "star" architects and their buildings, or they only address the history of architecture, featuring dead architects and their buildings. Architecture today seems to have no basis — not one that uses architectural traditions and analytic thought for today's designs. Students are taught by example that buildings of the past offer no lessons applicable to the contemporary built environment.

This book presents some ideas that I have explored in trying to discover the basis for architectural design. The search has led me to consider the application of science and mathematics to architecture. This approach has proved remarkably fruitful in establishing new and useful results. Most architects know of the historical application of ancient mathematics such as proportional ratios — but it is not this type of mathematics that actually governs general architectural form. Rather, it is the more recently developed mathematics of fractals, information theory, and complexity (concepts that will be explained in this book). I have presented these results in a manner I hope will be useful to practicing architects as well as to students who are seeking a greater clarity of how the physical world operates, and how this ties into architecture.

Each chapter consists of one of my published papers in architecture. It is my intention that collectively, these research articles can be used as a textbook for architectural design, or as supplementary material in a studio course. Individual chapters have indeed been used in this manner in many schools around the world ever since their initial publication. Their main message is that architecture can and should be based on principles that stand scientific scrutiny and experimental test. I present many new results, so no similar treatment of the principles underlying architectural design exists at the present time. My own architectural formation is due to my long involvement with Christopher Alexander in helping him to edit his monumental book, *The Nature of Order*, so, naturally, my work is profoundly influenced by and is complementary to his.

A student who sets out to study architecture should have a book that describes how to conceive and build an environment suitable for human activities. That is, after all, what everyone assumes that architects do. Design knowledge now resides solely in the minds of practicing architects and architectural academics. No clear guide exists to help the aspiring young architect deal with the physicality of form, founded on ideas open to questioning and verification. Instead, students are urged to use their imagination, though it is uninformed and limited. They are exposed to an extremely narrow stylistic vocabulary. When they look to the past (which is full of instructive examples) they are told to look to the future (which is unknown and thus of no educational value). "Approved" images seem to correspond only to each instructor's favorite architects, surely an insufficient reason to justify a lengthy education in architecture school. Even if it is to be followed by an apprenticeship in some architectural firm, this system does not train young persons to use a body of practical knowledge as principles of design.

All this seems anachronistic, and even dangerous. The reason is that a closed system of untested knowledge lends itself to corruption and dogmatism. Myths are created and perpetuated — the opposite of the openness of the scientific method, which seeks to demystify. Reflect for a moment on how scientific research is done. Someone announces the results of an investigation that links a cause with an effect, then his or her colleagues try their best to disprove them. The method by which they were obtained is scrutinized, as well as their ability to be verified by other researchers. If the results withstand this "trial by fire", then they are allowed to stand. When a result is verified independently of possible prejudices or of any agenda by those who proposed it, then it enters the permanent body of knowledge, at least until it is superseded by a more refined or more general result.

Architecture no longer works through any sort of empirical or experimental verification. This book represents my attempt to correct this condition, which is to me highly unsatisfactory. Architecture synthesizes a diverse body of disciplines in a manner that we react to directly. I did not write this book for scientists; I wrote it for practicing architects and students of architecture, in a language they can understand and apply. The task is so overwhelming, however, that it appears much more difficult now than when I first started on this project twelve years ago. This generation of architects has an abstract conception of architectural space, surfaces, structural coherence, and materials. As a result, contemporary architects are not often receptive to new knowledge about their discipline.

To achieve my aims, it is necessary to do the following, at the very least:

(*i*) Derive laws for how matter comes together to define buildings that give pleasure to human beings.
(*ii*) Explain, using scientific arguments, why people derive pleasure and satisfaction from some forms but not from others.
(*iii*) Find a basic commonality with past and present architects who have sought the same goals.

(*iv*) Explain why architects have not universally adopted known techniques that succeed in producing emotionally-nourishing buildings, and instead build structures that seem only to generate anxiety.

(*v*) Suggest how schools can train architects to create buildings that are emotionally and physiologically nourishing.

To work on any single one of these topics is daunting. Nevertheless, I have been forced to do all of these at the same time. The scientific results that I present contradict current architectural beliefs, and thus criticize architects who have ignored those results now and in the past. One of the explicit aims of modernism — and a major reason for its success — was to overcome nature through innovation. To do this, however, often requires doing the opposite of what is needed and what is natural. This violates people's feelings and our most basic instincts, because it goes against nature. Architects had to invent a new, "intellectual" justification for their forms, because they clearly contradicted our emotions and even our physiology.

It is essential in any serious analysis to explain what drives contemporary architecture, and why its objectives may be radically different from what architecture's aim ought to be. And who determines that aim? On the one hand, we have architects who argue in terms of images with an undeniable novelty supported by a volume of non-scientific writings; on the other hand we have the precedents of biological and natural structure, which are supported by traditional architectures. I cannot honestly present results that differ fundamentally from what is actually practiced today, without implying that present-day practices are misguided. This criticism has been unavoidable from a scholarly point of view. However unwillingly I take this iconoclastic stand, I defend it with the best arguments I can come up with.

People tend to trust figures of authority (such as prominent critics, "star" architects, and architectural academics in our top schools), who talk in the media about "architectural theory". I believe they are mistaken. What is currently labeled "architectural theory" — with few exceptions — is unverifiable, and hence not very useful for design. Not only does the architectural community not have a body of theory as such, but it is confused as to what a viable theory would look like. The professional organizations and bodies of accreditation, acting the role of watchdogs in other professions, seem to ignore this contradiction here. Nevertheless, young and sensitive practitioners are at long last seeking true architectural knowledge, welcoming science as their ally. Through computer applications, architects have begun to study a complexity of form and function hitherto undreamt of.

Courageous persons tried to achieve similar goals, but faced stiff opposition. Starting from my friend and mentor, Christopher Alexander, they include Léon Krier, Charles, the Prince of Wales, and the late Friedrich Hundertwasser. Each one, in his own unique way, has argued for a more humane architecture for our times. Each of these persons has spoken out against the dehumanizing effect of contemporary architecture, and each one has been criticized in the media (and, on occasion, harshly attacked and ridiculed). What they have to say has so far been kept out of architecture schools. However, as a result of the proliferation of the internet as a universal information source, the message is finally being communicated to young architects and students. This represents the beginning of an architectural revolution, or, as architects would say, a paradigmatic shift.

We have in our possession the means to build a new environment that equals the greatest architectural achievements of the past. People can once again experience architecture as something nourishing, instead of as a vehicle for novelty (often creating dysfunctional buildings that lead to anxiety and depression). It is just that today's architects are not informed about the natural laws for generating buildings with intensely human qualities, so that they might choose to incorporate them into their design. There is also resistance from the architectural establishment, and it is an ideological one. This is about to collapse, however. Once a new generation of architects emerges that is not beholden to outdated ways of doing things, and to unquestioning support of an entrenched power elite, it will be receptive to laws that enable an adaptive architecture. I predict a new architecture of unprecedented beauty, justly appropriate for the new millennium.

ACKNOWLEDGMENTS

I am indebted to Christopher Alexander, who inspired me to devote my research energy to understanding the built environment. Working with him on his book *The Nature of Order* during the twenty years prior to its publication taught me much of what I know about architecture and urbanism. He has generously encouraged me over all these years. More than that, he provided a solid point of sanity in an architectural world driven by images, fashions, and opinions. My work utilizes and expands on his ideas in many ways. A full appreciation of the material presented here can only come from reading his monumental work.

Many thanks to the Alfred P. Sloan Foundation for generously supporting my research into the scientific laws of architecture, through a grant during 1997-2001. My coauthors on four of the Chapters, Michael W. Mehaffy, Terry M. Mikiten, Débora M. Tejada, and Hing-Sing Yu, provided invaluable input. Individuals who contributed useful advice and comments on one or more chapters include Michael Benedikt, Carl Bovill, Alfonso Castro, Carl Davis, Ollivier Dyens, James M. Gallas, Dmitry Gokhman, Robert E. Hiromoto, Peter Hochmann, Wai-Kwok Kwong, David Miet, Terry M. Mikiten, John Miller, John C. Rayko, Lynn A. Steen, Gregory P. Wene, Sir Christopher Zeeman, and Mary Lou Zeeman. I thank all of them.

The chapters in this book are based on previous publications, and I am grateful to the various journals for their permission to use the published material. I started to write this book by publishing each completed topic as a separate research paper. It is only recently that I arranged these papers on different but related architectural topics into a comprehensive book.

Finally, Kenneth G. Masden II helped me directly in the demanding task of editing the individual chapters into a coherent monograph, in a way that would be useful to architects and architecture students. In addition to his careful reading of the text and numerous suggestions for revisions, inviting me to lecture from this book to his senior studio class generated valuable student feedback. Some sections were rewritten and expanded, the notation and terminology were made uniform, and explanations were added throughout the text. The result is a treatise that is much more coherent than the chapters as they appeared originally. Following his advice, the book also includes many new figures that were not present in the original articles.

Chapter One

THE LAWS OF ARCHITECTURE FROM A PHYSICIST'S PERSPECTIVE

1. INTRODUCTION.

It is my contention that architecture is an expression and application of geometrical order. One would expect the subject to be described by mathematics and physics, but it is not. There is as yet no clear and accepted formulation of how *structural order* is achieved in architecture. Considering that architecture affects humankind through the built environment more directly than any other discipline, our limited understanding of the actual mechanism that creates *structural order* is surprising. We have concentrated on understanding natural inanimate and biological structures, but not the systematic patterns reflected in our own constructions.

There exist historical buildings that are universally admired as being the most beautiful (see Section 2 in this Chapter, below). These include the great religious temples of the past (Fletcher, 1987) and the cultural wealth contained in various indigenous architectures (Rudofsky, 1964; 1977). Both were built by following some rules of thumb, which can be deduced from the structures themselves. One general set of empirical rules has been analyzed and collected in the *Pattern Language* of Christopher Alexander (Alexander *et. al.*, 1977).

Laws for *structural order* underlie both physics and biology, and I expect similar laws should hold for architecture as well. Alexander proposes a set of geometrical rules that govern architecture, derived from biological and physical principles (Alexander, 2004). They are based on the hypothesis that matter obeys a complex ordering on the macroscopic scale. *Structural order* requires only that forms be subdivided in a certain manner, and that the subdivisions be made to relate to each other. Even though forces such as electromagnetism and gravity are too weak to account for this, volumes and surfaces apparently interact in a way that mimics the microscopic interaction of elementary particles. Architecture can therefore be reduced to a set of rules that are akin to the laws of physics.

Structural order also refers to perceived form, and thus encompasses two components of architecture that have been segregated in the discussions of the past several decades: tectonic structure, and surface design. I don't wish to mix surface qualities with built structure; but our sensory mechanisms respond just as well to visual designs as to tectonics. Thus, *structural order* is due to both of these aspects of built form, which are distinguished simply by scale. This book spends considerable effort to relate scales to each other, and to human response. *Structural order* depends upon human perception, hence it cannot be judged strictly from abstract formal criteria. This is a concept familiar to physicists, where the observer becomes part of, and influences the behavior of, a quantum system. An underlying theme of this inquiry is that architecture exists in the universe of human beings, and cannot be isolated into an abstract realm of its own. The basic criterion may be stated as: "if we respond to it in any way, then it is a component of *structural order*".

Using analogies with the structure of matter, three laws of *structural order* are postulated here (Section 3). They are checked in three different ways: by agreeing directly with the greatest historical buildings of all time (Fletcher, 1987); by agreeing with fifteen properties abstracted by Alexander from creations throughout human history (Alexander, 2004); and by agreeing with physical and biological forms. This result represents a successful application of scientific analysis (i.e., the physicist's approach) to understanding and solving a highly complex problem, which has up until now resisted a scientific formulation.

The three laws of *structural order* can be applied to classify architectural styles in a way that has not been done before (Section 4). Whereas most traditional architectures follow the three laws, contemporary and modernist buildings often seem to be doing the opposite of what the three laws say. By modernist, I mean the architecture introduced in the 1920s, which led to "International Style" and minimalist buildings. This result categorizes traditional architecture into a separate group from the architecture of the twentieth century, which is not surprising, since their architects wanted their buildings to be different. It will be useful to get a clearer conception of the corresponding *structural order*. It appears that all buildings are created by a systematic application of the same three laws, whether in following them or in opposing them.

Thus far, the results do not distinguish which architecture is "better". Nevertheless, Alexander, in company with Charles, the Prince of Wales, prefers a more humane architecture, which is most often found in traditional forms. They believe that traditional architecture is more suited to humankind for fundamental reasons (such as human physiology and psychology) and not merely as a matter of taste. Section 5 of this Chapter presents arguments to support this view. The basis of those arguments is the sense of comfort one feels from a building and the universality of its *structural order*, which is the way the architecture hold together on a visual, physical, and tectonic level.

2. RULES OF BEAUTY AND ORDER IN PAST TIMES.

Every distinct civilization or different period in the past has left us a set of rules, usually implicit, that help produce the ultimate ideal in beauty. Each set of rules is relevant to the ornamental tradition of a particular time, the availability of indigenous materials, the local climate, or an underlying religious ritual, and defines architectural forms that are beautiful. What is important is that these very different buildings and objects are seen as beautiful by most people today, who live outside the time and culture that produced them. This implies the existence of universal laws governing *structural order*.

There is no difficulty in applying a traditional set of architectural rules to contemporary buildings. A Greek temple in Japan (as a bank), or a Chinese temple in the

United States (as a restaurant) can be beautiful, if built by following the rules appropriate to their particular form. Such rules tell us how to duplicate something from an earlier culture or different people. They cannot, however, be generalized or easily adapted to a different set of forces and circumstances. Rather what we need now, and what architects are always looking for, is a prescription for building something beautiful that is not constrained by a rigid and possibly irrelevant tradition.

Rules that are genuinely independent of any specific culture and time can be derived by approaching architecture as a scientific problem. I give three laws governing *structural order* that include, as special cases, most of the previous sets of architectural rules derived throughout history for creating beautiful buildings. I then show that the rules for building identifiably modernist structures simply do the opposite of what is needed to achieve *structural order* in architecture. This result singles out two distinct classes of structures in the history of human construction.

Different types of *structural order* also give rise to different experiences for a building's user. Many contemporary and earlier twentieth-century buildings (though certainly not all) that follow the industrial model are perceived as unpleasant by their users. This may be true for their visual aspect, and especially so for practical functions (entry and exit, working, circulation, etc.) that are supposed to take place in those buildings. It would be good to have some explanation for why this is, so we can fix it. Public reaction against certain architectural styles has been noted before (Blake, 1974; Wolfe, 1981), and is forcefully expressed by Charles, the Prince of Wales (Charles, 1988; 1989). Despite all these criticisms, however, the modernist aesthetic (which influences styles that succeeded modernism) remains deeply entrenched in our society, overriding questions of user reaction and comfort that might threaten to judge it as flawed.

Proponents of modernism have identified their credo with the technological progress of the twentieth century. In the minds of many people, post-war industrial progress is falsely linked to, if not outright due to, the expansion of modernist architecture, and for this reason they are reluctant to question it. It has become automatic for developing countries to build the most modern-looking buildings as the first step towards modernization. Nevertheless, it is now accepted that modernist building programs in the preindustrialized world have largely been disastrous in their urban and environmental consequences (Blake, 1974).

The widespread proliferation of modernist architectural typologies is a socio-historical phenomenon, and thus amenable to scientific analysis. Explaining modernism's extraordinary success occupies the last third of this book, Chapters 9 though 12. Though at the core of any theory of architecture, this topic cannot be studied using purely architectural reasoning; therefore, new techniques that utilize ideas from evolutionary biology had to be developed to explain historical events.

3. LAWS FOR ARCHITECTURE.

The following laws of *structural order* are inspired by and rely on Alexander's results; in particular, his "fifteen properties" in Book 1 of "The Nature of Order" (Alexander, 2004). They have grown out of my discussions and interaction with Alexander over the past twenty-two years. I tried to formulate a set of laws that might be easier to remember than Alexander's "fifteen properties". It is of course not possible to replace fifteen properties by only three laws, but hopefully my interpretation can help to bring Alexander's "fifteen properties" into sharper focus by approaching the problem of *structural order* from a slightly different, complementary direction.

Table 1.1. Three Laws of Structural Order.

Law 1.   Order on the smallest scale is established by paired contrasting elements, existing in a balanced visual tension.

Law 2.   Large-scale order occurs when every element relates to every other element at a distance in a way that reduces entropy.

Law 3.   The small scale is connected to the large scale through a linked hierarchy of intermediate scales with a scaling ratio approximately equal to $e \approx 2.7$.

The word "entropy" in Law 2 is the technical term for randomness or disorder. Although a standard term in physics, it does not commonly arise in architecture. In Law 3 above, e is a ubiquitous mathematical constant, the base of natural logarithms. I will discuss how to apply this number to design in this and the following two Chapters. Scaling in Law 3 relates components of different sizes, and "hierarchy" refers to the rank-ordering of all those sizes.

Several independent arguments supporting these laws are presented below. The first two laws govern the two extremes of scale: the very small and the very large; and the third law governs the linking of all different scales. Each law gives rise to several distinct consequences; together the three laws define a set of possible rules for architecture. They are validated because their immediate consequences appear to correspond to reality.

3.1. Order on the Small Scale.

I will establish an analogy with the way that matter is formed out of contrasting pairs of elementary components. From the vacuum in quantum electrodynamics arising out of virtual electron-positron pairs, to nuclei formed from bound neutrons and protons with opposite isospin, to atoms formed of bound electrons and nuclei of opposite charge, the composition of matter follows the same basic pattern. (All these examples are on the subatomic, atomic, and molecular levels). The smallest scale consists of paired elements with the opposite characteristics bound together. The binding is a result of complementarity. Coupling keeps opposites close to each other but does not allow them to overlap, because they would mutually annihilate (i.e., cancel each other); their close separation creates a dynamic tension. Keeping units of the same type next to each other does not result in binding.

Applying this concept to architecture gives us Law 1, which states: **"Order on the smallest scale is established by paired contrasting elements, existing in a balanced visual tension"**. Local contrast identifies the smallest scale in a building, thus establishing the fundamental level of *structural order*. This scale should be relevant to the observer — in regions where a person walks or sits or works, contrast and tension are needed at the smallest perceivable detail; in areas distant from human activity the "smallest" scale is much larger.

Structural order is a phenomenon that obeys its own laws. It connects built structure with visual structure on the human scale. Its fundamental building blocks are the smallest perceivable differentiations of color and geometry. Whereas visible differentiation on the small scale is not necessary to define physical structure, it is in fact necessary for *structural order*. This is demonstrated in architecture and in most objects made before the twentieth century. Classical Greek temples have marvelous contrasting details. This was also true of color, but the original coloration has been lost with time. To see the effective use of color contrast, look at the extraordinary fifteenth century tiled walls in Iran, Islamic Spain, and Morocco.

There are several important consequences of the first law.

(1a) Basic elements have to couple with each other. Like elementary physical components, the smallest fundamental units should have shapes that permit them to combine into more complex shapes (see Figure 1.1).

Figure (1.1)
Elements on the small scale
couple through contrast.

(1b) Basic units are held together by a short-range force, i.e., one that is very strong when objects are close, but has no effect when they are far apart. The only way to do this using geometry is to have interlocking units with opposite and contrasting characteristics. There are several ways to achieve contrast with materials: shape (convex-concave); direction (zigzags); color hue (red-green, orange-blue, violet-yellow); and color value (black-white) (see Figure 1.2).

31

Figure (1.2)
The small scale consists of contrasting coupled pairs.

(1c) The smallest units occur in contrasting pairs, just like fermions (a class of elementary particles). When these pairs of units repeat, the repetition is not of a single unit, but of a coupled pair, leading to alternation rather than simple repetition (see Figures 1.2 and 1.3). If one just repeats the same plain unit, it does not generate a pattern.

Figure (1.3)
Contrasting units alternate to interlock.

(1d) The concept of contrast recurs on different scales, thus actually preventing detail from filling all the space. A region of detail will need to contrast with a plainer region, and the two regions combine to form a contrasting pair (see Figure 1.4). In the same way, roughly built areas and finishes are necessary to complement those areas which are finely built or finished.

Figure (1.4)
High detail couples with plain, empty regions.

Consider the atomic nucleus, in which protons and neutrons are bound together by the strong force, which works via virtual pion exchange. This mechanism is constantly reversing the nucleons' identity. A neutron is able to become a proton, then switch back again. This switching back and forth is what actually binds them tightly to each other to form the nucleus: it is difficult to separate the protons from the neutrons inside the atomic nucleus, because one cannot tell which is which. A basic pair of complementary, contrasting units in a design, as described in consequence (1b), above, must also possess this duality. For an object and its surrounding space to be effectively bound into a contrasting pair, both the space and the object itself must have the same degree of structural integrity. Each component of a contrasting pair has to have a comparable degree of coherence and complexity. In the case of an object and its surroundings, each should shape the other, helping to endow it with complementary qualities. In the case of a building, coupling with its exterior space does not occur via a glass curtain wall, but through the geometry of its plan as it is formed so as to enclose outdoor space. This process leads to the definition of urban space.

I am going to revisit contrast from the physiological point of view in Chapter 4, *The Sensory Value of Ornament*, and from the architectural point of view in Chapter 5, *Life and Complexity in Architecture From a Thermodynamic Analogy*.

3.2. Order on the Large Scale.

In physics, when noninteracting objects are juxtaposed, nothing happens. An interaction, however, induces a rearrangement that leads to higher order for the large-scale structure, and therefore to a reduction of the entropy (disorder) (see Figure 1.5). Disorder prevents the formation of an integrated whole. The process of ordering could be as complex as the growth in a periodic crystal lattice, or as simple as the alignment of compass needles or iron filings in a magnetic field. This is the way that crystalline structures are formed, galaxies condense, etc. Action-at-a-distance, whether it is electric, magnetic, or gravitational, imposes a large-scale ordering characterized by geometrical connections that are not exclusively rectangular.

MORE ENTROPY

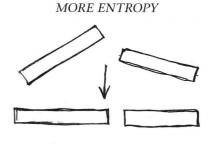

Figure (1.5)
Alignment along one axis reduces entropy (disorder).

LESS ENTROPY

One consequence of the process of organization is that similarities and symmetries appear between different visual subregions. This should be intentionally mimicked in architecture and used to tie the small-scale structures together into a harmonious whole. Law 2 states: **"Large-scale order occurs when every element relates to every other element at a distance in a way that reduces entropy"**. This basic prescription suffices to generate large-scale order in both color and geometry. Mimicking a long-range interaction via the intentional orientation and similarity of spatially separated units determines *structural order* (see Figure 1.6). I am not talking only of surface decoration, but about the genuine ordering of tectonic elements. Note the distinction with the first law: small-scale order comes from coupling units that are touching each other, whereas large-scale order comes from relating units that are not next to each other.

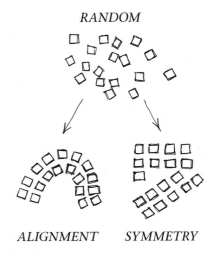

Figure (1.6)
Two distinct methods of reducing spatial entropy
(which includes both two and three-dimensional
objects).

RANDOM

ALIGNMENT   SYMMETRY

There is a very good reason for reducing the entropy, and it has to do with the way human beings perceive a structure. We find it very hard to grasp (consciously register) something that is disordered. By contrast, even a complex structure can be grasped perceptually if it is made more coherent by means of connections and symmetries. Then, we can conceive it as a whole, instead of as a multitude of unrelated pieces. Grasping a complex whole empowers us with knowledge about our environment, whereas confronting something that is too disconnected to grasp easily leads to frustration and anxiety.

Thermodynamic entropy relates different arrangements of the same number of particles according to their probability of occurring. Entropy applies to *structural order* in a slightly different way, because it relates different states with the same number of basic contrasting units. We are comparing rearrangements of the same pieces, some arrangements being more ordered than others. *Structural order* in architecture is inversely proportional to the entropy of a fixed number of interacting components. The higher the entropy (geometrical disorder) among the components at hand, the lower the *structural order*. Conversely, the lower the entropy, the higher the *structural order*. The entropy of a design could be lowered instead by reducing the local contrasts, but this also reduces the *structural order* — that would be analogous to eliminating the molecules in a gas (thereby reducing architecture to an empty minimalism).

The consequences of the second law are the distinct ways in which *structural order* is achieved on the large scale.

(2a) Large-scale ordering arranges basic units into highly symmetric combinations. As in crystallization, the entropy (disorder) is lowered by raising the number of local symmetries (see Figure 1.7). The smaller scales are therefore characterized by a high degree of symmetry, which is not required of the large scales, however (see Figure 1.8).

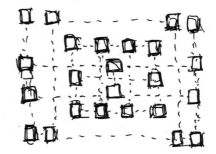

Figure (1.7)
Disorder is lowered by having many symmetries.

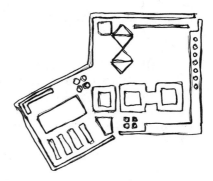

Figure (1.8)
Ordering generates multiple internal symmetries.

(2b) *Structural order* is also achieved by having units on a common grid (regular array), modeling them as in a crystal lattice (where the units are atoms at each intersection) (see Figure 1.9). Continuity of patterns across structural transitions raises the degree of connectivity. If one repeats the same nontrivial pattern on different regions, that ties those regions together.

Figure (1.9)
Units arranged on a rectangular grid.

(2c) In the absence of a physical force between areas, visual similarity connects two design elements (portions of a building) through common colors, shapes, and sizes. *Structural order* harmonizes local contrasts without reducing them in any way.

(2d) Insisting on visual "purity" can destroy the connection process, because connections represent smaller-scale structures. They may be misinterpreted as impurities, however, and eliminated. Therefore, imperfections are both useful and necessary; just as in a doped crystal such as silicon used in a transistor, where impurities enhance the structure and give it its useful properties as a semiconductor.

The second law makes it easier to understand the visual interaction of two objects placed near each other but kept separate, well known from optical illusions. The brain creates connecting lines that appear to tie the geometry of the two units together. Now, if we take two objects, draw the virtual connections that we see, on paper, then construct them from some material, the resulting structure will hold together against physical stresses. This establishes a physical relevance for a strictly visual phenomenon. It appears that the brain "sees" the proper physical connections for a coherent structure.

The entropy of a design is perceived by our innate ability to visualize connections. The main spaces of any building, and their relation to each other, are governed by the mutual interaction of all the walls and any other structural elements. Certain dimensions and certain combinations, will appear to "resonate" when all components interact harmoniously. These correspond to the states of least entropy. Making adjustments to a complex structure so as to lower its entropy conforms precisely to the process that gives rise to natural forms.

Entropy is discussed further in Chapter 5, *Life and Complexity in Architecture From a Thermodynamic Analogy*; and the formation of patterns in Chapter 6, *Architecture, Patterns, and Mathematics*.

3.3. The natural scaling Hierarchy.

The third law of *structural order* proposes the idea of scaling similarity, which is what links the hierarchy together. Law 3 states: **"The small scale is connected to the large scale through a linked hierarchy of intermediate scales with a scaling ratio approximately equal to $e \approx 2.7$"**. Surfaces interact; in so doing they create subdivisions of visual structure; all that one has to do is to establish structures at the appropriate scales, and link them together (see Figure 1.10). The different scales have to be close enough in size so that they can visually relate to each other, and the linking is accomplished through structural similarities, such as repeating forms and patterns (see Figure 1.11).

Figure (1.10)
Hierarchy links the small scale to the large scale.

Figure (1.11)
Repeating forms at different magnifications.

The physical reasoning here is that material forces are manifested differently on different scales. The shape of natural structures is influenced by stresses, strains, and fractures in solids, and by turbulence in moving fluids. Matter is not uniform: it looks totally different if magnified by a factor of 10 or more, and there is usually some perceivable structure at all possible magnifications. If we want the scaling ratio for which two distinct scales are still related empirically, however, this number is found to be around 3, and more specifically, be near 2.7. In fractal geometry, there are many different artificial fractals generated by algorithms and having different scaling ratios. The Koch, Peano, and Cantor self-similar fractal patterns that most closely resemble natural objects have scaling ratio equal to 3 or $\sqrt{7} \approx 2.65$ (Mandelbrot, 1983), supporting the universal scaling ratio of 2.7 that I propose here.

What is given here is only a prelude to a much more detailed discussion in subsequent Chapters. Hierarchy and scaling are the subject of Chapter 2, *A Scientific Basis for Creating Architectural Forms*; Chapter 3, *Hierarchical Cooperation in Architecture: the Mathematical Necessity for Ornament*; Chapter 7, *Pavements as Embodiments of Meaning for a Fractal Mind*; and Chapter 8, *Modularity and the Number of Design Choices*.

These arguments may at first appear totally subjective, and yet they reveal a basic scaling phenomenon seen in biological structures. The secret of biological growth is scaling, either via a Fibonacci sequence, or an exponential sequence (which is generated by $e \approx 2.7$). Ordered growth is possible only if there is a simple scaling so that the basic replication process can be repeated to create structure on different levels. Thus, different scales must exist, and they must be related, preferably by only one parameter. Using the scaling ratio e as this parameter fits both natural and man-made structures (i.e. buildings and artifacts).

Take one view of a building as a two-dimensional design. Then decide whether to measure areas, or linear dimensions, depending on the situation. Different substructures (subdivisions) of roughly the same size will group themselves into one scale, and different scales follow from distinct sets of elements at those sizes. The number of different scales will be denoted by N. Call the maximum scale x_{max} and the minimum perceivable scale x_{min}. A form with *structural order* will have n sets of subunits with sizes corresponding to every element of the following sequence of scales:

$$\{ x_{min} , e\, x_{min} , e^2\, x_{min} , \dots , e^{n-1}\, x_{min} = x_{max} \} \qquad (1)$$

These are the sizes of design components, arranged from the smallest to the largest. Equation (1) allows you to compute those sizes. The smallest scale has dimension x_{min}, the next larger scale $2.7\, x_{min}$, the next larger scale $(2.7)^2\, x_{min} \approx 7.3$ x_{min}, and so on, increasing by powers of 2.7 all the way up to x_{max}. It is possible to solve the last term of the sequence of scales in Equation (1), $e^{n-1}\, x_{min} = x_{max}$ for n (see derivation in the next Chapter). This relates the *ideal number of scales n* to the smallest and largest measurements (in the same units). We then have:

$$n = 1 + \ln x_{max} - \ln x_{min} \qquad (2)$$

Here, n is the nearest integer value. One measure of *structural order* is how close the *ideal number of scales n* given by equation (2) comes to the number N of distinct scales in a structure. The theoretical index n is my suggestion for the *ideal number of scales* in a building, whereas N is the number of scales that are actually built, and this could vary widely. Comparing how near N is to n indicates only if a natural scaling hierarchy exists; it does not determine whether similarities actually link the different scales together, which is also a requirement for *structural order*. Still, this number offers a dramatic insight into the design deficiencies of many buildings.

For example, a three-storey building with 2.5 cm (1 in) detail requires the *ideal number of scales n* to be about 7 (computed from equation (2), with 34 ft $\approx (2.7)^6$ in). In many buildings, however, N is nearer to 2, regardless of their size, because there are intentionally no structures in the small and intermediate scales. Those buildings tend to look "pure", in that they have large empty surfaces. At the other extreme, some buildings with unorganized structures of many different sizes might have N higher than the *ideal number of scales n*. That is not good, either. A building with a natural scaling hierarchy, regardless of what it looks like, should have N very close to the *ideal number of scales n*.

There are several consequences of the third law.

(3a) Every unit (subdivision, substructure) will be embedded into a larger unit of the next scale in size. This naturally leads to a very wide boundary or frame for each element in a design. The whole design is a hierarchy of wide boundaries within other boundaries.

(3b) As already mentioned, similarity of shape should link the different scales together; for example, the same curve or pattern repeated at different sizes.

(3c) The different scales can define a gradient through focusing similar shapes of decreasing size, as in the process of nesting. Each building requires an entrance gradient as well as other functional gradients, and these succeed better when they correspond to structural gradients defined by the scaling ratio.

(3d) A building must be placed into the environment in a way that fits the existing scaling hierarchy of urban dimensions. The surrounding nature and other buildings will then define the largest scales of the hierarchy.

The emergence of a wide boundary or frame, consequence (3a) above, defines an interacting object to have a boundary of similar size as the object itself. For example, a square embedded symmetrically in another square has a ratio of areas $A_2/A_1 = e$. This gives a ratio of the width of the border to the width of the smaller square as $w/x = (\sqrt{e} - 1)/2 \approx 0.32$ (see Figure 1.12). This is about 1/3. Another illustration comes from physics. The magnetic field around a spherical dipole magnet of radius R goes out to infinity, yet the effective region of strong field is comparable to the size of the magnet. The field strength along the axis falls to 1/10 of its surface value at $2.15R$, giving the thickness of field as 0.58 times the magnet's diameter (Jefimenko, 1989). Thus, a magnet's field defines such a wide boundary around the poles of the magnet.

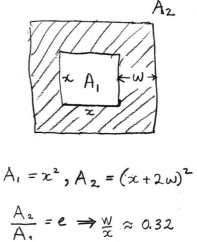

Figure (1.12)
A square embedded inside another square. The area of the smaller square is $A_1 = x^2$, whereas the area of the larger square is $A_2 = (x+2w)^2$. When the ratio of the two areas is $A_2/A_1 = e$, then the width of the frame w is about one-third the width x of the enclosed square.

$$A_1 = x^2, \quad A_2 = (x + 2w)^2$$

$$\frac{A_2}{A_1} = e \implies \frac{w}{x} \approx 0.32$$

4. A CLASSIFICATION OF ARCHITECTURAL STYLES.

The three laws of *structural order* presented here and their twelve consequences are revealed in historical buildings and artifacts from all over the world, throughout more than four millennia of civilization leading up to the twentieth century (Fletcher, 1987). This validates the above findings in an essential manner. I have used arguments from physics to obtain practical results for architecture that correspond to reality. The discussion of this Chapter confirms results already established by Alexander in a strictly architectural context (Alexander, 2004; Alexander *et. al.*, 1977).

Architects throughout history, including the early modernists, probably had some intuitive knowledge of the three laws proposed here. These general laws underlie the various forms and the basis of design and construction that mimic the beauty and *structural order* found in nature. Modernists, however, strove to produce human constructions that contrasted with nature. The shock value of something unnatural gives many modernist buildings their novelty. To achieve this, they tend to do the opposite of what the three laws say.

Twentieth-century buildings minimize certain components of their *structural order*. Some have a monumental overall symmetry, which is unwarranted, but none of the necessary small-scale symmetries. Often, both structure and function are deliberately disguised. Small-scale *structural order*, as expressed in ornament, is forbidden. There may not be any differentiation of the space; contrast between outside and inside, or contrast of busy with calm areas, or of areas having distinct functions. If there is any repetition, it is more likely monotonous and without contrasting components (see Figure 1.13). Most if not all parts of a building could exist in isolation, and not interact in any way. Connections between regions are often suppressed. Different scales are allowed only if the scaling ratio is 15 or more (thus hugely exceeding the recommended scaling ratio near 2.7), so the scales are visually disconnected (see Figure 1.14). There are no thick borders, frames, or connecting boundaries, since preferred surfaces are sheer and come to straight edges and sharp corners. Finally, any natural or existing order is usually razed before building, thus limiting a connection to the surroundings.

Figure (1.13)
Repetition without contrast does not connect.

Figure (1.14)
Too small of a jump between nested squares because the ratio of the interior's width x_2 to the frame's width x_1 is larger than 10. That is, $x_2/x_1 > 10$.

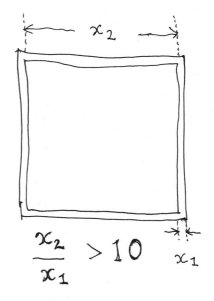

All architectural styles separate broadly into two groups: traditional and modernist (which includes successors to modernism). This distinction is based on whether they follow or oppose the three laws of *structural order* and has nothing to do with the age or historical context of the buildings. Many people instinctively separate modernist from traditional buildings based on their feelings, but, without a set of written rules, there was never a systematic way of doing this. It is even possible to judge a "mixed" or hybrid style by seeing which laws and sublaws it follows, and which it deliberately contradicts, and the degree that it does so. The best-loved modernist buildings reveal, on closer examination, to follow some of the laws leading to *structural order*.

Actually, it turns out that the classification of architectural styles is far more complex than I originally proposed when this Chapter was first published as an article. While most styles prior to the twentieth century do cluster in the same "traditional" region of solution space, there exists an infinite number of styles that move away from this region. Thus, there is no single "opposite" to traditional architecture. This point is analyzed in greater detail in Chapter 5, *Life and Complexity in Architecture From a Thermodynamic Analogy*, which develops a more sophisticated classification of architectural styles.

The architectural community distinguishes architectural styles according to the use of traditional materials such as stone and brick versus modern industrial materials such as steel, glass, and light-weight reinforced concrete. My results show this distinction not to be very relevant, since constructions that either obey or contradict the three laws are possible using any materials. It is true (and this point will be discussed in depth later) that industrial materials make it much easier to ignore the three laws, if that is the architect's intention. On the other hand, some of the most beautiful Art Nouveau buildings, which follow these laws, were made possible by modern industrial materials (Russell, 1979).

5. THE UNNATURALNESS OF CONTEMPORARY BUILDINGS.

This section discusses two criteria for choosing between competing architectural typologies: the emotional response to a building; and the deeper connection between *structural order* and nature. Modernism was invented in the 1920s by a group of men who championed extreme political and philosophical ideas (Blake, 1974; Wolfe, 1981). They were obsessed by the urge to break totally with any existing historical order. Their aim was to transform society by making constructions that defied nature, inadvertently going against people's instinctive feelings of beauty, and this is reflected in their buildings.

In Section 4, above, I argued that modernist architecture relies for its effects on rules that are logically the opposite of the three laws of *structural order*, which are found in traditional architecture. Nevertheless, modern physics was also a deliberate break from classical physics, but that was not a reason to dismiss either classical physics or modern physics. The crucial difference is that modern physics survived because of its agreement with experimental phenomena. Today, modern physics and classical physics coexist harmoniously. This comparison between physics and architecture identifies a deficiency in current architectural knowledge: the lack of an experimental basis or something analogous to it, which could validate what is important to the discipline and discard what is irrelevant.

5.1. The Emotional Basis of Architecture.

Successful buildings in any style have one overriding quality: they feel natural and comfortable. Human beings connect with their surroundings on the small scale (because it is more immediate) and need to feel reassured about any large-scale structure. There is a built-in human reaction to threats from the environment, and structures threaten our primeval sense of security when they appear unnatural. A building, regardless of shape or use, is perceived as beautiful when an emotional link is established with it, and that is possible only when the building has a high degree of *structural order*. The perception of *structural order* as a positive emotional state is independent of opinion, fashion, or style.

Emotional well-being can be used as an experimental criterion for judging a structure's effectiveness. We relate to the detail in a design or structure immediately, because connecting to the small scale is an emotional experience. On the other hand, perceiving the overall form often requires some thought, which is a more intellectual process. According to the three laws of *structural order*, our connection to architecture occurs via the smallest scale, through the intermediate scales, and finally to the large scale — and is successful only if all the scales are connected. Describing how scales are connected to each other occupies the next two Chapters.

The fundamental human need for small-scale *structural order* is manifested in almost every object and building made before the twentieth century. Modernist ideologues such as Adolf Loos, however, were relentless in attacking small-scale order as "criminal". This characterization represents an extreme and overblown reaction to nineteenth-century ornament. The solution to having too much decoration is not to banish organized detail altogether; it is to find the exact detail and small-scale ornament necessary for anchoring the larger forms and defining the *ideal number of scales* in a structure. Organized detail, properly placed, establishes emotional well-being because it contributes to *structural order*.

Certain architects downplay the basic human need for a comfortable mental environment in which to live and work, subordinating it to purely formal concerns. According to them, the individual has no right to expect emotional comfort in buildings. Those architects focused on introducing sharp corners, metallic edges, massive protruding overhangs, etc., as part of the industrial design vocabulary, and these create emotional discomfort. Their formal typology uncompromisingly insists on straight lines, even in situations where curves are clearly more appropriate. This is not always done for a functional reason, but often works against the functions in those buildings.

It is known from studies in environmental psychology that many twentieth-century structures make their inhabitants feel very uncomfortable. Human instincts towards the reduction of spatial discomfort try to reduce damage to the sense of well-being of the mind. We have mechanisms analogous to our instincts in avoiding physical pain, which protect our body tissues from damage. Architects have not paid serious attention to our need for emotional well-being in an architectural setting: something vital in human consciousness could well be damaged by an environment that ignores the three laws of *structural order*.

5.2. Uniqueness of Structural Order.

There exist two opposite conceptions of *structural order* in the world today. Most architects have been taught to think of "order" in early modernist architectural terms: large-scale bilateral symmetry, rectangular shapes, flat empty surfaces, straight edges and right angles, etc. That is a type of geometrical order based on simplicity and abstraction, as shown in popular images and built forms that we grew up with. This Chapter suggests that the *structural order* of our world, as revealed by science, is far more complex and is contradicted by the modern built environment. Logic cannot sustain two mutually contradictory definitions of *structural order*, which implies that the laws of *structural order* are unique. There is overwhelming scientific evidence supporting what I propose, thus any conception of *structural order* must agree with the points defined in this Chapter.

As pointed out earlier in Section 3, human beings can visualize connections intuitively. This innate ability has enabled us to develop architecture early in our evolution. The mind establishes patterns and connections not only between objects, but also between ideas and concepts. To a physicist, it appears that our built-in intuitive notions of *structural order* arise from the same source as our ability to reason and to do physics. This ability is no longer being nurtured, however. Either we inherit an innate conception of *structural order*, or we learn it from our environment. People in the late twentieth century are surrounded by structures that violate the three laws of *structural order*, yet they are constantly being reminded (by architects and the media) that those buildings represent the only "true" order appropriate for our age. If, as is claimed here, the laws of *structural order* are unique, then such buildings suppress the conception of *structural order* that we inherit (not from our culture, but in our physiological makeup). The consequence of this is to confuse our ability to perceive connections (and possibly, to irreparably damage it), which affects more than just architecture.

The structural and physiological basis of order is investigated further in Chapters 2 through 8. Ideas first expressed somewhat tentatively in this Chapter gave rise to research that generated the rest of this book. Fundamental questions raised here about *structural order* will be answered in the subsequent Chapters.

6. CONCLUSION.

Inspired by the work of Christopher Alexander, three laws of *structural order* were postulated from basic physical analogies. These laws were shown to have a scientific validity above and beyond any architectural fashion, opinion, or style. Natural forms have an ordered internal complexity that mimics interacting physical processes, and this is reflected in the world's great historical buildings and vernacular architectures. The three laws presented here are eminently practical and can eventually be applied to create buildings whose coherence is reflected in intense physical and emotional beauty.

At the end of the twentieth century, contemporary expressions of architecture spawned by modernist tenets dominate our entire world. This Chapter showed that such an architecture deliberately opposes nature by minimizing certain components of *structural order*, and in so doing, violates deeply-seated feelings that are an intrinsic part of human consciousness. Until now, people have been frustrated by the removal of *structural order* from their environment and the imposition of buildings that make us feel uncomfortable. The above results should convince people that their intuitive feelings of architectural beauty are correct, and that a nourishing man-made environment could once again be made possible.

Chapter Two

A SCIENTIFIC BASIS FOR CREATING ARCHITECTURAL FORMS

1. ARCHITECTURE AND HUMAN PERCEPTIONS.

Architectural design can be founded on scientific principles that are analogous to structural laws in theoretical physics and biology (Alexander, 2004). The set of rules presented in the previous Chapter applies to create novel forms having a common *structural order* with physical and biological forms, while encompassing most traditional architectural styles as well. By adopting them, the development of architectural forms can be divorced from specific images that define a particular style.

Human beings possess a basic instinct about forms that is linked to our ability to visually discern potential dangers as well as sources of benefit in our surroundings. Certain mathematical relationships implicit in a building's form, or their absence, will trigger either a positive or negative subconscious response. The presence of essential mathematical harmonies is perceived instinctively, and is emotionally fulfilling — this is the foundation of much of religious architecture. For several millennia, architecture was based on the user's emotional comfort. In our time, however, formal design criteria have taken priority over human feelings, so that many buildings feel unpleasant yet at the same time they are admired on an intellectual level (Sommer, 1974).

This Chapter develops a *scaling rule* that links human perceptions to geometry and materials. Using this *scaling rule* in design gives a result that feels instinctively closer to a natural structure than when the rule is violated. My objective is to connect buildings to human beings by means of a building's intrinsic design and internal subdivisions. This concerns a major aspect of architectural design: the exterior and interior appearance, and details. The proposed *scaling rule* says nothing about the plan or overall shape, nor the spaces in a building. It does dictate the subdivisions of the elevation, and it explains our connection to natural materials. What occurs in practice is that paying attention to scaling relations among design components prevents major errors, and narrows down the design to different choices that are equally supportive of human well-being. Different buildings can have different internal and external scales and still be perceived as unified. What is important is how each building's scales are related to one another.

Scaling coherence is achieved by two separate processes. First, a discrete hierarchy of different scales follows from the *scaling rule*, which is derived from physics and biology. Second, all the components in the natural scaling hierarchy are visually connected — forms are related on each individual scale, and an overall coherence is created by linking forms on the small scale to forms on the large scale (Alexander, 2004). How forms achieve *scaling coherence* was briefly discussed in Chapter 1. The present Chapter is devoted to establishing the natural scaling hierarchy and its *scaling rule*; the problem of connecting the elements is left to the last section of this Chapter (Section 11), which includes a helpful checklist intended as a self-contained practical guide for architects.

I believe that contemporary architecture can benefit from the approach presented here. Nevertheless, certain design conventions used today violate the proposed *scaling rule*. Therefore, we need to examine why contemporary design generates the particular forms it does. In Section 10 of this Chapter, the use of a scale model (such as the cardboard models architects use when formulating their ideas) in design decisions is singled out for special criticism, because such a small scale cannot reveal the natural scaling hierarchy. Suggestions are offered on what changes in the design process should be made in order to implement this program.

This Chapter and the following one develop the Third Law of *structural order* introduced in Chapter 1 of this book, giving a more detailed derivation and presenting the results in a manner so that they are more directly applicable to design. Using the Third Law in practice requires us to formulate two related but distinct concepts: the *scaling rule*; and the property of *scaling coherence*. The *scaling rule* was stated in concise form in Chapter 1, Section 3. Here, I provide practical formulas that architects can use to apply the *scaling rule* to their buildings. *Scaling coherence* is treated in Section 11 of this Chapter, and is discussed in much greater detail in the following Chapter, *Hierarchical Cooperation in Architecture: The Mathematical Necessity for Ornament*.

2. THE NATURAL SCALING HIERARCHY.

Nature connects to human consciousness through forms and colors, and also via a seldom recognized *scaling rule*. Empirical studies show that most natural objects exhibit a natural scaling hierarchy, starting from their largest dimension, down by approximately a ratio of 2.7 to the smallest perceivable differentiation. The number 2.7 is the scaling ratio between consecutive scales. Say a 15 cm rock or leaf has smallest details at 1 mm. It might have additional visible differentiations roughly of sizes 3 mm, 7 mm, 2 cm, and 5 cm. On the other hand, the smallest perceivable scale of a mountain could be 1 km, depending on how far away you are standing. The entire mountain could be 3 or 7 or 20 times the smallest visible detail at that distance (i.e., powers of 2.7).

An object with *scaling coherence* has differentiations starting from its largest dimension and decreasing by a scaling ratio of approximately $e \approx 2.7$ down to the smallest perceivable detail. As will be discussed later, the scaling ratio 2.7 is that ratio among many alternatives by which *scaling coherence* is established and understood. Buildings that obey this *scaling rule* share a coherence common to natural forms. The *scaling rule* is only one of several requirements for a design to appear "natural". Something appears "natural" if it is intuitively perceived to have a stable geometrical structure, to coordinate its component parts, and thus to offer the same genre of feedback as a stable physical structure found in nature. On the other hand, buildings that ignore the *scaling rule* are perceived as lacking an essential quality necessary for visual coherence. Recently, both architects and scientists have realized that architectural design can be understood in terms of the same laws of complexity as natural systems, although the exact connection has been elusive (Halliwell, 1995).

A building of 20 m height should have well-defined structures that are roughly 7 m, 3 m, 1 m, 30 cm, 10 cm in size, down by a scaling ratio of 2.7 to the smallest perceivable scale. Each scale is defined by similar units of the same size that repeat. When using traditional building materials and methods, the limited strength of the materials helps to generate these approximately correct subdivisions, though many architects intentionally suppress the intermediate and smaller scales for reasons of style. Stronger modern materials and methods of construction make it easier to avoid the natural scaling hierarchy entirely. If one does not deliberately incorporate the correct subdivisions as part of the design, then the structure is perceived subconsciously as contrasting with natural forms (Alexander, 2004).

Obviously, any man-made structure that does not explicitly copy a natural structure will contrast with natural forms. It is my contention, however, that there is a much deeper connection that follows not from the appearance, but from the underlying mathematical structure. If the way components are combined corresponds to that of natural forms, then a man-made structure will be perceived as natural, even when its appearance is clearly artificial. The great religious buildings throughout human history do not resemble any natural form, yet we feel perfectly at ease with their *structural order*. That is due to how their components cooperate to achieve visual and structural coherence. History tells us that human beings have a built-in need for structures with a natural scaling hierarchy.

Previous applications of mathematics to design theory have little in common with the approach of this Chapter. I apply modern mathematics such as similarity transformations and fractals, which go far beyond simple proportional ratios or fixed modules. The Golden Ratio $\Phi \approx 1.618$ was widely used in the past to define the proportions of rectangular forms (von Meiss, 1991). That determined either the overall form or the plan of a building, both of which are of secondary importance in the present theory (which focuses on the immediate visual connection to forms and surfaces). Scaling, as used here, governs the internal subdivisions of forms, which are found to be essential in natural systems. The overall shape and plan are left free by the method proposed in this Chapter, to be determined entirely by a building's practical requirements and the functional ordering of forms. Architects tend to work through the plan and grid systems, which I intentionally de-emphasize. Not that it is unimportant, but scaling coherence needs to arise from all the dimensions, and not just the plan. For example, the building's entrance needs to stand out while defining one of the scales in a natural scaling hierarchy.

According to Mike Greenberg (1995a; 1995b), the most fruitful advance in this work may be the choice for the scaling ratio as the irrational number $e \approx 2.718$, the base for natural logarithms. Modular systems of design — typical of the modernist ethic and modern technology, but also of traditional Japanese architecture — are based on integral multiples of some basic dimension. Fully modular systems tend to have a scaling ratio of exactly 2 or 3. The use of e as a scaling ratio prevents the rigidity and monotony that are often the consequences of a modular system. One cannot simply repeat a basic unit here, but has to define distinct forms at every new scale. This is the topic of Chapter 8, *Modularity and the Number of Design Choices*.

3. THE ORIGINS OF SCALING IN NATURE.

A building's design consists of components having different sizes, some of them repeating to cover a larger area. These sizes are our architectural observables, which define the perceivable ensemble of units and pieces. In quantum mechanics, observable energy states are quantized and not continuous. It turns out that architectural observables representing lengths and areas should also be quantized to some degree. A common feature of all natural forms is the existence of distinct scales. Pure natural forms without subdivisions on a macroscopic scale are extremely rare; most examples around us are man-made. The reasons for this are many and varied, yet the result is universal.

When an ensemble of objects has a continuous distribution of sizes, there is a chance of finding one or more of them of any given size, provided that it is neither smaller than the minimum, nor larger than the maximum. (One example is the length of tree branches found on the ground in the woods). In a quantized distribution, however, there exist several discrete sizes. All objects in that set can only be one of those sizes (for example, the lengths of pre-cut lumber in a hardware store). If we write down those sizes, arranged in ascending or descending order, then we establish a discrete scaling hierarchy. Despite what one might too hastily conclude from these examples, I am not advocating modularity for all components, but rather the breaking up of undifferentiated objects into smaller components. The scaling ratio decides the size of the subdivisions.

Material fractures due to stresses and strains create a discrete scaling hierarchy in solids (see Figure 2.1). Even in fluids, homogeneity is not possible, as moving fluids generate a hierarchy of substructures due to turbulence. For entirely different reasons, scaling is necessary for biological forms. Life is the result of complicated chemical and physical connections occurring at many different scales simultaneously. Metabolic and mechanical processes characteristic of living forms require a nested hierarchy of different structures on many scales. Biological forms therefore exhibit a discrete hierarchy of interconnected scales from the macroscopic into the microscopic level of structure (see Figure 2.2).

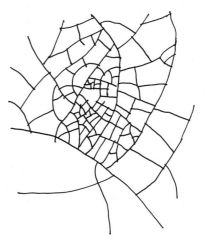

Figure (2.1)
Material fractures create a hierarchy of scales.

Figure (2.2)
Hierarchy of scales in human lung.

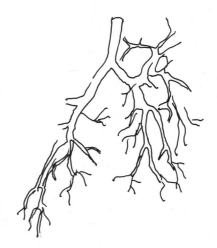

Suppose that a design has several distinct sizes of objects x_n , with the n-th scale defined by one or more objects of similar size to within a 20% spread. These units are identified by a definite shape, or by a clearly-defined edge. Objects don't have to be exactly the same size to be grouped into one particular scale. We can rank-order the components of a design from the smallest to the largest to obtain their hierarchy. Different components might be totally dissimilar; only their dimension is relevant for now. The simplest mathematical relation between them is for each scale size x_n to be related to the next largest size x_{n+1} by the same ratio k . (At this stage of the discussion, k could be any fixed number). Such a relationship gives an explicit formula for the size of the n-th component, with k a constant scaling ratio and x_{min} the minimum size. (Following mathematical convention, I will also denote x_{min} as x_0 , so as to label increasing sizes x_0 , x_1 , x_2 , x_3 , ...).

We thus have a formula for all the sizes in a design, given in terms of the smallest size x_0 and the constant scaling ratio k . It is a power law with successive powers k^n , $n = 0, 1, 2, ...$ of the same parameter k :

$$x_{n+1}/x_n = k \text{ , which implies that } x_n = k^n x_0 \text{ , with } k = \text{constant} \qquad (1)$$

A design with subdivisions obeying the simplest *scaling rule*, equation (1), will have the following property: some (though not necessarily all) parts of the design will have non-trivial structure when magnified by a factor of k . This process can be repeated n times to look at increasingly smaller details. This scaling property is most clearly shown in fractals, which exhibit some structure on every scale (Mandelbrot, 1983). An additional property of self-similar fractals is that successive magnifications have a similar design (see Figure 2.3). The fractal properties of diverse natural forms are becoming increasingly evident (Mandelbrot, 1983).

Figure (2.3)
Mathematical fractal with scaling ratio k = 2.

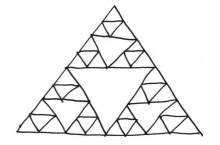

4. DETERMINING THE IDEAL SCALING FACTOR.

The validity of the above *scaling rule*, equation (1), is independent of the value of k; however, further arguments summarized below establish the ideal scaling ratio as being approximately equal to the logarithmic constant $e \approx 2.7$. It is this ideal scaling ratio that leads to *scaling coherence*. *Scaling coherence*, in turn, is a fundamental component of structural morphology (i.e., how internal structure influences the overall form of a complex object) in both inanimate and living forms, and is a property found throughout traditional architectures. Christopher Alexander originally established the *scaling rule* phenomenologically by measuring internal subdivisions in buildings, man-made artifacts, natural structures, and biological forms (Alexander, 2004). He gives a figure for the scaling ratio k as being somewhere between 2 and 3 (Alexander, 2004). I propose a single working value for the scaling ratio $k = e \approx 2.7$, based on the law of organic growth (discussed below).

The *scaling rule* that applies to endow architectural form with *scaling coherence* is thus very specific, and is expressed as the ideal ratio between successive scales in a building.

$$\textbf{\textit{Scaling rule:}} \quad x_{n+1}/x_n = e \approx 2.7 \qquad (2)$$

Before applying this *scaling rule* to design, I will justify it with some examples from nature. Exponential growth arises naturally if the change in size is equal to the size at that point. The relation $dx/dt = x$ for the quantity or measure x at any time t has solution $x = x_0 \exp(t)$, where x_0 is the initial value (and, in the case of exponential growth, the smallest value). The values of an exponentially-growing quantity x at integer time intervals $t_n = n$ obey the *scaling rule*, equation (2). Exponential growth is a fundamental law of nature. The growth of bacteria and ideal animal populations in time obeys the relation $x = x_0 \exp(at)$, a = constant (for the period of unconstrained growth). The same rule holds true for the shape of seashells and horns, whose form is described by an exponential curve known as the logarithmic spiral in polar coordinates (r, θ) as $r = \exp(a\theta)$, a = constant (Thompson, 1952). These examples indicate how the scaling rule applies to many situations outside of architecture.

Scaling coherence depends on the levels of scale being close enough to visually relate to each other, yet not so close that the difference in scale is indistinct. A scaling ratio k less than 2 fails to sufficiently distinguish between different levels of scale, so there is no discrete hierarchy. For example, a scaling hierarchy based on the Golden Ratio $\Phi \approx 1.618$ (such as Le Corbusier's Modulor) has its subunits too close in size, so they define more of a continuous gradient rather than discrete (quantized) scales. As a consequence, our perceptual apparatus cannot easily group structural units into a discrete hierarchy of scales, hence it cannot even begin to check whether the scales are spaced ideally or not. If, on the other hand, the scaling ratio k is much larger — say, 10 — structures that far apart in size are so unconnected that consecutive levels of scale fail to visually relate to one another (see Figure 2.4). This heuristic argument narrows the ideal scaling ratio to a number somewhere between 2 and 5, consistent with my choice of e for the *scaling rule* in equation (2).

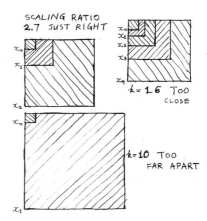

Figure (2.4)
Of the three scaling ratios, only one gives scaling coherence. With scaling ratio k = 1.6 the scales are too close. With scaling ratio k = 10 the scales are too far apart. With scaling ratio k = 2.7 the scales are spaced just right.

To illustrate what I am talking about, consider inserting a window in the middle of the wall of a small room. If the window is about 1/3 the width of the room, then it fits in perfectly well. The ideal width would be about $1/2.7 \approx 0.37$. This "rule of 1/3" predicated on using the scaling ratio $e \approx 2.7$ has been applied by master architects throughout history. If, on the other hand, one cuts the wall and inserts a window that is more than ½ the room's width, then one has changed the wall into a window — the integrity of the wall has been sacrificed to the window. There is no longer a hierarchy of "wall containing a window". This would certainly occur when using a window of width $1/1.618 \approx 0.62$.

Separate theoretical support comes from fractal patterns in mathematics. There is an infinite number of self-similar fractal patterns, each with similarity ratio $r = 1/k$. (Note that mathematics books use the "similarity ratio", whereas architects use its reciprocal, which is the scaling ratio). These fractal patterns have the remarkable property that any detail, when magnified by the scaling ratio $k = 1/r$, looks exactly like the whole. It is well known that self-similar fractals can be used to model natural structures such as mountains, coastlines, cauliflowers, and snowflakes. Of all the possible Koch, Peano, and Cantor self-similar fractals, those that correspond best to natural forms have similarity ratios $r = 1/3$ or $r = 1/\sqrt{7} = 1/2.65$ (Mandelbrot, 1983). If we had to pick a single universal value for the scaling ratio, these figures support the choice $k = 1/r = e \approx 2.7$ (see Figure 2.5).

Figure (2.5)
Mathematical snowflake with scaling ratio k = 3.

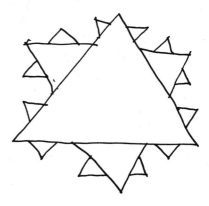

5. SOME CONSEQUENCES
FOR ARCHITECTURAL DESIGN.

The *scaling rule* explains why some asymmetric structures can appear surprisingly ordered in the sense of giving emotional satisfaction. Examples that satisfy it include buildings by Antoni Gaudí (Zerbst, 1993) and Lucien Kroll (Kroll, 1987). Also, some free-form "organic" buildings may appear strange to academic architects, but, if they obey the *scaling rule*, they undeniably give pleasure to their inhabitants (Day, 1990). Such buildings need not have Classical symmetry, nor follow any recognizable archetypes. According to traditional criteria that also govern modernist forms, buildings without any obvious overall symmetry are not thought to be ordered, as most people tend to identify "order" with symmetry, but that misses the contribution of a scaling rule. Those buildings that follow the *scaling rule* satisfy one of the several requirements for *structural order* in a design, independently of any symmetry (Alexander, 2004).

There is another point of considerable practical significance. Weathering patterns are due to fractures and stresses on materials. Morphological features in materials are generated by physical forces, which will tend to create a hierarchy of substructures that follows the *scaling rule* (Alexander, 2004). This is a remarkable observation, and it is consistent with the fractal development of material surfaces in time, which develop cracks, then smaller cracks between the cracks, and so on down into the microstructure (Mandelbrot, 1983) (see Figure 2.1).

All structures eventually develop morphologically towards a natural scaling hierarchy, regardless of materials used, or how they were initially put together. If a building's structural subdivisions (i.e., where forms join with and transition from one to another) fail to coincide with a natural scaling hierarchy, then the weathering patterns might cut across forms. It certainly doesn't make it easy to maintain the architect's original intentions. This process is clearly evident on large "pure" surfaces, which inevitably stain. In those cases where an architect pays attention and anticipates weathering by using smaller design components (subdivisions) to take up stains without showing, the result definitely obeys the *scaling rule*. Weathering tends to reinforce the design subdivisions of a building with *scaling coherence* that results from the *scaling rule*. For this reason, traditional architectures weather well, whereas modernist forms do not (Blake, 1974).

Going against the fractal staining of surfaces and refusing to subdivide them has led to the preference for materials that show weathering patterns in 10 years instead of 10 weeks. This is the reason we see a proliferation of high-tech — and very expensive — materials such as stainless steel, titanium, etc. These are not selected because of genuine architectonic needs, but simply from the desire to oppose the inevitable development of natural fractal patterns due to weathering. One reads about architects' quixotic, stubborn quest for a truly "modern" material that doesn't weather. Seldom is the basic stylistic/ideological motive behind this goal ever questioned.

6. A SEQUENCE THAT DEFINES DESIGN SUBUNITS.

Many architects are already familiar with theoretical descriptions of ratios in terms of the Fibonacci sequence. I will present the above results for the *scaling rule* in a practical manner, by giving a sequence consisting of powers of $e \approx 2.718$ rounded off to the nearest integer. Practitioners can then check that the subunits of their designs correspond approximately to the terms in the given sequence. The important point is not strict agreement with each number — these can differ widely in application — but one should make sure that no terms are missing. This is only a help and not a rigid rule. The following sequence of integers approximates the powers of e for $n = 0, 1, 2, \ldots$:

Sequence of scaling factors:

$$\text{Integer}\{\, e^n \,\} \approx \{\, 1, 3, 7, 20, 55, 148, 403, 1097, 2981, 8103, \ldots \,\} \qquad (3)$$

There are two ways to use this sequence of scaling factors, which gives the entire range of relative sizes of subunits in a design. The first way is to choose the smallest architectural detail x_{min} (also labeled x_0), and then multiply it by the terms of the sequence of scaling factors, equation (3), to obtain the sizes of all the larger units. These sizes must coincide with what are already established sizes from functional requirements, otherwise one has to redefine x_{min} and start all over. Alternatively, one may start with x_{max} as the largest overall size (i.e., the biggest dimension of a room or building), and divide by the terms of the sequence of scaling factors, equation (3), to obtain the sizes of all the subunits. Again, one must recover the correct intermediate sizes that are determined by functional requirements, otherwise x_{max} has to be adjusted. Deciding which method to apply depends upon which dimension, x_{min} (the smallest) or x_{max} (the largest), is fixed. Either progression — small to large, or large to small — will generate a natural scaling hierarchy that satisfies the *scaling rule*, equation (2). This method can help to find scaling relationships that can bring harmony to a building. Note how all scales are interrelated, and one cannot change one without ideally affecting all the scales in a building.

Certain readers will recognize that the sequence of scaling factors, equation (3), initially corresponds approximately to the alternate terms { 1, 3, 8, 21, 55, 144, 377, 987, 2584, 6765, ... } of the full Fibonacci sequence. The correspondence becomes progressively worse for larger terms. Alternate terms of the Fibonacci sequence have scaling ratio $k = \Phi^2 \approx 2.618$ in the limit as the terms become large, whereas the sequence of scaling factors, equation (3), is an integer approximation of a sequence of numbers with fixed scaling ratio $k = e \approx 2.718$. As the scaling rule is only approximate, this resemblance is useful and of considerable practical interest..

7. THE NUMBER OF DIFFERENT SCALES IN THE HIERARCHY.

In principle, *scaling coherence* defines an infinite number of decreasing levels of scale in any design. For practical purposes, however, I impose a low-end cut off for the minimum detail that we want to show in a building. Taking this lower limit to be 6 mm $\approx$ (1/4) in provides a useful rule for estimating the total number of different levels of scale. If x_{min} is the smallest size of a design subunit (corresponding to $n = 0$), and $x_{max} = e^{n-1} x_{min}$ is the largest overall size, then we can solve for the *ideal number of scales n* , by taking the logarithm of both sides of this expression. This is what we need. Rounding off to the nearest integer value, the *ideal number of scales n* is computed as follows (see also Section 3.3 of Chapter 1, where the *ideal number of scales* was originally derived):

$$n = 1 + \ln x_{max} - \ln x_{min} \qquad (4)$$

Here, x_{max} and x_{min} must be expressed in the same units. For example, if we are going to measure the overall dimension x_{max} in meters, then choosing $x_{min} = (1/4)$ in $= 6.4 \times 10^{-3}$ m gives the *ideal number of scales n* in terms of the building's largest size x_{max} only:

Ideal number of scales:

$$n = 6 + \ln x_{max} \text{ (measured in meters)} \qquad (5)$$

A building of height or width x_{max} meters therefore needs to have distinct subunits of exactly *n* different sizes — the *ideal number of scales n* given by equation (5) — in order to appear coherent. If a building has either significantly fewer levels of scale, or significantly more, it will appear incoherent. Equation (5) for the *ideal number of scales* tells us that the majority of buildings, which range in size from a short building with $x_{max} = 5$ m to a tall building with $x_{max} = 50$ m, have to have 8 to 10 distinct levels of scale if their smallest detail is going to be $(1/4)$ in (where I have used the values $\ln 5 \approx 1.6$ and $\ln 50 \approx 3.9$). Even when a building has the required number of scales, the relative sizes have to further obey the *scaling rule*, equation (2) in this Chapter. The degree of *scaling coherence* will of course depend on the similarities and wide boundaries of all the different scales (as discussed in Section 11 of this Chapter, below).

8. CONNECTING TO THE HUMAN SCALE.

Starting with Vitruvius, writers underline the necessity for architectural forms to have features on a scale to which human beings can relate (Licklider, 1966). There are two independent problems of scale here. The first is use and physical contact: a building's components and dimensions must accommodate people, their anatomy, movement, and tactile sense. Room sizes, staircases, banisters, placement and dimensions of doors and windows, door handles, etc. have to be carefully fixed for maximal ease of use. A sensitive architect fits the geometrical forms and accessible features of a building to activities on the human scale.

The second problem is how a design's subdivisions are actually perceived, and it is solved by establishing the natural scaling hierarchy. At any given distance, a person will connect to design components that correspond to the entire human structural scale: the whole body; an arm's length; a foot; a hand; a finger's width; etc. (Licklider, 1966). This impression is visual and relative, and depends on the changing distance between the viewer and the structure. It is necessary to define designs that have the complete range of internal subdivisions, regardless of the viewer's distance. Only a building with *scaling coherence* from top to bottom provides the complete range of human scales to an observer at any distance, and from any perspective.

The smallest perceivable size obviously depends on the distance between the observer and the object. If a portion of a building can only be experienced from a large distance, then the smallest perceivable scale is rather large. Some structure should be defined on that scale, but more detail is going to be wasted. Buildings tend to have unnecessary precision, or expensive materials, where they cannot be experienced. That wastes resources that are better spent on areas accessible to human contact. In many situations, the user can move closer or further away from a region, so the smallest perceivable scale is changing continuously. In that case, there must be detail down to the smallest of the "smallest perceivable scales". The detail will be lost at larger distances, but will re-appear when needed at the closest approach.

This principle of connected scales at every distance makes a dramatic difference to a user's experience of larger buildings. If a large building is connected to the range of human scales through a natural scaling hierarchy, it will be perceived in psychologically positive terms. It could then be described as awesome, grandiose, and impressive, in a way that is largely independent of other attributes. On the other hand, if a building disconnects from the human scale by eliminating the smaller scales in the scaling hierarchy, it detaches and is perceived in psychologically negative terms. Independently of other design factors, it will be felt as aloof, severe, or it might even appear so alien as to be oppressive. Some architects deliberately strive for such an aloofness.

9. CONNECTING TO BUILDINGS VIA MATERIAL SURFACES.

If we don't stop it at 6 mm, the natural scaling hierarchy has no rigidly-defined lower limit. The smallest perceivable size depends on the distance to the viewer, and at the closest approach goes down to less than 1 mm. In humans and animals, the most expressive forms are highly detailed: e.g., the eyes, nose, and mouth. Here the details indeed go down to below 1 mm. Note that distinguishing details occur locally, and focus attention onto a small region: the same degree of detail does not usually spread over the entire form. It is the existence of detail where it can be experienced that is important, and not its profusion.

Architecture connects to the human consciousness via the smallest details, whether those buildings are in a traditional, modernist, or any other style. The psychological need for detail at the smallest perceivable scale is illustrated by the widespread use of natural surfaces such as polished wood and stone, whenever it is economically feasible. Such surfaces provide an emotional connection to details well below 1 mm in size. The eye actually perceives the natural structures that characterize real wood or marble, even though they are at the limit of visual perception. One is not easily fooled by Formica even at a distance. Using known materials establishes a personal, emotional connection because we feel related to their microstructure.

Here is where one of the great disconnections in twentieth-century architecture occurred. Surface qualities were thought of as separate from tectonic form, even though both are merely expressions of form and pattern on vastly different scales. All the polemics against architectural ornament in the twentieth century clouded the basic issue of scale connectivity. There are good forms and patterns on both the large, and on the smallest scales. Great buildings succeed because they manage to unify their largest scale (overall forms and patterns) with their smallest scale (surfaces, details, and ornament). Paint on a wall may be 1/10 mm in thickness, yet it can play a major role in how we connect to that wall through color and quality of surface. Just because it is much easier to replace the paint than the wall itself is no reason to dismiss its connective role. At the same time, Formica totally lacks the ordered microstructure of real wood (thickness, grain, and reflective properties), which reveals it to be fake.

It is possible to highlight the connection between an observer and the microscopic structure of materials, obtained via the natural scaling hierarchy. From the human scale on down, there exists an infinite hierarchy of decreasing scales connecting us to the basic components of matter. This downward scaling links us to the microcosm, and is just as important as the more obvious connection to the larger scales. We establish a strong connection to materials that have a clear hierarchical microstructure, but not to featureless materials that are either amorphous, transparent, or highly reflective.

Materials lacking in natural qualities often result in unresponsive surfaces. That is in part due to the ways they are employed. Industrial materials (synthetic or composite), which as a rule have no ordered microstructure, are not liked because we cannot relate to such surfaces. They can establish an emotional connection only when the natural scaling hierarchy is used to create scaling through pattern, and this has to occur on the macroscopic scales. The process has to be deliberate, because the result is harder to achieve than with natural materials. One needs to differentiate surfaces and to articulate subdivisions much more than with materials whose microstructure follows a natural scaling hierarchy. That might involve combining matte with shiny materials, and re-introducing detail and color. I do not advocate superficially copying the attributes of natural materials, but rather finding expressive means to utilize each material's own intrinsic capabilities.

10. THE USE OF MODELS
IN ARCHITECTURAL DESIGN.

Whereas a design model or a drawn plan pays attention to detail at the smallest perceivable scale on the model or plan, this becomes far too large when built. A building consequently loses its crucial levels of scale. The reason is that the different scales in the natural scaling hierarchy increase exponentially, and therefore lie much closer together at the smaller scales (see how small the difference is between the first terms in equation (3) of Section 6, above, compared to how big the difference is between the larger terms). Say, a typical model of a 40 m tall building shows 3 levels of scale before the detail is lost. We automatically lose the smallest 7 levels of scale, which are those that we connect to most strongly. The full-size building, however, will have 10 levels of scale if the built detail goes down to 5 mm (from equation (5)). Take x_{min} = 5 mm and multiply by the ten terms of the sequence of scaling factors, equation (3): 5x1 = 5 mm, 5x3 = 15 mm, 5x7 = 35 mm, ... ending up with x_{max} = 40 m as the largest size. When working in drawings or models, we normally cannot show those scales, thus they don't make it into the final building.

The design process generally begins on an intellectual level, using a set of ideas to plan a new structure. A building's functions should determine the initial design, though in many cases those are subordinated to the building's image. What ultimately defines the success of a building is a set of emotional responses arising from forms at the full built scale, when we can experience all the smaller scales directly (Alexander, 2004; Day, 1990). Nevertheless, it is the reduced plans and miniature model that are routinely evaluated by the emotions they produce, and these can be misleading. The user's experience of the final building is totally different, yet commissions, prizes, and grades are awarded on the basis of these small-scale models and drawings.

A model may be judged by its novelty; its overall symmetry; how it fits pieces together; how it resembles familiar forms; if it has "clever" parts. Those decisions rest on factors that are specific to the model's actual scale. When the building is built, one's experience of the forms changes dramatically, and the original judgments based on the model are no longer relevant. Because of the perspective, the way that large forms fit together cannot be easily perceived at the full scale. The building's overall shape usually doesn't matter to a user inside. Any similarity between the total plan and familiar forms is apparent only from an airplane. Things that look "clever" in a model might turn out to be oppressive and dysfunctional when built.

Critical decisions depend on feedback that cannot be triggered by a small-scale model. The only way to determine this accurately is from the interaction between a user and the full-scale structure and its subdivisions. This has to be anticipated during the design phase. A drawing that shows all the smaller scales has to be at or near actual size. Moreover, the success of architectural forms depends on the viewpoint of the observer: points close-by to a pedestrian are the most important, and points far away the least important. Relying too narrowly on a scale model reverses these priorities, ignoring the immediate spaces, and emphasizing large areas and forms that are invisible or inaccessible to a user. Fortunately, today we can mimic the full-scale experience in a building through virtual reality techniques using virtual reality simulated environments.

In practice, one uses a small, cheap-to-make model for getting the large forms in place, but should be constantly imagining how those spaces are going to be experienced from the inside and by an approaching pedestrian. Selected regions with which a user will come into close contact need additional sketches and partial models at a larger scale. Full-size mock-ups built from inexpensive materials such as cardboard and styrofoam can help decide on the impact the full-size structure will have on the user, in those crucial regions of immediate contact.

These ideas will be of utility to readers given the interest in finding guidelines in a built environment that is often unresponsive, and is becoming increasingly chaotic and anarchic. There is a comfort in a natural scaling hierarchy. Computer-aided design offers the potential to assist in producing a three-dimensional design that satisfies the natural scaling hierarchy, but this has yet to be fully integrated into current practice and education. Given a generous tolerance in dimensions, one can determine if any particular scale is missing. This gives a "spell-check" to highlight particularly bad scale relationships before they are built. I will not attempt to describe the vast number of decisions encountered in designing thoughtful buildings. The rules introduced here provide a useful criterion that helps to narrow down the possibilities.

11. A CHECKLIST FOR
ACHIEVING SCALING COHERENCE.

The natural scaling hierarchy establishes the proper subdivisions, and the relationship between the different scales in a building. "The small scale is connected to the large scale through a hierarchy of intermediate scales with scaling ratio roughly equal to $e \approx 2.7$" (the *scaling rule*, equation (2) in Section 4, above). To achieve *scaling coherence*, however, it is necessary to go one step further and link the distinct scales together via similarity techniques as discussed by Alexander (2004) and in the first Chapter of this book. The following list summarizes how to connect the different levels of scale to each other — these are suggested means and should not be taken as absolute.

Table 2.1. Rules for achieving scaling coherence.

1. Define recognizable units through contrast in color and geometry at all scales in the natural scaling hierarchy.

2. Tie different units together through symmetry, overlapping designs, a common grid, complementary shapes, and matching colors.

3. Every unit needs a thick boundary (frame) that is itself a unit on the next-smallest scale — sequential units should couple visually with adjoining units.

4. Units of different size can link with one another by having a similar shape, so the same pattern repeats at different magnifications.

5. Similar patterns of decreasing size can be nested to define a geometrical focus, and this should coincide with a functional focus.

I am now going to discuss these five rules, and suggest how they apply to architectural design.

Rule 1 in the above list opposes the elimination of intermediate scales found in buildings that project a purist image (i.e., embody a minimalist geometry). Such buildings may have subdivisions, but they are often deliberately disguised or made too subtle, and so fail to differentiate the form's outline or frame. Many contemporary designs go to great lengths to disguise ordered structure at the small and intermediate scales, trying to achieve uniformity by eliminating components. Visual and textural contrast is necessary because it establishes the different scales we connect to. *Scaling coherence* harmonizes obvious components, which requires all the components of a design to be clearly articulated.

Rule 2 emphasizes the need for multiple symmetries in architecture. Reflectional (mirror) symmetries and translational symmetries (repetition along an axis) tie together groups of elements. The natural scaling hierarchy guarantees that symmetries can be defined independently on each level of scale. A building with *scaling coherence* has an enormous number of internal symmetries: there is one overall scale, and an increasing number of components populating each scale of decreasing size; symmetry can act on all of these scales. The number of smaller elements could be vast (see Figure 2.6). (With the elimination of the smaller scales, however, the only possible symmetry is an overall bilateral symmetry).

Figure (2.6)
Increasing number of units on smaller scales.

Rule 3 in the list helps to achieve *scaling coherence* by tying the different scales together through visual and physical contact. When a form's frame or thick boundary is the next-smallest term in the natural scaling hierarchy, and the boundary's boundary is the second-smallest term, and so on, then successive forms in the natural scaling hierarchy are paired geometrically. It is not enough simply to have forms of the right size according to the hierarchy: they must also be touching each other in the proper sequence. If sequential units are not tied together by proximity (something that fails to happen when an isolated small scale is juxtaposed with a large scale), then there will be a perceptible discontinuity in the scaling connection. It is the ordered progression of scales that leads to *scaling coherence.*

Proximity of scales means that units must be connected by intermediate borders. This "wide-boundary" concept is due to Alexander (2004), and is found in buildings throughout history (i.e., baseboard framing walls; trim framing ceilings, windows, and doors, etc.). Traditional materials having limited strength usually make a boundary whose size is comparable to what it bounds unavoidable, and many historical buildings deliberately accentuate this effect. For example, carved Romanesque doorways have a frame or trim that is as large as the door itself (see Figure 2.7). One normally has to work against the materials if one wants to minimize or disguise the connective boundaries in structures. On-site cutting of materials has a wide tolerance, making trim necessary to cover inaccuracies and gaps. Insisting on removing all trim to satisfy a stylistic dictate leads to vastly increased costs in off-site precision cutting of materials. Going off-site is one step towards modularity and fixed standard sizes, which can never adapt a design to local conditions.

Figure (2.7)
Wide frame on doorway intensifies it.

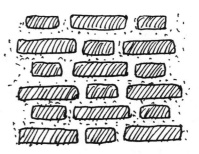

Figure (2.8)
Thick grout between bricks gives scaling coherence.

Sheer walls and large plate-glass windows in today's buildings do not contain the necessary scaling hierarchy. Historically, the thick grout between bricks defined a wide boundary for each brick, but modern bonded brickwork minimizes the mortar (see Figure 2.8). As a consequence, contemporary brick walls embodying a minimalist style lack *scaling coherence* and feel oppressive. In the same way, as long as glass could only be produced in small panes, the supporting framework provided the proper subdivisions; this contribution towards *scaling coherence* is entirely absent from large panes of industrial plate glass. Glass walls emphasize a technological advance that one cannot relate to, making us feel anxious because we sense a wall that is not there.

In our present technological condition, we still require the requisite scaling. We must imprint our buildings with the natural scaling hierarchy, no longer because of the weathering or failure of traditional materials, but because of the inherent need human beings have for *scaling coherence*.

Going now to the larger scale, a building has to fit harmoniously into its environment. The relationship of an object to its surrounding space is determined by the natural scaling hierarchy. A building's boundary — which is a region of comparable size as the building itself — should couple with the building to define the next-higher level of scale. Therefore, the building's outer border requires the same definition and connections as the building's internal subdivisions: the border must be an identifiable region. A proper boundary region connects the building to its surroundings. A building that draws attention to itself by either ignoring, or clashing with its surroundings is ultimately unsuccessful (Gehl, 1987).

Sometimes the boundary *is* the building, as in Medieval Cloisters and Islamic Madrassas. These work by focusing an intensely-detailed surrounding structure onto a central courtyard. Here, a complex boundary intensifies the open space (see Figure 1.4 in the previous Chapter). The coupling of two complementary opposites — the courtyard together with its bounding structures — creates a coherent unit. Coupling also occurs between randomness and highly-ordered detail. Some Mosques and Madrassas couple strictly-ordered ornamented walls to the courtyard's deliberately irregular paving stones (Blair & Bloom, 1994). This is an extremely sophisticated coupling between plainness/randomness and surrounding ordered detail. Louis Sullivan's banks use bricks with random variations in color and texture to contrast with a regular design in the surrounding border (Weingarden, 1987). This is the same idea of coupling opposites.

Rule 4 recalls that the simplest way to link distinct scales is to repeat a unit at different magnifications. Linking via the property of "self-similarity" is shown in many mathematical and biological fractals, and is a technique employed by master architects as well.

Rule 5 establishes a necessary link between built structure and function that is all too often ignored in contemporary buildings (Alexander, 2004). The use of gradients (such as found in a hierarchy of scales with increasing and decreasing sizes) to lead the pedestrian towards a focal point is extensively utilized in Hellenistic and Roman colonnades, later imitated during the Renaissance. Other applications include staircases that become narrower as they ascend, and doorways that focus one's movement through a sequence of concentric arches. Approaches and entrances that connect to the user in a positive and natural way make an enormous difference to a building's use.

12. CONCLUSION.

A *scaling rule* comprises part of a design theory proposed by Christopher Alexander. I have elaborated on this rule and provided some theoretical backing. The practical method described here is intended to produce buildings that connect subconsciously to users. By controlling the size and similarity of internal subdivisions, the design can be made to generate the same positive emotional response as natural forms. The *scaling rule* derives from physical and biological forms, so buildings designed using this *scaling rule* have an intrinsic structural similarity to natural forms, even as their shape need not resemble anything in nature. The *scaling rule* is independent of architectural style or particular building shape.

It is useful to summarize here all the new terms introduced in this Chapter. The existence of discrete measurable scales is a necessary but not sufficient condition to achieve *scaling coherence*. Two additional requirements towards that goal are that successive scales should obey the *scaling rule* with scaling ratio $e \approx 2.7$; and that each scale somehow links with every other scale (this is the topic of the following Chapter, *Hierarchical Cooperation in Architecture: the Mathematical Necessity for Ornament*). A structure with *scaling coherence* will exhibit the natural scaling hierarchy and will also have the *ideal number of scales*.

Buildings with *scaling coherence* look and feel very different from contemporary and earlier twentieth-century buildings. Architects wishing to adopt this Chapter's proposals will have to overcome a familiar and accepted way of building things. Many practitioners automatically strive for a "look" that eschews *scaling coherence*, without realizing what they are doing, and why they are doing it. The images that drive contemporary architectural design largely ignore the *scaling rule*. Following my analysis, a thoughtful architect will know what points to emphasize in developing innovative designs that have *scaling coherence*. My goal is a level of emotional satisfaction and human engagement from buildings in those places where little or none exists today.

Chapter Three

HIERARCHICAL COOPERATION IN ARCHITECTURE: THE MATHEMATICAL NECESSITY FOR ORNAMENT

1. ATTEMPTS TO FORMALIZE THE DESIGN PROCESS.

There have been numerous attempts to formalize the design process in architecture and in other fields. In the 1960s, there was a flurry of activity applying mathematics and *systems theory* to architectural design, starting with Christopher Alexander (Alexander, 1964). Also relevant is the work of Bruce Archer (Archer, 1970), Bill Hillier (Hillier, 1996; Hillier and Hanson, 1984), Christopher Jones (Jones, 1970), and Horst Rittel (Rittel, 1992). Sophisticated mathematical tools were utilized in setting up general models to handle the design process. The early work is summarized by Broadbent (1973). Many architects today believe that this effort ended in failure, as *systems theory* never entered into mainstream architecture.

It is true that the initial promise of a formal theory of architectural design based on mathematics never materialized. Nevertheless, such an approach found more fertile ground in engineering and programming, where it is now established as a major topic of research (Booch, 1991; Cross, 1989). Some of the above authors eventually expressed reservations that a comprehensive design theory was at all possible. This Chapter, which is based on Alexander's later work (Alexander, 2004), does not attempt to formalize a design method. It is a design constraint, which leaves the actual design and all its details up to the architect.

In offering a design constraint, I am in keeping with Hillier's prescription for a theory of design:

"What is needed are theories ... that are as nonspecific as possible to particular solutions in the generative phases of design in order to leave the solution field as large and as dense as possible, and as specific and rigorous as possible in the predictive phases in order to be able to deal predictively with unknown forms where the need for effective prediction is greatest." (Hillier, 1996: p. 68).

In the previous two Chapters, I introduced the notion of *scaling coherence* and the natural scaling hierarchy. I used examples of biological growth, fractals, and the natural weathering of materials to support my results. Much stronger and independent support for incorporating these concepts in design comes from *systems theory*. Now that the importance of *scaling coherence* in architecture has been established in Chapter 2, I will focus in this Chapter on how different design scales should link with and reinforce each other. This mechanism, denoted here as *hierarchical cooperation*, can be understood using *systems theory*.

Hierarchical cooperation is perfectly consistent with Hillier's requirement. It is necessary for achieving *scaling coherence*, but it does not dictate the overall form of a building or its specific design details. Except for Alexander, the explicit notion of *hierarchical cooperation* is not emphasized by other authors who applied *systems theory* to architecture.

Why did that early body of work have little lasting impact on architecture itself? It could be that much of the work was just too scientific for architects to accept. Architecture schools don't teach the higher-level mathematics needed to understand *systems theory*, and architecture students are not required to learn advanced science. Architects tend to be visually oriented, working through images and from formal rules, while being unaware of rules implicit in natural ordering systems. It is difficult to communicate a design method unless it can be done in intuitive terms, and *systems theory* was never presented to architects in a sufficiently intuitive manner. Also, the application of those early theories did not lead to any significant improvement of buildings, even in test cases. Scientific formalism was useful in comprehending the complexity of the problem, but was incomplete as a practical design tool.

Modernism offers a remarkably simple universal constraint on built form, which is easy to apply to any type of building. This is the root of its success, more so than any political or philosophical ideology. Its down side is that it is highly specific (hence not very adaptive) in the initial design phase, and narrows the solution space considerably, by reducing the number of possible building forms and types (see Chapter 5, *Life and Complexity in Architecture From a Thermodynamic Analogy*). Even critics of modernism have to admit that contending theories and styles hoping to displace the modernist style have not offered anything so simple. The present notion of *hierarchical cooperation* is slightly more complicated than pure, rectangular forms. This could indeed provide opportunities to innovative architects wanting to build according to the spirit of the times. That should be no problem in our computer age.

2. FORMS WITH AND WITHOUT HIERARCHICAL SUBDIVISIONS.

In the early 1920s, a preference for unadorned Platonic solids — such as simple cubes, cylinders, spheres, etc. — was established as one of the principles of the "new" architecture (Le Corbusier, 1927). Many people at the time assumed that regular shapes are somehow ingrained within the human consciousness, so that the mind is programmed to prefer them. We now know that this is false (Bonta, 1979). Human beings have to be trained to recognize Platonic solids, which are a purely intellectual concept (Fischler & Firschein, 1987; Zeeman, 1962). What *is* built into the human consciousness is a recognition mechanism based on hierarchical subdivisions, irrespective of the structure's overall shape.

The artificial preference for Platonic solids eventually became part of the twentieth century's architectural tradition. In fact, one may argue that modernist architecture owes its success to the fact that Platonic solids are almost never seen in nature as large-scale macroscopic forms. A building with a pure, abstract shape contrasts with the natural environment and therefore stands out. The sun and full moon

— both exceptional cases of perfect disks — were worshipped by ancient peoples. The same was true for monoliths. Humankind throughout history has built unnatural structures such as the pyramids assert humankind's dominance over nature.

Such simple forms lack *hierarchical cooperation*, but can appear exciting by virtue of being unfamiliar. That feeling, however, is not the emotional elation experienced inside a Medieval Cathedral. And yet, because they provoke a similar intensity of response, we often fail to distinguish between an uneasy, distressing excitement, and a deeply satisfying, nourishing visual excitement — which are totally different in their psychological effect. Thus, we neglect to question how each is produced in buildings. Environmental psychology clearly distinguishes the two cases (Nasar, 1989). Nevertheless, confusion still reigns in this topic, which provides the basis for architecture's impact on people. Our multi-dimensional emotional space is wrongly compressed by many architects onto the single dimension of arousal. Both modernist and Classical buildings are rationally understandable, and visually and emotionally evocative, but in almost opposite ways.

An architect chooses whether to follow or to ignore certain conceptual rules (whether explicit or innate) that relate a building to natural forms. All complex systems — natural as well as artificial (i.e., cathedrals, computers, electrical grids) — have distinct scales that cooperate hierarchically to define a coherent whole. A design constraint comes from *systems theory* and leads naturally to *hierarchical cooperation*. It also happens that this rule is built into the human consciousness. The underlying argument is based on the following three observations:

- Inanimate natural forms (such as rock formations, weather systems, and rivers) and biological organisms are complex systems that are hierarchically organized.

- Systems in engineering and computer science (such as large-scale electrical networks, computer chips, and software) have been found to follow the same hierarchical organization rules as natural systems.

- The human mind evolved in order to recognize and analyze hierarchical structures in nature, so artificial structures that are not hierarchically organized are perceived as alien.

Architecture creates artificial complex systems. In order to achieve emergent properties, architecture must organize matter according to hierarchical system rules (presented in Section 7, below). An emergent property is something that is not present in the components. All great architecture shows this. The exaltation felt in a Gothic Cathedral is not felt when standing in front of the piles of stones before their assembly. Evidence for this conclusion is presented throughout this Chapter, yet the truth of my claim is evident to any observer. If we can detach ourselves from our biases, which are culturally based, then we can test our favorite objects, buildings, and designs against this set of rules. Buildings and urban regions that satisfy *hierarchical cooperation* resonate with our own built-in perceptual mechanism for recognizing *structural order.*

Confronted with a man-made object or structure, we grasp all the different scales at once, automatically discerning its scaling hierarchy. In cases where the scales are ambiguous, our perception of *structural order* is frustrated. The scaling ratio and degree of similarity between successive scales determines whether the ensemble achieves *hierarchical cooperation* or not. If the scales are spaced the same way as in natural structures (i.e., obey the natural scaling ratio), and if they also correlate with each other via connections and similarities, we perceive the structure as a coherent whole. This subconscious process determines a building's impact independently of such traditional concerns as shape, form, and overall proportion.

Independent support for this theory comes from the science of cognition (neuroscience and the physiology of vision), though experimental psychology is not used as the primary argument here. There are two reasons for this. First, the nature of human perception has never been completely described, and is still a subject of much investigation. Second, the critical experiments that would demonstrate this phenomenon directly have not been performed, and the evidence, while supportive, is scattered and circumstantial. (See the next Chapter, *The Sensory Value of Ornament*, where I probe further into cognitive support for *structural order* and *scaling coherence*). Readers often confuse the need for symmetry (as manifested by the mental completion of missing regions of regular figures) with a non-existent predilection for Platonic solids.

3. ARCHITECTURAL SCALES.

Natural complex systems have a hierarchical structure, regardless of whether they are biological or inanimate (Simon, 1962; Smith, 1969). Most inorganic materials are crystalline (the exception being supercooled liquids such as glass). Material stresses create fractures that show as regular patterns, thus preventing a long-range ordering from continuing throughout macroscopic forms (Smith, 1969). Smoothness and uniformity (which are the visual manifestations of long-range ordering) are alien to natural materials, because they do not survive on the largest scale. In nature, structural features exist on different levels of scale, from the macroscopic to the microscopic, through all intermediate scales. We see in our environment physical forms that have a natural scaling hierarchy as a result of internal and external forces.

Biological forms also exhibit a definite scaling hierarchy. In decreasing order of size some examples are: communities of organisms in an ecosystem, organisms, organs, tissues, cells, organelles, membranes, molecules, atoms, and elementary particles, with many possible intermediate scales to these (Miller, 1978; Passioura, 1979). At different sizes, structurally coherent units will define a particular scale. The scales are distinct, yet they are also nested in a complex structure that exists in the large scale (see Figure 3.1). The same is true for built forms. Architectural scales arise from the materials, structure, and functions of a building, and their distribution expresses an architect's organizational ideas.

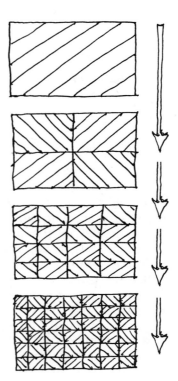

Figure (3.1)
More structure as the scale becomes smaller.

Methods used throughout the history of architecture to define scales include symmetry, as manifested through shape, fenestration, and columns. For example, windows — if they are of the same size — create a distinct scale. They can be repeated in a symmetrical pattern to define a larger scale. Subdividing a window into panes creates a smaller scale. Massing and monumentality define the largest exterior scale. Colonnades define several scales: the column's width; the inter-column spacing; and the column's base and capital (with fluting generating yet one more smaller scale). Interior scales are created by window and door frames, baseboards, and trim in various sizes, aided by contrast in materials, surface texture, and color.

Design units cooperate to achieve *scaling coherence* when a distinguishing characteristic connects them visually: if they have some portion of design in common, and if they have a similar texture or color. Although existing design methods can organize materials on a particular scale, there is no accepted procedure of how to space the scales themselves via a *scaling rule*, nor of how to correlate the different scales into a natural scaling hierarchy. (That's the reason I introduced a general theory of *scaling coherence* in Chapter 2). And yet, most human creations prior to the twentieth century (urban spaces, buildings, artworks, artifacts, tools, and machines) satisfy *hierarchical cooperation*. They achieve a balance between different design units according to their size. My objective is to cast this process into scientific terms so that it can be applied consciously and deliberately.

I now present four examples of natural and architectural structures and discuss the degree (either weak or strong) of *hierarchical cooperation* in each case.

Example A (strong). *Spanish Oak Tree.* Despite the apparently amorphous character of the tree, it is in fact subdivided into distinct scales. The trunk and main branches have a narrow distribution of lengths and roughly the same width. The secondary branches are about 1/3 the width of the main branches. Leaves are grouped into clusters that are about the same size as the width of the trunk; the leaves are distributed neither uniformly, nor randomly. The inter-leaf spacing on twigs tends to be regular. This hierarchical structure is evident once one looks for it. Organized detail goes all the way down to the microscopic scale. The size of leaves, twigs, acorns, and bark articulations define one or two scales, while their fine structure defines many scales smaller than these. There exists *scaling coherence* from the height of the tree at several meters, down to details below 1 mm (see Figure 3.2).

Figure (3.2)
A tree has a hierarchy of scales.

Example B (weak). *Small Bedroom.* The largest scale of a small room in the author's old apartment, painted white throughout, is 4 m. Two windows built together define a scale at 180 cm. The width of each window equals the door's width, which defines another scale at 75 cm. The window trim and door frame are both 7 cm wide. There is no other scale until we get down to 3 mm surface detail in the faint wall texture. Altogether, we have five scales (four obvious scales and one barely distinguishable) labeled x_i at { $x_0 = 0.3$ cm, $x_1 = 7$ cm, $x_2 = 75$ cm, $x_3 = 180$ cm, $x_4 = 400$ cm }. These are the distinct sizes of the room's components. It is instructive to compute the ratios x_{i+1}/x_i between consecutive scales, which yield approximately $x_1/x_0 = 23$, $x_2/x_1 = 11$, $x_3/x_2 = 2.4$, and $x_4/x_3 = 2.2$. As explained in Chapter 2, the first two numbers, 23 and 11, reveal the room's poor hierarchy, because those scaling ratios are far too big for *scaling coherence*. (A good ratio between consecutive scales has been established to be around 2.7).

Example C (strong). *Piazza San Marco, Venice.* This is one of the world's great outdoor urban spaces. It has been diagrammed, replicated, but its success is still incompletely understood. Here, a hierarchical explanation is proposed. Each surrounding building has subdivisions at roughly 1/3 its overall size, and further subdivisions at roughly 1/7, 1/20, etc. Richly-articulated detail is evident from all directions. The plaza itself is subdivided through the use of contrasting floor paving (Moughtin *et. al.*, 1995). Each building has *scaling coherence*, and the strongly established individual hierarchies link across space to create a coherent whole. It is the geometrical subdivisions, or architectural scales, of the disparate and visually dissimilar buildings around the plaza, that cooperate with each other and with the pavement to make us experience this space as a magnificent ensemble (this is an example of an emergent property).

Example D (weak). *Grande Arche de la Défense, Paris.* The pavement in front of and inside the arch does not relate to any other structure through scaling or similarity, because it has minimal features and subdivisions. The arch itself has very few distinct scales; by far not enough components to connect the structure internally through its design subdivisions, or to connect to a pedestrian, or to the plaza. Overall, the deliberate avoidance of hierarchy leads to the failure of the parts, despite their studied simplicity, to unify into a whole. The structure is of such enormous size that it is imposing, monumental, and under favorable weather conditions exciting; nevertheless, the entire range of human scales is missing so this excitement turns to a threatening sensation. A viewer cannot avoid feeling isolated. One searches in vain for hierarchical subdivisions. This structure is meant to impress and intimidate, but does not satisfy the human need to feel connected.

4. SIMPLICITY, FRACTALS, AND IMAGE COMPRESSION.

A design with a natural scaling hierarchy influences the viewer because it facilitates the process of human cognition. We are able to perceive a complex structure easily by reducing it to a number of distinct levels of scale. The more design subdivisions, the more scales there are. Human beings have a basic biological need to organize complex distributions of units into hierarchies as a means of avoiding information overload. First, the mind groups similar units of approximately the same size into one scale (Fischler & Firschein, 1987). Then, it looks for similarities or links between all the different scales. Since the mind has evolved in response to patterns found in nature and the natural scaling hierarchy, a certain set of rules for recognizing *hierarchical cooperation* is "hard-wired" within our perceptive mechanism (Fischler & Firschein, 1987).

The idea behind proposing the Platonic solids as fundamental in the early days of modernism was an effort to find simplicity and purity in design, and to apply it to new built forms. Inevitably, the notion of simplicity that belongs to ancient science is outdated: modern science has overturned our understanding of simplicity. This is of the utmost relevance to architecture, and is best discussed in the context of mathematical image compression: an image is simple if it requires the least amount of information to specify. There are many different ways of encoding an image, and I show how two of them imply radically different notions of simplicity.

The first method, called the "Graphics Interchange Format" (GIF), is commonly used for storing pictures electronically on the World-Wide Web. The algorithm divides an image into pixels on a rectangular grid, and looks for both horizontal and vertical repetitions. A repeating sequence on one row is coded compactly by entering the repeating group, along with its multiplicity. Thus, a horizontal line requires about the same information to represent in GIF as a single pixel. Horizontal lines that are the same do not need to be coded more than once; the same line is multiplied. In this way, any horizontal or vertical regularity is compressed. More sophisticated connections, ones that are seen automatically by the eye, pose serious problems for this particular algorithm of pattern recognition in wishing to emulate human perception (Fischler & Firschein, 1987). This rectangular compression scheme is not efficient at compressing complex, curved, and detailed images.

A newer, more powerful method is called "Fractal Image Compression" (FIC), and works much more closely to the way the mind itself works (Barnsley & Hurd, 1993; Fisher, 1995). Roughly speaking, fractal image compression identifies self-similarity at different distances and at different scales. It deals with pieces of the picture rather than individual pixels. Repeating units of the same size along any direction or directions are encoded as one design scale. Similar units that differ only by scaling are also grouped (corresponding to a cooperation across scales). This method works very well to encode faces, trees, and natural scenes. According to the general notion of "simplicity", natural, intrinsically fractal images are simple when encoded by the FIC compression scheme. Simple objects are not necessarily plain and rectangular, thus overturning the principal motivation behind visually empty modernist design typologies.

Neither GIF nor FIC can simplify random textures, because those have no spatial regularities. The information contained in a random array cannot be compressed. Every pixel is unrelated to every other pixel, so an encoding system has to identify all pixels separately.

In the first method (GIF) plain rectangular forms are the simplest, requiring the smallest amount of information to encode. In the second method (FIC), plain rectangles are simple, but so are fern leaves, snowflakes, and rock cliffs. Any structure that is hierarchical and self-similar (resembling the well-known pictures of fractals (Mandelbrot, 1983)) requires very little encoding. By contrast, rectangular GIF compression cannot handle such complex scenes well. This Chapter proposes an architecture that reflects the much more sophisticated simplicity associated with fractals, and which moreover has a far deeper connection to both natural and artificial complex structures, and to our own perceptual mechanism.

5. DIFFERENT SCALES IN A DESIGN.

What determines the visual and emotional impact of a building? Some factors, such as form and color, are obvious; just as important, though perceived only subconsciously, are its architectural scales. In a building (already built, or in the process of being designed), the architectural scales are determined by the size of all clearly-defined substructures. Different situations might require different measures such as area, width, or length. Any unit of measurement (cm, inch, foot, or meter) may be used as long as features of all sizes are measured in the same unit. We have to estimate the size of curved sections, the idea being to group similar units according to size.

All such measurements depend on clearly articulated differentiations of the structure on a particular scale. Distinct units arise only by contrasting against their adjoining units and background. There are several means of achieving this: sharp differences in grayscale value or color hue; an outline; a change in texture and materials; relief; etc. (see Figure 3.3). In those cases where the background or boundary also defines a unit, then those units will occur in contrasting pairs (see Chapter 1, Section 3). Vague or indistinct articulations might work to define a boundary when seen close-up, but that is insufficient to distinguish a unit when viewed at a distance. Intentionally subtle design transitions work against a natural scaling hierarchy by concealing or blurring the scales. Doing that removes a major factor contributing to design coherence.

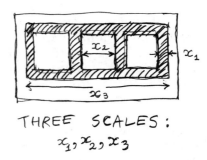

Figure (3.3)
Contrast is essential to define each architectural scale. Three scales: x_1 , x_2 and x_3 are shown.

One can measure either the width or the length of similar repeating units, depending on which is repeating. It frequently happens that two or more different types of units have the same size but different characteristics, and these will define coincident scales. Units could be aligned with translational, rotational, or reflectional symmetry, but that is not necessary for defining their own particular scale. An overall symmetry defines a new *higher* scale. (Units related by a similarity transformation — which occurs when a similar form is scaled up or down in size — do not form a scale, because they don't have a measurement in common; this is instead a method for linking different scales together).

Levels of scale have been defined with great care in the architecture and human artifacts of the last several thousand years. The concept of "modularity" is anchored in the fundamental need to perceive distinct architectural scales. A molding used throughout a building ties the entire space together through repetition. The possible scales in a building's scaling hierarchy arise from the physical structure, materials, and the need to accommodate physical stresses. Moreover, the result is crucial to how that building is perceived. Some of the greatest buildings in the world (Parthenon; Hagia Sophia; Dome of the Rock; Palatine Chapel; Phoenix Hall in Kyoto; Konarak Temple of Orissa; Salisbury Cathedral; Baptistry of Pisa; Alhambra; Masjid-i-Shah; Maison Horta; Carson, Pirie, Scott store; etc.) succeed in good part because they integrate their different subdivisions into a hierarchy of interconnected scales.

6. THE EMOTIONAL IMPACT OF ARCHITECTURAL SCALES.

How clearly architectural scales are defined, and how closely they correlate with each other, are now consequences of design decisions based on very different concerns. Those concerns are not geared towards establishing *hierarchical cooperation*. Contemporary design styles promote hierarchy reversal. Such buildings intentionally ignore the natural scaling hierarchy, defeating the organizational process that generates complex coherent forms. In a minimalist design approach, whole scales of articulation are removed. This minimizes complexity by trivializing forms. At the opposite extreme, both hierarchy and integration are prevented through the randomization of substructures (by intentionally making and shaping units so they don't relate to each other); this disorganizes the complexity so that it eludes human comprehension (Simon, 1962).

Either of the above extremes will result in a structure that lacks *hierarchical cooperation*. Up until now, that has seemed a viable design option justified by the application of a formal scheme, or the desire for innovation. In the first case, if one seeks a pure, regular geometric shape, then one does not want any internal structure. An architect desiring to express a Platonic solid in its purest state is led to an empty form. What happens more often is that this notion is appropriated by contractors to build a big-box building as cheaply as possible. Removing *hierarchical cooperation* from the environment changes it in a fundamental manner, and in a way makes it more vulnerable to inevitable changes. It also affects the emotional and physical state of the people in that environment, creating a source of anxiety and unease.

There is mounting evidence from experimental psychology supporting this phenomenon, though this work is far from complete (Alexander *et. al.*, 1977; Küller, 1980; Mehrabian, 1976; Sommer, 1974). One explanation is that the human mind has developed to recognize natural and living forms by analyzing their *hierarchical cooperation*. Any form that lacks those qualities creates alarm and so raises the adrenaline level. An unnatural, alien form attracts attention and uses up the brain's energy as it tries to figure out the form's organization. There is no comfortable state of coexistence with such a form: it goes against the ordering processes inherent in the mind, so it can never be experienced as visually (and psychologically) comfortable.

The model presented here is consistent with Gibson's theory of "direct perception" in psychology (Gibson, 1979; Michaels & Carello, 1981). According to that view, pattern perception does not begin with information input, then follow along a sequence of steps that processes the information according to different sets of criteria by turns; instead, patterns are perceived at the same time as they are seen. That is because the brain is closer to a massively parallel computer than to a sequential computer (Fischler & Firschein, 1987). The mechanism involves a kind of resonance established between an external structure and the internal structure of our cognitive system. Because this process is almost instantaneous, it is usually unnoticed by the observer. The effect itself is noticed, but not how it was reached.

The organization of a building into distinct scales (or lack thereof) has an immediate emotional impact on the user, which supports the Gibson theory of cognition. In the past, this effect of direct perception usually — though not consistently — created a definite positive emotional state. Our experience of traditional and vernacular buildings is instantaneous, and usually generates positive emotions. Nowadays, the reaction to many of our new buildings tends to be negative. We often face the contradiction of a building validated by formal design criteria, but which makes us feel uneasy. The imposition of alien qualities on buildings, however, is quite deliberate. Contemporary architects create images according to a particular style that ignores the natural scaling hierarchy and its integration in coherent structures.

I will illustrate what I mean by describing the opposite: how *hierarchical cooperation* is avoided, since this negative effect is more readily recognizable in contemporary buildings. Three different methods are shown, which may be summarized as follows:

Table 3.1. Three methods of avoiding hierarchical cooperation.

(a) *Too large a gap between scales.* This occurs when substructures intermediate in size between large forms and the smallest natural detail in the materials are suppressed. In buildings that depend on very fine detail, the median and smaller scales are often missing. An exaggerated jump from the larger to the smallest scales is felt immediately, creating a strongly negative reaction in the user. Boundaries between obvious subsections are usually removed or camouflaged, and this prevents the visual subdivision of larger forms into discrete components on an intermediate scale (see Figure 3.4).

Figure (3.4)
I compare the number of scales up to a magnification of 1,000 corresponding to different scaling ratios. For scaling ratio k = 1.6 there are fifteen different scales, too many for human memory to grasp. For scaling ratio k = 2.7 there are eight scales, which are easily related, since their number is around the number of digits in a telephone number. For scaling ratio k = 10 we have four distinct scales, which are too few to relate structures at such a magnification.

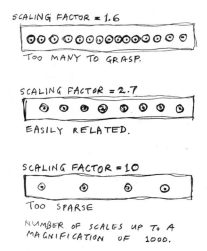

(b) *Elimination of the smaller scales.* Architects who promote a minimalist style tend to favor amorphous, homogeneous materials such as glass and concrete that have no intrinsic substructure at any scale, and especially no ordered microstructure. These are then employed in such a way that no smaller scales ever arise. A building is allowed to have very few scales, all of them large. Brutalist use of concrete removes the lower end of the scaling hierarchy (because it defines a rough surface devoid of organized details), leaving a user without any visual structure to focus on at arm's length.

(c) *Scales that are too closely spaced.* Blurring the distinction between scales destroys the scaling hierarchy. This results from too busy a design; one that includes many different non-matching units of not quite the same size.

Repetition and rhythm are essential for defining architectural scales, but these can be deliberately prevented through random variations. A natural scaling hierarchy is impossible to achieve when the scales themselves are indistinct, and even if scales are defined but they are randomly distributed. Some architects plan "randomness" very carefully, but it occurs more often through a lack of cooperation among different components that is a result of neglecting this component of design altogether (Figure 3.4).

For a building to be perceived as coherent, it needs a distribution of clearly defined architectural scales that satisfy *hierarchical cooperation* (see Figure 3.5). Whereas shape is purely a matter of choice in design, its subdivision into a scaling hierarchy is not. Just as in biological systems, the smaller scales are relevant because they support and anchor the forms on the larger scales. Internal coherence is possible only if all the subunits cooperate, therefore, anything that fails to cooperate should not be included. A form or detail is irrelevant if it doesn't integrate into the whole. While we find many examples of incoherent structures (in both traditional and modern styles) where large and small units fail to correlate to each other, the greatest buildings depend fundamentally on their details.

10 m

3.7m

1.4m

50 cm

20 cm

7 cm

2.5 cm

1 cm

⅓ cm

1 mm

Figure (3.5)
A two-storey building must have ten obvious scales.

7. HIERARCHICAL SYSTEMS AND EMERGENT PROPERTIES.

I now turn to the interdependence of different levels of scale in a structure. This topic has been extensively developed in *systems theory* and complexity theory, with significant recent applications to computer science and biology (Kauffman, 1995; Mesarovic *et. al.*, 1970; Passioura, 1979). The general properties of hierarchical systems (also called layered systems) can be summarized as follows. These rules apply to any discipline that deals with complex structures, and according to the thesis of this Chapter, also to architecture. My terminology is that a lower scale has the smaller units, and the higher scale has the larger units.

Table 3.2. Hierarchical system properties.

1. Units on a particular scale have their own type of interaction, which is independent of those in the other scales. Each scale has to be strongly defined before different scales can be combined to create a whole.

2. Higher scales result from constraints (expressed in terms of the higher scale) being imposed on lower scales. Many small units combine to make up a big unit (on a higher scale).

3. The interdependence of scales is only one-way: a higher scale requires all lower scales in order to function, but not vice versa. Large pieces depend on their small components.

4. Interaction across scales leads to correlations among all the different scales, and this process generates a coherent whole. Connecting different scales creates a system.

5. Emergent properties add new properties of structure to a complex, organized system, making it greater than the sum of its parts. The interactions among all the different pieces add something new to the whole.

Life generates hierarchical systems as observable organic structures (Miller, 1978; Passioura, 1979). Computer programs are hierarchical information systems with distinct, interconnected scales that have to cooperate (Booch, 1991). The increasing complexity of man-made systems has made it necessary to organize them internally in some practical manner, simply in order to understand them (Mesarovic *et. al.*, 1970). As a consequence of their complexity, these totally artificial entities have evolved a structured hierarchy that has many common features with natural forms, showing how the underlying rules are the same (Booch, 1991).

The significance of a unit in a complex structure is clarified as we view it from different scales in the scaling hierarchy, trying to grasp its organizational role in the whole. The need for any given unit may not be fully understandable on its own scale: it could be a necessary component supporting the structure on a higher scale (Mesarovic *et. al.*, 1970; Passioura, 1979). In an organized structure, every scale in the hierarchy contributes, with the downward dependence of larger on lower scales, yet the total effect is an effect of the system. A complex system does not depend solely on any single scale; neither can any scale be neglected or eliminated. Each scale has its own particular goal, which is indirectly supporting the organization of the whole.

The complex whole represents something not found in the isolated parts alone. A hierarchy links units together in ways they could not achieve on their own. When units of one scale combine to form the next-highest scale, a new and in some ways unexpected component of the total structure emerges; this is referred to as an "emergent property" (Kauffman, 1995; Miller, 1978). Those units combine into something not explainable in terms of the lower scale. A more encompassing whole includes the contributions of all the lower scales, while adding its own organizational principle (see Figure 3.6).

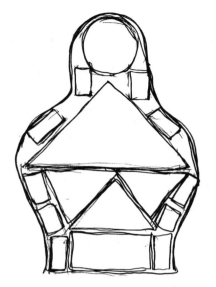

Figure (3.6)
A whole emerges from, and transcends its parts.

This point is really at the heart of my thesis, and links architecture with the new science of nonlinear phenomena. The assumption of nearly all nineteenth century mechanistic physics is that a complex system could never be more than the sum of its parts. In the last few decades, however, we have discovered a score of important phenomena that have emergent properties: properties of the system as a whole which cannot be traced back to any of its isolated constituent parts (West, 1997; West & Deering, 1995). That is, many complex systems are irreducible. This Chapter argues that the greatest architectural achievements are in fact characterized by emergent properties. Thus, my discussion is aimed at understanding what is happening in a great building that has achieved emergent properties so that it can be successfully applied to new structures.

Since it is impossible to guarantee positive emergent properties, it is also impossible to impose them in design. And yet, in architecture, the emergent properties, as experienced from the finished whole, establish our primary response to a building. Emergent properties that result from the interaction of all the components in unanticipated ways can result either in a positive effect (the awe experienced inside a Cathedral) or a negative effect (a piece of complex software that does not function as expected). Top-down design misses emergent properties, yet they are the most important component of great architecture. We need to recognize that our design capabilities are limited to the lower orders in the hierarchy of scales, and the overall effect is largely outside our control. We experience order from all the scales coming together, but can neither rigidly design this higher order, nor entirely quantify it (see Chapter 10 of Salingaros (2005)). I believe that the scaling ideas outlined here provide a basis for positive emergent properties, by making them possible and facilitating their emergence.

LARGE SCALE

Figure (3.7)
Lower scales are necessary for
higher scales to work.

SMALLEST SCALE
= FOUNDATION

All lower scales are necessary for the higher scales of a hierarchical system to work (hierarchical system property number 3 in Table 3.2, above) (see Figure 3.7). In plant physiology, this explains the effect of a herbicide (Passioura, 1979). A chemical blocks the working of a lower scale, and that is sufficient to sabotage (and kill) the organism. Similarly, a lower-scale bug crashes a big computer program. The same might be said of viruses and germs for the animals. In architecture, this principle implies a fundamental role for details. If a lower scale is lost, this sabotages the emergent properties.

8. THE MATHEMATICAL NECESSITY FOR ORNAMENT.

Natural scaling hierarchies arise from structural and functional reasons. We show a misunderstanding of nature if we interpret those hierarchical structures from our own, human viewpoint, as a visual style or effect. The marvelously complex hierarchy of a leaf or spider web has nothing to do with its aesthetic perception by humans (even though they appear beautiful to us): those structures existed long before human beings did, and actually helped to influence the way our mind developed. A hierarchy of distinct scales is a fundamental component of *structural order* that precedes humankind's emergence as a dominant species, because in nature hierarchy follows function (as demonstrated in the spider web).

This is obvious in much of architecture itself. For example, a Greek theatre is correctly subdivided into a hierarchy of cooperating scales, from its diameter down to the height of a step. Every one of those architectural scales has a functional basis. The ensemble happens to be beautiful, thus beauty is an emergent property of the utilitarian concerns (and is not something designed from the beginning). One can also find details that continue the scaling downwards from 30 cm (the height of a step) right to the smallest limit of visual perception (about 0.5 mm at arm's length). Some readers might argue that these smaller scales are irrelevant. Nevertheless, all the larger and intermediate scales arise out of functional requirements, and are therefore necessary, yet they are part of the same hierarchy as the smaller scales.

According to *systems theory*, the higher scales depend in an essential manner on all the lower scales (hierarchical system property number 3 in Table 3.2, above). If we eliminate any architectural scale for which we can think of no obvious functional argument, then we deny the coherence of the structure as a whole. There is a range of scales that is hard to justify from functional needs. These are the scales between 30 cm and 3 mm, and which exist most often in traditional architectures as ornament (Alexander *et. al.*, 1977). And yet, these scales — perceived as visually and emotionally correct in their original creative context — are necessary in order for the system to achieve the emergent properties that give it its coherence.

The same can be said for the even smaller scales defined in the materials' microstructure. Ancient Greek architects had very good reasons for choosing marble as the building material for their theaters, because its crystalline microstructure can be clearly perceived. The same strong connectivity through vision and touch cannot be achieved when one substitutes concrete, which lacks the visual scale in its structure. Most architects would love to be able to use natural textured surfaces whenever possible. Ironically, materials with a richly-ordered microstructure were also preferred by early modernist architects, at the same time that they eliminated the ornamental scales (3 mm to 30 cm) from their buildings. The question is again one of scales and the scaling hierarchy: if the scales exist, and whether they cooperate. The smallest scales can play a major role in how a building is perceived, completely disproportionate to their size.

At present, architectural theory lacks this argument entirely, and as a consequence leaves an important visual and psychological component out of the design process. If an architect feels either justified, or obliged by the prevailing style to eliminate any scales in the natural scaling hierarchy, then inevitably some scales necessary for the building's coherence will not be included. Twentieth-century architecture's neglect of *hierarchical cooperation* has severely compromised the coherence of buildings and urban regions. Where does one determine the lower cut-off at the smallest scale? Careful thought shows that there really is no smallest scale; all scales must decrease by steps until they meet the natural texture of the materials, which is at the limit of visual perception.

9. SYMMETRIES GENERATE THE HIGHER SCALES.

Higher scales arise from the geometrical ordering of lower-scale units. They could be aligned along a straight line or curve; or to form a pattern having a simple or complex symmetry. A constraint acts on the units of the lower scale, and is expressed as symmetry in the language of the higher scale. Translations repeat a unit in a straight line; rotations repeat a unit in a circle; reflections double a unit and tie it together with its reflection; and glide reflections (which combine translations with reflections) move a unit, then reflect it (Washburn & Crowe, 1988). All of these can act on different architectural scales, as seen in buildings throughout history. Out of an incredible wealth of mathematical symmetries, contemporary buildings tend to utilize only bilateral symmetry in rectangular forms, and often restrict this to the largest scale. Ironically, some form of symmetry is essential on all scales except the largest one.

There is no reason for symmetry on the maximal scale, as most of the functions of a building reside in the intermediate and smaller levels of scale (see Figure 1.8 in Chapter 1). Nor is a prominent large scale necessary from *systems theory*, because of the downward dependence of higher scales on all the lower scales. Symmetries and connections on all the lower scales are necessary to define the larger scales, but no symmetry is required of the largest scale. Great buildings and urban ensembles throughout history (with some notable exceptions) have a relaxed, complex overall shape as in the Piazza San Marco and the Masjid-i-Shah in Isfahan, which are approximately symmetric, or not symmetric at all. The rigidly symmetric exceptions are those cases where monumentality is desired, and it is frequently achieved at the cost of internal functions. Such buildings express authority and power, and some intensify the largest symmetric scale by suppressing the intermediate and smaller scales altogether. Examples include the pyramids; Fascist architecture; buildings around the world during the so-called "Heroic Age" of modernism; Canary Wharf; La Grande Arche de la Défense, etc.

Some architects disguise architectural units (the visual subdivisions of a building) through the use of empty surfaces, thus preventing *hierarchical cooperation* of scales; or they do the opposite, which is to arrange units in a way that avoids any symmetry. When units are spaced or aligned randomly, that region becomes incoherent. It can still be incorporated into a scaling hierarchy by a very wide boundary that itself has internal coherence, so that the two contrasting regions (inner/random and outer/ordered) couple to become a whole. For this to happen, the boundary has to be as large as the region it bounds (Alexander, 2004). The same effect integrates a large empty surface or space — for example the void in a Roman arch or Romanesque doorway — into the scaling hierarchy. This solution is avoided by contemporary styles, which shrink frames (i.e. the door or window trim) to an ineffective size for what they enclose, thus excluding anything that could act as an integrating boundary for a region.

10. COOPERATION AMONG DIFFERENT SCALES.

Individual units of design define a scale, and each scale has its own identity. Methods of *hierarchical cooperation* determine how the different scales are made to link. Specific coupling techniques given below guarantee the connection between distinct scales (see also Table 2.1 in Section 11 of the previous Chapter).

Table 3.3. Three methods of achieving hierarchical cooperation.

(*a*) Coincident scales (i.e., two scales that are defined by different units of the same size) link through contact, adjacency, and contrasting color or shape. The clustering of coincident scales helps in establishing contrast, which is an essential component of design coherence. Units having complementary shapes and colors can alternate in one or more directions to provide rhythm, and this is seen in patterns and buildings throughout history (Washburn & Crowe, 1988).

(*b*)   Different scales can be linked by similarity: the higher scale units being scaled-up versions of the lower scale units (see Figure 3.8). It is not necessary to duplicate the entire unit; a portion of it will do, as long as the similarity is recognizable. Many fractal patterns are completely self-similar. That is, the units of different scales are similar to each other, so that the whole design is just a combination of an infinite number of scaled-down copies of the same generative unit (Mandelbrot, 1983). It is for this reason that designs with fractal properties — such as natural scenery — are easily compressed by a fractal image compression program (see discussion in Section 4 earlier in this Chapter).

Figure (3.8)
The same shape repeats at different magnifications.

LINKING SCALES

(*c*)   The relative abundance of units on each scale leads to a statistical link between any two scales. This scaling is apparently perceived as a visual balance between the scales. Elsewhere (Salingaros & West, 1999), I have used entropy arguments to derive an inverse-power scaling law for architectural units. This scaling law is a multiplicity rule, which states that the number of components increases geometrically as one descends from the largest to the smaller scales (i.e., there are very few components on the large scale, several components on the intermediate scales, and very many components on the smaller scales) (see Figure 3.9). The correct multiplicity of units in each different scale helps towards achieving cooperation among the scales themselves, but in a manner totally distinct from geometrical similarity. Here we have similarity in numbers versus similarity in form (and the two usually act together). The same process is apparently ubiquitous in both natural and man-made phenomena, with the multiplicity rule being satisfied by DNA sequences; laws of economics; the evolution of ecosystems; word frequency in linguistics; and the population of cities (West & Deering, 1995).

Figure (3.9)
Multiplicity rule for the distribution of sizes.

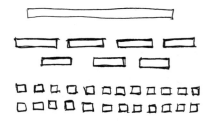

Rather than apply formal rules of *hierarchical cooperation*, we should in practice use the built-in capabilities of the human mind, which has evolved precisely so as to recognize *hierarchical cooperation* in natural forms. It is obvious just by looking at two scales in a structure if they cooperate or not, unless we have an intellectual override. We might be sidetracked by what we are taught to like; what provokes us; what reminds us of something else, etc. Nevertheless, this direct visual method is still the most powerful and comprehensive method we have to judge *hierarchical cooperation*, and to achieve coherence among design scales.

11. PRACTICAL CONSIDERATIONS FOR DESIGN.

The architect's role is to organize inanimate matter consisting of building materials to create functional spaces. A complex coherent whole that has emergent properties can be achieved only via the hierarchical organization of different scales.

The technique established here, and expanded by Alexander in his book (Alexander, 2004), uses feedback from the structure at each stage of its construction in deciding what to do next. This presupposes a certain freedom in design that is not currently part of the building process, although it was previously so for several millennia. At every point, the architect has to visualize what step will enhance *hierarchical cooperation*. A building process that is too rigid — that doesn't allow for alterations during construction — does not permit the evolution of *scaling coherence* that is necessary for emergent properties. In allowing the design to evolve and adapt during construction, we can approach the quality inherent in the great buildings of the past, without having to copy either their form or their details. While this approach is straightforward, and at first sight can be seen as helping existing design practice, in fact it challenges much of what we have accepted unquestionably in the twentieth century about good design.

We want an adaptive design method: one that adapts form to human needs (and not to formal criteria), to the site and to surrounding structures, and to itself. The building's and the user's functional needs should determine its internal design, as well as portions of the external form. It is an advantage to give the final design freedom to evolve. A rigid preconceived design imposed onto a building or a site constrains all the functions to fit into that particular form, with varying and unpredictable degrees of success. Furthermore, a simplistic overall design prevents the emergence of a natural scaling hierarchy. The process by which *hierarchical cooperation* triggers emergent properties is summarized by Alexander as: "every time a scale is created, it must link both to a higher scale and to a lower scale" (Alexander, 2004). The conditions for achieving *hierarchical cooperation* in built structures therefore depends on two design criteria: first, the ability to define architectural scales; and second, creating them so that they link via the rules for complex systems.

Materials and surfaces should be chosen primarily for structural, functional, and climatic considerations, and not exclusively for stylistic effect. The materials and structural subdivisions by themselves create obvious architectural scales, which can be intensified by some (but not excessive) intervention. Remember that contrast is an essential tool for defining compositional units. One adjusts the sizes of units so that they correlate with each other, and contribute to the natural scaling hierarchy. It will be necessary to add units that enhance an existing scale, or create a scale that is missing altogether. The architect should be ready to create a missing scale in a building simply because it is required by the natural scaling hierarchy. There may be a functional justification for it if the architect looks hard enough, but maybe there is none, especially if it is a small scale. It will probably cost more to build that new scale with materials rather than leaving empty surfaces, but it will help the building in the long run.

Allowing the design to evolve at every stage of construction guides the whole towards an emerging internal coherence (Alexander, 2004). The design process will itself be facilitated by paying attention to the hierarchical subdivisions. During the process of deciding on the scales, one checks them by computing their successive ratios. To achieve *hierarchical cooperation*, the ratio should be roughly the same between consecutive scales, and not too different from 2.7 — in practice, any number from 2 to 4 is adequate. It is essential, moreover, that subdivisions be continued downwards so as to create the smallest scales near the limit of visual perception. If there is any texture in the chosen material surfaces, then the man-made scales ought to continue down to this level of detail; otherwise, one can stop at 1 cm or 3 mm. Within this criterion, the architect has complete freedom in the overall design.

12. THE ANALOGY WITH ECOSYSTEMS.

In Chapters 1 and 2, I proposed that consecutive scales in the hierarchy satisfy a scaling ratio given approximately by the constant $e \approx 2.7$, the base of natural logarithms. This corresponds very closely to the spacing of scales found in psychologically comfortable structures. Measurements of the most successful buildings — including the great buildings of the past, and ordinary buildings from vernacular architectures — reveal a discrete distribution of scales. Plotting the different scales on a logarithmic graph, we find an evenly-spaced distribution, with roughly one scale or group of coincident scales for each integer 1, 2, 3, etc.

On the basis of this *scaling rule*, the room discussed as Example B at the beginning of this Chapter (Section 3) fails because its scales are insufficiently differentiated, and many of the smaller scales are missing. Recall that the actual room's scales were at {0.3 cm, 7 cm, 75 cm, 180 cm, 400 cm}. Ideally, a 4 m room should have eight clearly-defined scales measuring approximately {0.3 cm, 1 cm, 3 cm, 7 cm, 20 cm, 50 cm, 150 cm, 400 cm} (see the discussion in Chapter 2). Two stylistic features detailed earlier contribute to degrade the *scaling coherence* of this room: the elimination of, or just not bothering to define, the smaller scales at 1 cm, 3 cm, and 20 cm; and the almost complete lack of contrast (all the room is painted white).

The theory laid out in this Chapter has a remarkable parallel in animal populations. Hierarchical concepts have found an especially fruitful application in studying the evolution of ecosystems (Allen & Starr, 1982; Salthe, 1985). Ecosystems exhibit a quantization of sizes. Animals comprising a one-dimensional ecosystem define a discrete sequence, in which the mass of each different animal type increases geometrically. An ecosystem cannot support animals with body masses that are too close, so one of them may be eliminated by competition. On the other hand, a large gap in the distribution of body masses will be filled by some animal evolving either from above or from below. Plotting all the animals' weights on a logarithmic plot reveals a discrete evenly-spaced distribution (May, 1973), exactly like the logarithmic plot of scales in a building with *scaling coherence*. The actual scaling ratio for animal body mass has been determined in one case to be roughly equal to 2 (Hutchinson, 1959). Body mass can be compared directly to the size of architectural units: the distribution is indeed discrete, and depends on a fixed scaling ratio.

The analogy with ecosystems can be used to illustrate a point in a dramatic manner. If one level of a functioning hierarchy is removed, then all the higher levels will die out, since the animals that are no longer there are the food supply for larger animals. To avoid this extinction, there will have to be a drastic rearrangement of the hierarchy, with the evolution of existing levels either up or down the hierarchy so that the correct spacing between scales is reestablished. Otherwise, new complex food chains have to be established, with drastic changes in the ecosystem. I have argued that a building's *scaling coherence* is severely compromised by the removal of a single architectural scale from its hierarchy. The crucial difference between architecture and ecology is that human beings can be taught to accept incoherent structures, whereas nature does not. We can build while violating the natural scaling hierarchy, but ecosystems are ruthlessly efficient at eliminating incomplete units.

13. CONCLUSION.

The organization of complex systems inevitably leads to a scaling hierarchy, and to emergent properties that are not present in the individual components. We are able to understand the world precisely because it is hierarchical; those aspects of it which are not hierarchical elude our understanding and observation. This Chapter applied the rules of hierarchical systems, developed to describe any complex structure, to aspects of architectural design. *Systems theory* relates the organizational mechanisms underlying design to analogous processes taking place in biology, physics, and computer science. Cast in this scientific setting, architecture can profit from results already established in *systems theory*. Style is a matter of choice, but *structural order* is of profound importance to the human experience.

Buildings with a quantized distribution of scales predominate until we come to the twentieth century, when some of the architectural scales were either suppressed, or were distributed randomly. Those practices, originally introduced as innovative, in fact prevent the emergent properties that characterize the most coherent known structures. This result has a remarkable parallel in population biology: the laws governing the distribution of architectural scales in a building are analogous to the laws governing the size distribution of animals in an ecosystem. This framework provides practical design rules based on scientific principles that go much further than present-day architectural theories.

Chapter Four

THE SENSORY VALUE OF ORNAMENT

1. INTRODUCTION.

This Chapter argues that ornament is valuable for us to experience architectural form in a positive way. Chapter 3 presented mathematical reasons for why ornament is necessary. The visual coherence of a complex form, as defined by *systems theory*, requires ordered substructure on all scales: from the overall size of the building, down to the detailed grain in the materials. Natural structures have this (essentially fractal) property. If a man-made form lacks ordered structure on one or more obvious scales, it is perceived by human beings as being visually incoherent, and consequently as alien to our conception of the world (which is based on visual consistency). A building's visible substructure on the range of scales from 1 mm to 1 m has been achieved in the past through traditional ornament and detail.

Our neurophysiology is set up so that we expect visual input from our surroundings to contain many of the characteristics of traditional ornament. Human visual and mental make-up is linked through evolutionary processes to the informational richness of our environment. This biological background helps to explain some aspects of why human beings create ornament. Going deeper than the usual "artistic" analysis of architectural ornament, I try to place it within the context of shared biological mechanisms. It is part of human nature to order our world and establish scaling relationships so as to better understand our relationship to it. Here, I will present several rules derived from our cognitive mechanism — these rules are intended to help understand how we conceive a form as visually coherent, and thus meaningful. I then discuss the relationship between cognitive rules and the creation of ornament.

Altogether, eight "cognitive rules for *structural order*" can be established. They represent the neurophysiological equivalent of the three laws of *structural order* presented in Chapter 1, together with detailed rules for achieving *scaling coherence* given in Chapters 2 and 3. It is remarkable that the concept of *structural order* can be reached from three entirely different viewpoints: we can use science to discover how structures are put together coherently; we can use art and architecture to do the same thing; and we discover that our own mind works in precisely the same way. This reveals a universality for all the concepts discussed in this book — a level of validity that cannot possibly be dismissed as accidental.

Table 4.1. Summary of the Eight Cognitive Rules.

1. A region of contrast, detail, or curvature is necessary.
2. The center or the border should be well-defined.
3. Attention is drawn to symmetric ornamental elements.

4. Linear continuity orders visual information.
5. Symmetries and patterns organize information.
6. Relating many different scales creates coherence.
7. We connect strongly to a coherent environment.
8. Color is indispensable for our well-being.

I propose two arguments against both the minimalist design, and the random design of built forms. The first is that both cause anxiety and physiological distress, because they inhibit human mental connection with a given structure, normally experienced when meaningful information is available. Minimalist design omits aspects of warmth and comfort from our surroundings. A geometrically pure space can generate anxiety. The second argument centers on a concern about a very disturbing similarity. Minimalist and disordered built environments resemble the perception of a normal, visually complex environment by persons with a damaged perceptual apparatus or cognitive mechanism. I shall discuss how different types of injury to the eye and brain result in precisely the same effects offered by either minimalist or intentionally disordered design. This coincidence is serious because our body is programmed to respond to and so avoid perceptual and cognitive damage, and environments that are deliberately conceived in this manner are often triggering a reaction of distress.

The broader implication is that architecture adapted to human beings requires ornament for a sense of well-being. To prove this in a fully rigorous fashion is outside the scope of the present Chapter. I acknowledge other factors that influence the appreciation of architecture, including past experience, cultural formation and environment, and upbringing. Other authors argue for innate preferences for certain types of physical landscape, giving convincing reasons based on the environment's fractal qualities, which support the necessity for ornament and detail. At the same time, however, it has been shown that innate preferences are displaced by factors such as familiarity and psychological conditioning. It is probably true that living life in a minimalist architectural environment will make a person more familiar with it, yet such types of structure are not in harmony with our neurophysiological make-up.

2. VISUAL MEANING.

A form's visual organization communicates information to people through the surfaces and geometry it presents. Environmental experience is based upon an intimate interaction of human beings with surfaces and spaces, as it relates to our senses. This influences our emotions and physiological state, and consequently our actions. A building's exterior and interior surfaces either "connect" in an emotionally positive manner with the user; remain neutral by having no effect; or act in a negative fashion so as to repel. This interaction resides in the information content of space and the transitions from one region to another, and is independent of cultural bias. Even though surface qualities are usually assumed to be separate from the spatial geometry in a building, the two are in fact interdependent, and both contribute to how people respond to their surroundings.

Traditional architecture uses organized information to establish a positive connection with human beings. Throughout history, nonfunctional architectural components were deemed necessary for a building to offer a pleasant environment, and thus to enhance its attractiveness and use. Moldings, color, decoration, and richly-textured materials serve this purpose. Traditional architectural environments are inconceivable without such psychological design enhancements. Their architects were extremely sensitive to the need of appealing to and satisfying human psychological responses.

In the twentieth century this connective mechanism was abandoned to focus on pure geometrical form. Nevertheless, the emotional link established between people and built structures had led us, through feedback, to produce traditional ornamented structures. Human emotional response is based on neurophysiology and information input. It should not be undone for the sake of any particular architectural design style that eschews ornament. An environment lacking in texture, color, and ornament (in the form of organized detail) can be punishing for a human being, as exemplified in the design of prisons throughout history. Going to the other extreme, an environment that is supercharged with uncoordinated visual stimuli (the geometrical analogy of musical cacophony) — such as the Las Vegas strip lit up by neon lights — exceeds the visual input that can be consistently tolerated.

We seek intelligibility and meaning from our environment and are repelled by environments that convey no meaning, either because they lack visual information, or because the information present is unstructured (Klinger & Salingaros, 2000). The need to interpret environmental information has driven human evolutionary development: both vision and intelligence developed to increase our capacity for processing information. The eye and the brain form a single mechanism (Hubel, 1988). Design is itself a product of human vision and intelligence, therefore the organized complexity of traditional designs seems to parallel cognitive structures of the human brain. This observation makes the underlying reasons of why we build complex things less of a mystery. People are motivated to build so as to extend their consciousness to a wider domain outside their own mind.

3. HOW THE EYE SCANS A PICTURE.

In classic experiments on human eye motion while scanning a picture (Hubel, 1988; Noton & Stark, 1971; Yarbus, 1967), the eye is observed to focus most of the time in the regions of a picture that have the most detail, differentiations, contrast, and curvature (the experiments referred to did not include color). These are clearly the high-information regions in the picture. Eye fixations establish a fairly narrow "scan path" where the eye spends about one-third of its time, with random excursions to low-information (i.e. plain) regions of a visual image. The brain thus selects informative details such as convoluted, detailed contours and contrasting edges for recognizing and remembering an object. Our visual system is built to select those items of concentrated information that can provide the most complete response in the shortest possible time. (Color is extremely important in this process, playing a principal role in the realm of visual stimuli, and will be discussed separately in Section 7, below).

The information content of visual images lies precisely where the eye spends its energy scanning; the rest of the picture is easily reconstructed by extrapolation (Nicolis, 1991). That is, empty regions don't need to be stored since they are all the same. This is how the brain stores information via a compression algorithm (a concept discussed in Section 4 of Chapter 3). Selective weighting of information to minimize coding also provides the basis for information storage in artificial systems such as computer graphics (Klinger & Salingaros, 2000). We comprehend an object by seeking to define its boundaries and any characteristic details within the boundary. Note, however, that a discontinuity or sharp interface such as occurs when two edges (of flat empty surfaces) come together has no width or dimension, and so does not provide any detail. A precise straight edge has no information. A frame has information, and so does a curve. The more complex a frame or a curve are, the more information they contain (see Figure 4.1).

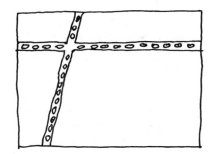

Figure (4.1)
The eye is drawn to regions of
high contrast and detail.

Detail is nothing more than contrast on the smallest scales. In principle, therefore, contrast coupled with hierarchy is necessary for detail. Nevertheless, as the concept of hierarchical scales is not widely known, I will continue to discuss contrast and detail as separate entities.

There is another reason why our eye/brain system has evolved to perceive detail, and that is our capacity to predict future events (Llinás, 2002). An intelligent, mobile animal focuses on details that give it crucial information about an adversary during combat; about changing physical conditions crucial to survival; the recognition of familiar animals and their facial expression; visual cues from a prey being hunted; etc. This is an adaptive trait that is essential for species survival. All of this information comes directly from telling details. Our cognitive system normally has no time to process all available visual information in those instances, and has to rely on first input in order to make almost instantaneous decisions.

Recent work (VanRullen & Thorpe, 2004) suggests that a first, rough image is created using only the salient parts of a retinal image — that is, regions of high contrast and detail. In this first burst of signals, it is contrast that encodes sufficient information to make a decision on our need to respond. The rapidity of this first image, which is entirely subconscious, is faster than our motor response time (see Figure 4.2). For example, a person will stop suddenly in front of a camouflaged snake, reacting to the brain's clear but non-visual message "snake" long before the image of a snake has fully formed. Sometimes, we react to the message but have to search very carefully before we can distinguish the animal from the background. This is an absolutely necessary feature, which makes possible a rapid response to any potential threat while the full image is still being processed. Our "instinctive" response to a form is therefore based on contrast and selected detail. Further information from the retina is processed more slowly, and any kind of rational analysis of the form can begin only after the retinal image itself is completed.

Figure (4.2)
High contrast and detail
determine first response.

First response depends on an incomplete image that somehow has enough detail for recognition. With more processing time, the image progresses to evolutionary higher levels of the midbrain, where single neurons can recognize complex wholes. Islands of such neurons capable of sophisticated pattern recognition exist at the same level as islands of neurons responsible for seeing fine detail. The ability to recognize detail is thus an advanced cognitive skill that the brain has developed over time. It is now established experimentally that the first, rough image is processed via different channels of the brain than the slower, more complete image (Johnson, 2004). The point is that our body responds viscerally to forms and textures in our environment in a way that we have no control over, and we are hardly aware of what triggers those responses.

The above considerations suggest two cognitive rules on how we perceive our world. I propose that artificial structures in general should follow similar rules, precisely because our perceptual apparatus (i.e., our eye) has evolved to use them. The following two rules are the cognitive analogues of the first law of *structural order* in Chapter 1, Section 3, consequences 1b, 1c, and 1d. Understanding how our cognitive mechanism works implies that we use analogous rules for constructing the man-made world.

Rule 1. Every structure should have at least one region with a high degree of contrast, detail, and curvature. That corresponds to high values of the first and second spatial derivatives (i.e., the change over a short distance).

The mathematical derivative computes the difference in surface qualities such as articulation along a given direction, whereas the second derivative computes the difference of the difference, i.e. the curvature.

Let me discuss Cognitive Rule 1 through its contradiction. Large, plain objects or surfaces disturb the observer by presenting little or no information — the most disturbing being surfaces of glass or mirrors that prevent the eye from even focusing on them. Glass is great for looking through, but terrible for looking at. Those structures have a low degree of contrast, detail, and no observable curvature. We instantly look for reference points, either in a form's interior, or at its edge, because our physiology is programmed to do so (Zigmond *et. al.*, 1999). We need to comprehend a structure as quickly as possible, to make sure that it poses no threat to us. Large uniform regions with abrupt, ill-defined boundaries such as an infinitesimally thin line generate psychological distress (which then has negative physiological consequences) as the eye/brain system seeks visual information that isn't there. This frustrates our cognitive process.

Rule 2. Plain surfaces require either their interior regions, or their borders, to be defined through contrast and detail.

Rule 2 reminds us of the principles involved in message transmission. In sending a message, it is necessary to indicate its limits. For example, a one-dimensional piece of information needs to be identified as such by noting where it begins and ends. This requires additional coding for the message's boundaries (limits). Without those boundaries, the receiver has no idea of what it is receiving, and cannot distinguish a message from other portions of a signal. In ordinary writing, a sentence begins with a capital letter and ends with a period. In any computer language, encoded text — even if it consists of no words at all — is always bounded by BEGIN and END tags. In architecture, this is best described by door trim or window trim used to transition between wall and open space. Every place where the condition changes from solid to void, from inside to outside, needs these well-defined transitional borders (see Figure 4.3).

Figure (4.3)
Transitions require defining
boundaries (limits).

END   BEGIN

message boundaries

internal boundary

external boundary

4. NEUROPHYSIOLOGY OF THE EYE/BRAIN SYSTEM.

Starting from a light-sensitive spot on protozoans and primitive worms capable of judging direction, the primitive eye developed a sense for various degrees of light intensity so as to perceive distance, or the shadow of an aggressor. Movement detectors, requiring first and second derivatives of the signal in time, were among the first to appear during evolutionary development. Finer and finer tuning corresponds to an increase in the brain's information channels and capacity. Researchers believe that the brain developed concurrently with the eye in order to handle the increasingly complex optical information input from the evolving eye (Fischler & Firschein, 1987). Some accept the co-evolution of the left/right reversal of functions in the two brain hemispheres, and the left/right reversal of an optical image on the retina, as proof of the concurrent evolutions of the eye and brain.

Geometrical uniformity is decoupled from our neurophysiology, because a majority of cells in both the retina and visual cortex will not fire in response to a uniform field (i.e., an empty region with no identifiable features) (Hubel, 1988; Zeki, 1993). Visual receptors in the retina (either single cells, or groups of cells) compare the characteristics of adjacent regions — they spatially differentiate the signal. Color wavelength is determined by comparing the output from three different types of cone cells due to the response from a single point. Neurobiologists have identified specialized neurons and clusters of neurons that perceive angles, curvature, and contrast (Hubel, 1988). The latter work via lateral inhibition (i.e. signal comparison) and are successfully simulated in artificial (computational) visual systems to achieve edge detection (Fischler & Firschein, 1987). The eye/brain system is thus idle in a visually homogeneous environment, the lack of stimuli reducing the need for activity.

Particular brain cells, and some groups of cells, have a preference for all possible oblique orientations in addition to vertical and horizontal. The directional preference of successive cells in a cortical region distinguishes between angles of 10 to 20 degrees (Hubel, 1988; Zeki, 1993). The existence of orientation-specific cells in the visual cortex proves the importance of angular information, since such a cell will fire only when confronted with diagonal lines at the particular angle the cell is created for. None of these neurons will fire in a strictly rectangular environment, thus diminishing the sensory connection to it.

In addition, "end-stopped" cells in the visual cortex respond to lines of a distinct orientation up to a small maximum length, beyond which their response drops to zero. These are neurons that exist only to recognize detail and differentiation. End-stopped cells are biological receptors that are directly sensitive to corners, curvature, and to discontinuities in lines. All these brain cells are again inactive in a visually homogeneous environment, which supports Cognitive Rules 1 and 2. Our brain works much like a scanner, which spends the bulk of its processing energy copying the highly detailed areas of an image.

Figure (4.4)
Cortical neurons respond directly
to ornamental elements.

More impressive is the finding of individual neurons in the cortex that are optimized for complex shapes. Experiments show that such cells preferentially fire when presented with complex symmetrical figures such as concentric circles, crosses with an outline, stars of various complexity, and other concentrically-organized areas of contrast (see Figure 4.4) (Zigmond *et. al.*, 1999). Furthermore, these neurons coexist with "silent surrounds", which help the neuron to recognize a complex figure better when that figure stands out in a plain background. From all appearances, our brain has ornament recognition built right into it. I therefore propose another cognitive rule:

Rule 3. Our visual attention is immediately attracted to symmetric ornamental elements, such as star shapes, concentric circles, crosses with an outline, etc.

Our eye/brain system evolved to perform a very specific function, and this suggests that human beings, as the animals that can create the greatest variety of physical structures, reproduce in artifacts what stimulates our brain directly. It is no coincidence that the elementary ornamental elements mentioned above appear on pottery, bone designs, non-representational paintings, and textiles over a period of several millennia (Washburn & Crowe, 1988). Early people represented visual aspects of their environment in an effort to codify it, and thus gain better control over it. Symbolic representations aided in ordering elements of cultural and physical landscapes, and therefore helped to understand the unknown. Cognitive Rule 3 is analogous to Consequence 1a of the first law of *structural order*, and to Consequence 2a of the second law given in Chapter 1.

Neurophysiological findings link our ability to recognize ornament with our evolutionary development. Complete visual information (not the fast, approximate image used to detect danger) is processed hierarchically in the brain, moving through different regions in succession. Two features point to increasing complexity. First, as one progresses forward into the brain's major processing pathway, there is a progression of the complexity and the critical visual detail needed to activate certain individual neurons (Zigmond *et. al.*, 1999). That is, as one progresses into the more advanced regions of the brain, more complex patterns are required as visual input before certain neurons will respond. Second, the relative numbers of neurons that are selectively driven by a complex pattern increases.

Minimalist surfaces and edges negate the way human beings have evolved to process information. It is known that when we go against our neurophysiological make-up for whatever reason, then our body reacts with physical and psychological distress. Such effects are measurable, and include raised blood pressure, raised level of adrenaline, raised skin temperature, contraction of the pupils — all symptoms of triggering our defensive mechanisms against a threat. When it recognizes a threat, the eye/brain system initiates physiological actions in order to protect the organism. Stress is an adaptive reaction to disease, injury, or toxins. The same mechanism extends to cope with unpleasant sensory input from the environment (Mehrabian, 1976).

The opposite effect — depression — results from understimulation. Studies of sensory deprivation show that we require above a minimum threshold of informational load from our environment in order to function normally (Mehrabian, 1976). I would like to see more experiments to measure human physiological response to different architectural environments. Already, studies by environmental psychologists tend to confirm what is proposed in this Chapter (Klinger & Salingaros, 2000). Depressing work environments are a result of poor architecture. Conversely, people are more productive in environments rich in ordered fractal information, such as is provided by trees and plants.

Degradation of our ability to see fine detail signals the onset of different pathologies of the eye itself rather than the brain. The first group of problems occur with the lens — either the lens can no longer focus, or it becomes opaque due to a cataract. The second group of problems have to do with the retina; in particular, with the macula, the central region of the retina where cone cells that are responsible for seeing fine detail and color are concentrated. The retina can be damaged by detachment, or the macula can degenerate because of inadequate blood flow. The loss of visual information cuts us off from our environment, and creates anxiety by lowering our ability to respond to it. These pathologies make us experience normal, informationally-rich environments as if they were minimalist environments.

All of this strongly suggests that we become uneasy in architectural settings where we experience a reduction of perceptual or cognitive input. This is unsettling because the circumstance of being unable to define our surroundings makes us feel helpless and lost. Those environments mimic signs of our own pathology. Are we subconsciously reminded of a failure of our visual system when we spend time in a minimalist environment? Such a response is probably so deeply-seated that it can only be overridden via a concerted conscious effort, if at all.

The brain has novelty detectors, which have alerting functions as consciousness. Unfamiliar patterns or constructs (not found in nature or traditional artifacts) trigger an immediate response that is physiologically based. This makes sense given our evolutionary development, which had to learn to protect us from potential dangers. People who are taught (i.e., have had to be trained) to look at novel constructs without alarm have undergone psychological conditioning, which establishes aesthetic preferences that contradict their basic instincts.

5. VISUAL ORDERING AND PATTERNS.

Cognitive Rules 1, 2 and 3 explain the necessity of visual information. Now we turn to the opposite problem: the case when there exists too much information. The first three cognitive rules are by themselves not sufficient to explain the geometry of form, since they say nothing about how visual information may be ordered. We know very well, however, that our cognitive system craves structured information and is overloaded with disordered (i.e. random) information. Information overload causes distress. Too little information has no meaning, and too much information also has no meaning. We can comprehend a lot of information when it is ordered. Ordering via patterns is discussed in (Klinger & Salingaros, 2000), where a complexity index is used to measure visual coherence. This leads to additional cognitive rules that govern how visual information can be organized. The easiest way to order information is to group objects along a curve or straight line (see Figure 4.5).

Figure (4.5)
Visual information may be ordered
via linear continuity.

Rule 4. Visual information can be ordered
efficiently via linear continuity.

This corresponds to the simplest grouping, lining up high-contrast objects on end; not necessarily always in a straight line, but it could also be on some sort of curve. The units do not need to repeat to be connected in Cognitive Rule 4 (one could align different objects). What this lining-up does is to significantly narrow the scan path that the eye needs to follow in order to grasp the information encoded in the components, since now there are fewer excursions to visual regions away from the line. Lining-up corresponds to a condensation of two-dimensional information.

It is probably no accident that we read text that is organized on a line. Also, artists know the advantages of a pencil line sketch in capturing information — as in a quick portrait sketch — as opposed to the more difficult task of representation by means of shaded areas without abstracted linear information. A successful line sketch (which contains reduced but still fractal information) can represent an object or person's portrait just as well as a photograph, because it has captured the essential physiognomic details, and those are linearly ordered.

There exist other techniques of organizing information spatially without condensing it along a line. The alternative is to organize high-information units using symmetry, which leads to patterns in two dimensions. A further savings of effort is accomplished in visual compression, by repeating a similar unit. Repetition can give rise to the wide range of traditional symmetries, such as reflectional, rotational, translational, and glide symmetries (Washburn & Crowe, 1988). High-contrast objects on the small scale can be spatially arranged in a symmetrical pattern, and the smaller units made similar so as to cut down the total amount of information. This leads us to:

Rule 5. Symmetries and patterns organize visual information, significantly decreasing the mental computational effort.

A well-defined unit (with coherent internal geometry and boundary) that is repeated does not need to be processed by our cognitive mechanism each time we encounter it. We apparently have the means to recognize similarity very easily, so the eye/brain system can encode a pattern in terms of one or more basic units, plus their positional distribution. If the units are repeated in some symmetric fashion — i.e., the units' positions are themselves symmetric — then only a little additional information is needed to specify the pattern. For this reason, patterns tend to be preferred over a random distribution of repeated units (Klinger & Salingaros, 2000). In the absence of any symmetry or ordering, our eye/brain system has to compute the position of each unit separately, which increases effort and comprehension time. Cognitive Rules 4 and 5 relate to the second law of *structural order* in Chapter 1.

It is now established that we have a built-in preference for symmetry, and this is singled out as the key visual characteristic that determines how we choose a mate. Symmetry on the large scale is thus linked to human attraction.

Organization structures information and endows it with meaning, which in turn connects that object with the human mind without the need for conscious reflection. Here is where *scaling coherence*, the topic of Chapter 3, comes into play in an essential manner. A symmetric arrangement of units is perceived on a higher level of scale than the units themselves (see Figure 4.6). Together, the smaller units define some pattern — a cognitively coherent whole that is larger than, and has more information than its components alone. As soon as one starts to do this, then recursion can be applied to define increasingly higher levels of scale, with each coherent arrangement on a particular level being very easily comprehended.

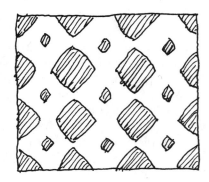

Figure (4.6)
A symmetric arrangement of units
defines a higher scale.

This nesting of patterns within patterns has occupied mankind for millennia (Washburn & Crowe, 1988). One could even claim that it forms a significant percentage of creative output over the history of the human species. It is seen in architectural ornament (especially Islamic), oriental carpets and traditional textiles, geometric designs on pottery, etc.

Readers will undoubtedly note a relationship between the cognitive rules proposed here and the well-known Gestalt laws of perception from psychology (Fischler & Firschein, 1987), as follows. Cognitive Rule 4 relates to the Gestalt Laws "Proximity" and "Good Continuation", while Cognitive Rule 5 relates to "Similarity", "Closure", and "Symmetry".

Failure to perceive patterns indicates a pathology of the brain; in particular, the failure of different specialized regions and mechanisms that process visual information to integrate their functions (Zeki, 1993). Specific causes of such disintegration include Carbon Monoxide poisoning and cerebral lesions due to strokes. In what is known as "visual agnosia", a person perceives detail but cannot integrate this information to recognize an overall form. This could be manifested as an inability to recognize objects or faces. Such afflicted persons can see but cannot understand their environment, and the trauma makes them anywhere from mildly to severely dysfunctional.

Agnosic patients can draw an artifact so that others can recognize it, but which they themselves don't. They are found to copy pictures strictly according to their local structure (i.e., their details), without a grasp of the global structure (i.e., the overall shape) (Zigmond *et. al.*, 1999). Their drawings lack an overall coherence, and they will classify two pictures differing in only a minor detail as different objects. Some patients with brain damage complain that their environment appears fragmented; components are isolated and they cannot discern any meaningful spatial relationship among them.

I conjecture that, presented with an environment that deliberately breaks patterns and large-scale visual coherence, human beings will instinctively react in a manner similar to feeling an internal loss of integration; namely the different pathologies I just described.

6. HIERARCHICAL COOPERATION.

In order to identify exactly what it is that successful ornament achieves, I need to discuss the many ways it serves to connect and integrate structures with humans. The first way is the most obvious one — ornament connects spatially separated regions by giving them a informationally similar surface. That is, using the same ornamental design on opposite walls connects them in the mind of the observer. This is an application of translational symmetry. Without having an identifiable similar design or geometry somewhere on them, two disconnected, separate surfaces are not likely to appear as being related.

The second way in which ornament connects is through *hierarchical cooperation*. This is a term introduced in Chapter 3 to summarize part of what is a fundamental theory of "wholeness" developed by Christopher Alexander (2004). In the previous Section of this Chapter, I mentioned how patterns within patterns define different scales of structure. The existence of a natural scaling hierarchy is not sufficient, however. The different scales must cooperate visually in order for the ensemble to appear coherent. One way to achieve this is to have scaling symmetry, in which a design is repeated at a higher magnification. The eye/brain system thus perceives a connection between the two different scales.

Practical methods of *hierarchical cooperation* utilize scaling properties of fractals. Establishing *scaling coherence* plays a fundamental integrative role. Linking different scales in this manner serves to make a large-scale structure appear internally coherent. It also provides an easy point for external connection at every scale. Since all scales are visually connected to each other, then a person connecting to one scale will immediately connect to all the scales. This is the purpose of the mechanism of *hierarchical cooperation* — to make possible an effortless human connection to a structure defined on several different levels (see Chapter 7, *Pavements as Embodiments of Meaning for a Fractal Mind*). These points may be summarized by two additional cognitive rules:

Rule 6. Visual coherence occurs when each scale is related to many different scales — it is often necessary to introduce new structures on the smaller scales to create a hierarchy of connected scales.

Rule 7. Human beings connect to their environment on a number of different scales, and the connection is strongest when the environment is visually coherent.

Human beings establish a critical dialogue with artifacts that have been formed by the human hand — or with natural objects that exhibit geometrical substructure on that range of scales 1 mm to 1 m (see Figure 4.7). The exact reasons are unknown. One can guess, however, that it has to do with the more intimate matching of scales that the human body itself possesses, and is also greatly influenced by our tactile sense. This is far more important than is usually assumed in discussions of aesthetics, where the role of the tactile sense is undervalued. Since tactile connections exist purely on the smallest scales, this favors the smaller scales in the overall scheme. Our sense of touch helps to connect us to the smallest scale of a building. Cognitive Rules 6 and 7 reflect the third law of *structural order* from Chapter 1, which was developed into the rules for *scaling coherence* in Chapters 2 and 3.

Figure (4.7)
Human beings connect to
geometrical structure through details.

A study of the neurophysiological mechanisms whereby we connect to our environment reveals that concurrent mental processes operate at different perceptual scales (see Chapter 7, *Pavements as Embodiments of Meaning for a Fractal Mind*). The visual cortex is organized in a hierarchical fashion, and signals proceed up the hierarchy through a processing stream traversing several cortical areas (Zigmond *et. al.*, 1999). At the same time, at all stages in the pathway, connections tend to be reciprocal, feeding back processed signals from later regions (which respond to complex visual stimuli) into earlier regions (which respond to basic stimuli such as edges and orientation). This creates an iterative loop among hierarchically-organized clusters of neurons that parallels the linking among the components of a hierarchically-organized complex pattern.

I emphasize connectivity and integration because I believe it to be a central factor in experiencing our environment (see Chapter 7, *Pavements as Embodiments of Meaning for a Fractal Mind*). Visual coherence at all scales is perceived as "beauty". Descriptions of this effect are found more often in philosophy and religion than in science — a harmonious environment is considered connected on all scales, and we experience peace (i.e., psychological and physiological well-being) when we ourselves connect to it. Once we establish what is behind this effect, then we can analyze the various mathematical methods that are responsible for connectivity.

Although there is insufficient experimental confirmation on this topic, it is believed that intelligence, thought, reasoning, and consciousness, are emergent properties — products of an enormous number of ordered connections. Intelligence is measured by our ability to establish a connection between thoughts. Drawing a very broad analogy between neurons, individual thoughts, and physical structures, we mimic our own mind when we create coherent objects and buildings. While this conclusion is conjectural, it nevertheless offers a way of understanding the human urge to connect designs on artifacts and the built environment in many different ways. It helps to explain our instinctive need to integrate or "harmonize" our surroundings.

Rodolfo Llinás (2002) posits that 40 Hz coherent oscillations observed in the brain are related to consciousness. He offers this mechanism as one possible explanation of the observed phenomenon of spatial coherence, in which different groups of perceptual functions interlock. Perceptual unity links together independent sensory components, in what is called "cognitive binding". This represents a synchronous neuronal activation during sensory input. It is indeed observed that neural mechanisms operating independently in the spatial domain, each responsible for separate processing of sensory stimuli, link physiologically. Whether it is driven by the observed 40 Hz oscillations or not, cognitive binding is irrefutable.

The breakdown of integration, when it occurs due to a pathology in our own brain, diminishes our ability to function at the full level of a human being. It is not clear what happens when an analogous breakdown is intentionally imposed on the built environment, by suppressing both perceptual components, and the possibility of their integration. Nevertheless, I cannot help but think that willfully disconnecting a sentient being from surfaces and structures has strongly negative implications.

7. COLOR AND INTELLIGENCE.

Color vision represents a significant information increase over monochromatic vision found in otherwise intelligent animals such as dogs and cats. The sensation of color resides just as much in the computational part of the brain as it does in the optical mechanism of the eye (Hubel, 1988; Zeki, 1993). This is shown by "color constancy", which is the ability of the eye-brain system to adjust a biased color illumination and reconstruct a faithful color image. In the experiments of Edwin Land, a color painting or collage illuminated by red, green, and blue lights together appears the same to us regardless of the relative intensities of the three different lamps used for illumination. Color photographs of an object under different lights, however, look very different (everything is either too red, too green, or too blue). An enormous amount of computation is taking place in the brain to help us maintain the same experience of color under widely different circumstances.

Color perception evolved to support higher cognitive processes occurring in the human brain (Llinás, 2002). This is shown by the well-known evolutionary tradeoff between sensitivity to dim light, which is necessary to detect movement, and sensitivity to color, which is useful for identifying and classifying objects. For most animals, it is more important to be able to detect objects (a lower-level function) than to identify them (a higher-level function) (Fischler & Firschein, 1987). This tradeoff is present in our own eyes, where the most color-sensitive central fovea is not very good at detecting a wide range of grayscale contrast, whereas this situation is reversed in the peripheral regions of the retina (which detect contrast well but color poorly).

Color perception takes place in the most evolutionary developed region of the brain's cortex, so color perception is related to intelligence. We know that from direct experiments. Positron Emission Tomography (PET) can measure the varying blood flow to the most advanced cortical regions, which correlates with the level of neuronal activity corresponding to the eye's input sensation of color. Blood flow to the region of the brain responsible for color vision increases by threefold when subjects first view a picture only in shades of gray, then again in full color (Zeki, 1993). This corresponds exactly to what one would expect from an increase in information due to jumping from one sensory dimension (grayscale) to the three color dimensions.

Three different types of cone cells are needed in order to perceive color hue or wavelength, and to distinguish color intensity from white (colorless) (Hubel, 1988). Interestingly, the cone cells in the retina responsible for color vision are also responsible for our ability to see fine detail (Hubel, 1988), thus linking color with geometry in our perceptual apparatus. Contrary to what is frequently assumed, therefore, color and linear design are intimately related. This leads us to the final cognitive rule.

Rule 8. Color is an indispensable connective element of our environment.

Three arguments support this claim: first, our highly-developed color sensitivity; second, the neurophysiological coupling between our ability to see detail — something that is necessary for our survival — and our ability to see color; third, psychological experiments demonstrating how colors affect us profoundly. Not only does color have the ability to change our mood (with the greater pleasure offered by the more saturated hues); it can also directly affect our physiological state (Mehrabian, 1976). Finding the appropriate color, however, is a very difficult problem, which will not be treated here. A significant portion of the world's economy — that driven by the advertising and fashion industries — is based on the emotional connection between human beings and color.

Cognitive Rule 8 reveals a more profound role for color than was originally anticipated in Chapter 1. While color helps to define contrast in the first law of *structural order* (consequence 1b), and also to define harmony in the second law (consequence 2c), it appears that color is by itself responsible for an intense, different, and independent connection of humans to their environment (Alexander, 2004).

For a long time, the importance of color in architecture was dismissed because it is normally so easy to change. One can build with very expensive naturally-colored stone, but it is much easier to paint a wall with the pigments of one's choice. Even though wall coloration affects a building's users to a remarkable degree, the ease by which this major emotional effect can be changed has led to its being classified as "interior decoration" and not architecture. It is also felt to be outside an architect's control, since this is the single component of a building that a user can alter without problems. We see architects going to extraordinary lengths in an effort to maintain their hegemony over color. Such measures include forbidding users from painting their own walls; deliberately using colorless surfaces made from materials that are very difficult to paint over; and coming up with false philosophical arguments whose only purpose is to prevent people from expressing their need for color.

Color vision is an essential tool for acquiring knowledge about objects and the physical world. As pointed out by Semir Zeki (1993), consciousness and the acquisition of knowledge are inextricably linked to those neural organizations concerned with color vision. Indeed, he defines a system that can see and experience color as being "conscious".

Common color-blindness (inherited retinal achromatopsia) is experienced by about 8% of the male population. This is a common though not debilitating condition. People who are color blind lead normal lives, but have persistent problems in negotiating their world because their color perception is reduced from three color dimensions to only two color dimensions.

Total loss of color occurs in a pathology known as "cerebral achromatopsia" (Zeki, 1993). Cortical lesions in the specific region of the brain responsible for color vision destroy the ability to see in color, usually as a result of a stroke. Alternatively, transient achromatopsia can be caused by inadequate blood supply to this region. This is an experience well known to jet pilots who fly in high-G aircraft. As a consequence, the world is seen entirely in shades of gray, but the ability to distinguish detail is not affected. Patients who are permanently stricken with this condition describe their surroundings as "drab" and "depressing", and frequently live lives of despair after their injury (Zeki, 1993). Organic objects (such as foods and person's faces) are now repellent. A gray coloration is normally associated with decay and death.

These findings are so powerful that I am surprised they are not known by architects. In flat contradiction, we see an infatuation with drab, gray surfaces of raw concrete. Everyone I ask (with the notable exception of some architects) finds such surfaces morbid and depressing; and yet architects keep building them. Even worse, they go to great lengths to prevent their users from painting them with color so as to stop the deadening effect. Where paint is allowed to be used, again it is often restricted to depressing shades of gray. This is in stark contrast to historical and vernacular architectures around the world. The greatest buildings of the past are very colorful (or were before their color faded from weathering). Owner-built dwellings employ all the color they can find to intensify visual response from wall surfaces. Color appears to satisfy a fundamental human need, as shown by children's art (before they are conditioned to a gray industrial world) and folk art.

8. THE VALUE OF ORNAMENT.

Ornament helps to connect us to our environment. In order to satisfy the eight cognitive rules given above, buildings should have either a continuous swath of high-density visual structure that the eye can follow in traversing their overall form, or focal points of intense detail and contrast arranged in the middle or at the corners of compositional regions. These contrasting elements could include a thick border or edge of the building; a thick boundary (frame) around openings and discontinuities; concentrated and detailed structure in the centers or corners of walls; etc. (Alexander, 2004). The visually-intense framework should organize information via patterns and symmetries.

Color has three distinct functions. First, it can help to define visually-intense regions due to the sensation of color intensity. Second, complementary colors can be used to define contrasting regions. Third, a common color can appear throughout the structure, and help to define an overall visual coherence.

The above cognitive rules would seem to have influenced architecture from around the world up to the beginning of the twentieth century, including Art Nouveau. Note, however, that key examples of the world's architectural heritage have lost their original bright coloration (which has never been restored because of the stylistic prejudices of today's architects who are in charge of restoration). It is far easier to classify those examples that do not comply with these rules, which happen to be primarily buildings from the twentieth century. Starting from the perspective of well-being, ornament seems a valuable factor in realizing a human architecture (Alexander, 2004; Bloomer, 2000). This Chapter argues that our neurophysiology requires us to resurrect the ornamental element of architecture that was arbitrarily condemned a century ago.

My conclusion also challenges a basic assumption of twentieth-century architects: that a building could be conceived in an abstract design space unrelated to physical space and to human beings. In fact, people actively seek perceptual connection with their physical environment to satisfy a fundamental physiological need (see Chapter 7, *Pavements as Embodiments of Meaning for a Fractal Mind*). This is consistent with the view of buildings and people forming a unified, interacting system (Alexander, 2004). Buildings do not exist in isolation from nature; the complexity of natural structures establishes the level at which information is valued. This threshold is part of our physiology. A building is successful or not after it is erected, for many different reasons. In addition to its strictly utilitarian aspects, "liking" a building depends on establishing visual and tactile connections with it.

Ornament is an indispensable part of this connection, but people today, after a century of doing without it (and hearing that it is somehow immoral), have almost forgotten how to generate ornament. Architects who reject ornament for ideological reasons are quick to point to unsuccessful, visually detracting examples of applied decoration to justify their decision for eliminating ornament altogether.

Since we no longer think about ornament as an integral part of architecture, most ornament created today fails in its task. Ornamentation that does not aim at coherence produces its opposite — incoherence. Garish or uncoordinated ornament is not satisfying, and could be visually disturbing. Ornament produced within the design canon of minimalist architecture is equally ineffective because it does not register with us. Its detail is too small or indistinct, and its differentiations are too faint or excessively subtle. On the other hand, sometimes effective ornamental components are used in contemporary architecture, but they are intentionally randomized so as to avoid coherence. This also makes them ineffective, because it frustrates our attempts to comprehend them in the context of the whole.

Successful ornamentation requires the recursive capacity (i.e., the ability to analyze images at different levels, then to synthesize that information) of only the most highly-developed brains, those of human beings. Different types of recursion include rhythm and repetition that generate translational and rotational symmetries; the iteration of geometrical structure on smaller and smaller scales that generates fractal patterns; and iteration on the same scale that generates denser and denser connections (Alexander, 2004; Bloomer, 2000). The human capacity for spoken and written language is in fact made possible by our capacity for recursive logical thought.

Students ask me how a building that already embodies a natural scaling hierarchy — which includes built structure on the ornamental scales — can accommodate additional ornament in the form of paintings, vases, plants, etc. That is no problem whatsoever, since a natural scaling hierarchy will simply extend to include those new objects. Too many decorative objects in a room may eventually lead to clutter because they will define too many uncoordinated scales, but that is strictly up to the user, and has nothing to do with the architecture.

9. ORNAMENT AND WRITING.

Ornament presents organized information that is entirely distinct from text as encoded in letters and signs. Ornament does not communicate a message in written language, but instead something equally as relevant in a subconscious language. I will use the example of typography to discuss this difference. When early typeface fonts for printing were cut by hand, they were created with the aim of having maximal legibility, guided by aesthetic considerations. Those were serif fonts (in which open lines end with a dot or T-stroke) like present-day Times and Garamond, which are more pleasing to the eye.

The introduction of radically new typefaces at the beginning of the twentieth century confirms that removing the ornamental serifs also removes a level of meaning. Sans-serif fonts such as Helvetica were popularized along with the modernist Bauhaus design style. They were promoted for their mathematical simplicity. It has been experimentally established that sans-serif fonts degrade legibility. People's reaction to these stripped-down typefaces was strongly negative; so much so that the first sans-serif font was named "grotesque" by the Berthold foundry, which introduced it commercially (the sans-serif typeface Berthold Akzidenz-Grotesk eventually gave rise to Helvetica).

Figure (4.8)
Demonstration of how ornament improves a typeface. On the left, the serif letter is the result of highly complex nonlinear operations on the basic design. In the middle, the overly simple sans-serif typeface is neither as attractive nor as legible as the serif typeface. On the right, adding substructure in the wrong places further reduces legibility.

Typography and text formatting ought to provide the simplest possible interface between information encoded in a text, and the mind of the reader. Everything should ideally facilitate the transmission of the text's message. Any imposition of visual elements or ideas as "design" extraneous to the text's meaning can easily degrade this transmission. Such is the case, unfortunately, with much of typography nowadays, where a "contemporary" visual appearance characterized by sans-serif fonts, grey ink, and paragraphs not separated from each other with either space or indentation takes precedence over the information in the text itself. By contrast, traditional fonts and text formatting evolved towards optimal legibility and psychological comfort, so as to enable reading without visual or emotional distractions. These practices facilitate the transmission of the text's meaning, and moreover produce a complex visual appearance that is aesthetically beautiful.

The transition from sans-serif to serif fonts shows clearly how ornament works to make form clearer, sharper, hence more distinguishable. Classic serif fonts go much further in establishing a positive emotional connection with the reader. In Chapter 3, I support the necessity of detail from arguments based on the properties of hierarchical systems. It is not just any added detail that improves the legibility of the font, however. Adding dots or small cross-strokes anywhere other than at the terminals of open lines (and even there, at some arbitrary angle) would degrade the font (see Figure 4.8). This provides one of the clearest illustrations that successful ornament is integral to the form, and is not merely "added on".

Ornament organizes detail in a very precise and sophisticated fashion in order to make a larger form more comprehensible. Adjustments are necessary for a better comprehension of letters. The most effective serif fonts are vastly more complex mathematically than a similar sans-serif font. They show substructure on a hierarchy of decreasing scales. A serif typeface doesn't simply add end-strokes; the entire font is adjusted so that new, more detailed elements cooperate to define a coherent whole. The font's line thickness is everywhere different. Correcting an old misunderstanding, ornamentation does not superimpose unrelated structure; rather it is a subtle operation that generates highly-organized internal complexity. It therefore has to be extremely precise in order to be effective.

10. CONCLUSION.

This Chapter reviewed results from neurobiology and experimental psychology, which together provide evidence of an informational connection between people and the built environment. Visual information input helps to create a physiological state in the user, triggered by the design of the environment. Eight cognitive rules for *structural order* were given that facilitate this. The quality of information and its organization affects the emotional connection that human beings establish with forms and surfaces. Traditional architecture sponsors the interaction between human beings and environmental information, connecting people with a building. Detail, differentiations, curvature, and color appear necessary in at least some part of a building, implying that ornament is a valuable component of our environment. Without it, buildings tend to be perceived as having alien qualities.

Architects in the twentieth century created a visual condition similar to the environments experienced by brain-damaged patients, most certainly without knowing the physiological conditions of eye and brain pathologies that reduce human visual and spatial perception. The architecture of the twentieth century successfully reproduces the spatial experience of persons with eye conditions such as cataract, retinal detachment, and macular degeneration. It also recreates the experience of patients with cortical lesions, who suffer from visual agnosia, cerebral achromatopsia, and other causes of neurophysiological disintegration that destroy the ability to integrate visual information. Architects did this in their quest for pure expression, and in an effort to impose a certain conception of order on the built environment. With the knowledge we now have, it is appropriate to reconsider the effects architecture has on us, and how architectural education and practice can use this information to make more human buildings.

Chapter Five

LIFE AND COMPLEXITY IN ARCHITECTURE FROM A THERMODYNAMIC ANALOGY

1. INTRODUCTION.

Architecture affects humankind in a predictable way in terms of physiological comfort level. An analysis of architectural forms distinguishes three different aspects: the small scale, the large scale, and linking all the intermediate scales together through *scaling coherence* and *hierarchical cooperation* (as detailed in Chapters 1, 2, and 3). This Chapter examines how the small and large scales contribute to the success of a building independently of the hierarchical mechanisms of coherence. I present a method of quantifying architecture according to geometrical and visual content. This makes it possible to compare two buildings based on intrinsic, computable values of their design. More important, I claim that these values influence the value and feeling of the building; i.e., its architectural quality as determined by how good and comfortable it feels to its inhabitants.

Returning to Laws 1 and 2 for *structural order* from Chapter 1, I give a practical method of applying these laws to design. After having discussed the Third Law (dealing with scaling and hierarchy) at length in Chapters 2 and 3, it is time to focus on the other components of design such as detail, entropy, organization, etc. Chapter 4 set the neurophysiological background for why detail, contrast, color, symmetry, and organization are necessary in our environment. The present Chapter gives more architectural tools for dealing with and understanding the organizational component of design.

We can systematize intrinsic qualities that govern the geometrical coherence of architectural forms by setting up a simple mathematical model, which draws on analogies with thermodynamics. This is a totally innovative approach to design. The first part of the model identifies two distinct qualities and suggests how to measure them. Small-scale structure is described by what I label here as the architectural temperature T. The higher the architectural temperature, the higher the intensity of the design and the degree of visual stimulation — the more color, differentiations, detail, and curves (Section 2 of this Chapter, below). Another measure, the architectural harmony H is then identified with the degree of symmetry and visual coherence of forms, and measures visual organization, i.e., the absence of randomness (Section 3). This is a property of the larger scales. The architectural harmony H carries its traditional architectural meaning, whereas the architectural temperature T is a new way of describing familiar concepts in architecture.

The second part of the model relates the perceived "architectural life" and "architectural complexity" to different combinations of T and H. The *architectural life* L is defined as $L = TH$ (Section 4), and the *architectural complexity* C as $C = T(10 - H)$ (Section 5). The "life" refers to the degree that one recognizes in a building those intrinsic qualities that make it seem "alive". These are the same qualities that connect us with a building in the same way that we connect emotionally to trees, animals, and people (Alexander, 2004). If I stand in front of or inside of a building with a high degree of "life", I feel comfortable, relaxed, and at ease. Independently of its "life", a building's "complexity" as already understood by architects will also be computed using the model I define here. The feelings generated by a high degree of "complexity" correspond to interest, excitement, and anxiety. Two of the principal emotional responses to architectural forms are thus formalized in this Chapter. The *architectural life L* and *architectural complexity C* are two independent measures that determine how we feel about a building.

This establishes a connection between scientific quantities based on measurements, and intuitive artistic qualities based on feelings. Although it is usually difficult to quantify subjective statements, people tend to agree on the ranking of the emotionally perceived "life" of structures, and what I measure here as the *architectural life L* (Section 6). I emphasize the model's predictive value in differentiating buildings on a graph of C (complexity) versus L (life), which is presented later as Figure 5.6 in Section 6. The graph reveals a pattern independent of personal preferences, in which one can follow the historical development of architecture in terms of intrinsic qualities rather than styles. To my knowledge, no comparable analysis of the evolution of styles has ever been presented.

The third part of the model reveals how to imbibe a building with "life". The method suggests how to judiciously adjust the individual constituents of forms. By providing a coherent theory on how to do this, the model becomes an extremely valuable tool for both analysis, design, and construction. The process that raises the *architectural life* is entirely independent of particular styles, or what the forms look like. This model can help someone to understand and control the interplay between *architectural life* and *architectural complexity* in any novel structure.

Section 7 discusses the model's origin from an analogy with thermodynamics (of interest to architects seeking a more scientific understanding). The quantity H represents something analogous to a negative entropy. In defining L and C , the model mimics the thermodynamic potentials used in physics to describe the state of a system. Like them, the *architectural life* and *architectural complexity* are relative and not absolute values. This analogy suggests that similar physical principles underlie organization and disorder in all structures, thermodynamic as well as architectural.

The final section (Section 8) investigates the link between biological life and architectural forms. For example, self-similar fractal patterns have high architectural life, which is why they are widely successful in modeling natural forms (Mandelbrot, 1983). The values of L and C correspond to the organization of matter in living forms. This resemblance generates the emotional responses in humans to structures with different architectural potentials L and C . Buildings are created by living beings, who have a basic need to instill *architectural life* into inanimate structures. A building is as successful as the degree to which it reflects this, independently of its character and individuality.

2. TEMPERATURE IN ARCHITECTURAL DESIGN.

Several factors contribute to the perceived qualities in architectural design, and my first task is to distinguish them. The most obvious is the departure from uniformity. A form is either plain and empty, or it is differentiated in terms of the geometry and color. In physics, uniform states in fluids and gases are normally associated with low temperatures. Raising the temperature often breaks the uniformity, leading to gradients and convection cells. Independently of this, heated metals acquire a coloration by radiating.

If we draw an association with those physical processes, this suggests that we refer to the degree of detail and small-scale contrast (obtained through differentiation) in a design as the architectural temperature T. (There is a loose analogy between the architectural temperature and the thermodynamic temperature times the particle number density; see Section 7). The architectural temperature is determined by several intrinsic factors such as the sharpness and density of individual design differentiations; the curvature of lines and edges; and the color hue. Even though people think of architecture as being concerned with the form only, color is an integral part of experiencing a form's surface (Chapter 4 of this book; Alexander, 2004).

I propose a very simple method of measuring the architectural temperature T. It will provide us with a statistical measure of a structure's informational richness. This approximate guide is by no means the only possible prescription; it is the first step to handling an extremely complex topic. I will distinguish five elements T_1 to T_5 that contribute to T. Each quality is measured on a scale by assigning a value of 0 to 2 according to the rough judgment: very little or none = 0, some = 1, considerable = 2. The different components are listed as follows: the first three contributions come from geometrical substructure, whereas the last two come from color.

Table 5.1. Components of the Architectural Temperature.

T_1 = intensity of perceivable detail
T_2 = density of differentiations
T_3 = curvature of lines and forms
T_4 = intensity of color hue
T_5 = contrast among color hues

The architectural temperature T is the sum of all these estimates (the subscripted quantities). As each component assumes values between 0 and 2, the quantity T will range from 0 to 10. We have:

$$T = T_1 + T_2 + T_3 + T_4 + T_5 \qquad (1)$$

Let me now discuss how to estimate each component of the architectural temperature in turn.

(T_1) — The limit of perceived differentiations in material texture at arm's length is roughly 1 mm. Well-defined detail at any comparable size in surfaces that a person can touch, regardless of whether the detail is localized or spread over the entire region, suggests we assign a value of 2 for T_1 . On regions farther away, textural differentiations that contribute to T_1 should be much larger so as to appear the same size as detail would be at arm's length. Coarser, or less sharply-defined detail assigns a 1 for T_1 . Detail is defined by the width of a substructure or differentiation. Detail that is too small or is faintly-defined assigns a 0 for T_1 . Smooth or textured monochromatic surfaces rate a 0; to count, detail must be articulated against the background. High-tech precision should not be confused with detail. The interface where two edges come together has no width or dimension, thus it does not define a material line. Detail is not defined by a single discontinuity or sharp interface.

(T_2) — T_2 measures how much substructure and variety is presented to the viewer. I will treat every geometric differentiation such as a relief or color pattern as having the same effect as its grayscale value. T_2 of a colored relief is therefore judged in terms of a flat black-and-white photograph. (This is done because color is a separate measure). In this projection, any differentiation or texture is perceived in terms of its grayscale contrast, or by the shadows it casts. A high density of sharp differentiations assigns a 2 for T_2 , whereas a plain surface assigns a 0 for T_2 . The color value itself, which represents a particular shade of grey, doesn't contribute to T_2 directly.

(T_3) — T_3 measures the smallness of the radius of curvature of lines and forms (a smaller radius corresponds to greater curvature), and also how many curves are present. A curve can be approximated by a very large number of small straight-line segments. Any curve and inflection (for example, the graph of a higher-order polynomial; or a zigzag) has a higher architectural temperature than a straight line. The architectural temperature is proportional to the curvature of lines and forms. Curved forms on the intermediate scales (that is, between detail and the overall size) assign a 1 to T_3 ; if they have a high degree of curvature, or if there are many curves, we assign a 2 for T_3 . Straight lines and rectangular forms assign a value of 0 for T_3 .

(T_4) — T_4 estimates the chromatic depth of any color present: high for a vivid, intense color, but low for a dull, grayish, muddy color. A richly colored building, even if it is of one color (say, all red), has a higher temperature than a grey building (which assigns a 0 for T_4). A design with some color overall suggests a value of 1 for T_4 ; an intense though not necessarily bright color assigns a 2 for T_4 . The actual color (i.e., yellow, green, red, blue, or purple) is immaterial.

(T_5) — T_5 measures the interaction among several distinct colors. The architectural temperature is increased further by having complementary colors, for example, yellow next to violet, orange next to blue, or red next to green. It is also high for black-and-white contrast. If there is any contrast among colors, assign a 1 for T_5 ; if there is a great variety, or the contrast is particularly vivid, assign a 2. Having either a uniform color or no color at all assigns a 0 for T_5 .

In different cases, the architectural temperature T , which is the sum in equation (1), will depend on each factor T_i to a greater or lesser extent (see Figure 5.1). While there have been periods and cultures that have been more restrained in their detail, curvature, contrast, and color than others (i.e., whose architecture is defined by low values of T), the predominance of buildings and artifacts with high architectural temperature throughout history suggests that this satisfies a profound innate need in human beings (Alexander, 2004).

To illustrate how the model works with actual examples, I have estimated in Table 5.2 the architectural temperature T of twenty-five famous buildings covering a spectrum of architectural styles and traditions spanning the entire world over several centuries (Fletcher, 1987). The numbers given are very approximate, and their derivation is discussed in Section 6, below. To obtain these estimates, I have used a variety of published photographs, coupled in some cases with my personal recollection of those buildings in the list that I have experienced first hand. Table 5.2 also includes computed values for the architectural harmony H, the *architectural life L*, and the *architectural complexity C*, whose derivation is discussed later in this Chapter.

Table 5.2. *Twenty-five famous buildings and their values. Buildings are numbered in chronological order. The third and fourth columns are computed from the first and second columns as L = TH , and C = T(10 − H).*

Building	Place	Date	T	H	L	C
1. Parthenon	Athens	–5C	7	8	56	14
2. Hagia Sophia	Istanbul	6C	10	8	80	20
3. Dome of the Rock	Jerusalem	7C	9	9	81	9
4. Palatine Chapel	Aachen	9C	7	9	63	7
5. Phoenix Hall	Kyoto	11C	7	9	63	7
6. Konarak Temple	Orissa	13C	8	8	64	16
7. Cathedral	Salisbury	13C	7	9	63	7
8. Baptistry	Pisa	11/14C	7	8	56	14
9. Alhambra	Granada	14C	10	9	90	10
10. St. Peter's	Rome	16/17C	9	6	54	36
11. Taj Mahal	Delhi	17C	10	9	90	10
12. Grande Place	Brussels	1700	9	7	63	27
13. Maison Horta	Brussels	1898	8	7	56	24
14. Carson, Pirie, Scott	Chicago	1899	7	8	56	14
15. Casa Batlló	Barcelona	1906	8	5	40	40
16. Fallingwater	Bear Run	1936	4	5	20	20
17. Watts Towers	Los Angeles	1954	10	4	40	60
18. Corbusier Chapel	Ronchamp	1955	3	2	6	24
19. Seagram Building	New York	1958	1	8	8	2
20. TWA Terminal	New York	1961	3	4	12	18
21. Salk Institute	San Diego	1965	1	6	6	4
22. Opera House	Sydney	1973	4	5	20	20
23. Medical Faculty	Brussels	1974	7	4	28	42
24. Pompidou Center	Paris	1977	6	4	24	36
25. Foster Bank	Hong Kong	1986	3	7	21	9

3. RANDOMNESS AND HARMONY IN ARCHITECTURAL DESIGN.

Randomness is measured by the entropy (disorder). Because entropy is not a traditional concept in architecture, I introduce the architectural harmony H to measure its opposite: the lack of randomness in design. *Architectural harmony* is a traditional concept associated with visual organization, but it has never been measured. (The relationship between H and a negative architectural entropy is discussed later in Section 7). Design information may be organized so that it leads away from randomness. Where the individual details and shapes relate to each other, the architectural harmony H is high. Symmetrical forms and patterns have high architectural harmony. The architectural harmony H is a property of the whole structure, due to the correlation between the parts on all the distinct levels of scale.

3.1. Estimating the Architectural Harmony.

The proposed model depends on direct measurements from perceivable surfaces and forms, i.e., walls, doorways, passages, etc. When thinking about symmetries, most architects immediately look at a building's plan (von Meiss, 1991). The plan, however, is not directly perceivable to a user, therefore it is not relevant to this model. In a break with both traditional and current practice, I will ignore the aerial view: this model doesn't cover the formal organization of spaces; only the immediate impressions of elevations and surfaces from a human viewpoint.

The architectural harmony H is constituted as five components, each of which assumes a value of 0 to 2. Again, this is only an expedient that gives very approximate numbers. I will use the same scale: very little = 0, some = 1, considerable = 2. The architectural harmony H ranges from 0 to 10, and is the sum of the five components described as follows:

Table 5.3. Components of the Architectural Harmony.

H_1 = reflectional symmetries on all scales
H_2 = translational and rotational symmetries on all scales
H_3 = degree to which distinct forms have similar shapes
H_4 = degree to which forms are connected geometrically one to another
H_5 = degree to which colors harmonize

The architectural harmony H is the sum of these five estimates:

$$H = H_1 + H_2 + H_3 + H_4 + H_5 \qquad (2)$$

The following discussion clarifies how to estimate the different components of the architectural harmony.

(H_1) — An average numerical value has to be assigned for the presence of symmetries on all scales, not just for the largest scale. Moreover, the quantity H_1 actually depends on the orientation of the symmetry axis, because gravity defines a preferred direction for both life forms and materials. Of the possible axes for reflectional symmetry, the vertical one raises the architectural harmony the most. For having many vertical symmetries on distinct scales, assign a 2 for H_1 , whereas a vertical symmetry on a single scale assigns a 1 for H_1 . Symmetry about a diagonal axis clashes with natural symmetries created by gravity, and the ensuing imbalance lowers the architectural harmony to 1 (i.e., the leaning Campanile of the Cathedral at Pisa). Lack of reflectional symmetry on different scales leads us to assign a value of 0 for H_1 . In plain surfaces with no distinguishing elements, H_1 is defined by the edges; if they are parallel, then assign a 2 for H_1 .

(H_2) — The contribution H_2 measures translational symmetries (and the less common rotational symmetry) on walls, doors, and windows; not on a building's plan. If the same element is repeated in a regular pattern along one or two directions, then assign a 2 for H_2 . Elements repeated randomly lower H_2 , assigning it a 0 instead.

(H_3) — Self-similarity raises the architectural harmony, by scaling up the same figure to several different sizes, then aligning all the scaled copies. The contribution H_3 measures the similarity of overlapping or spatially-separated figures occurring at different sizes. For example, a group of parallel lines or similar nested curves is related by a scaling transformation, so in that case we assign a 2 for H_3 . This mechanism works when the windows have the same proportions as the entire wall or façade, in which case we also assign a 2 for H_3 . Pieces with markedly different shapes do not harmonize with the whole, and we assign a 0 for H_3 .

(H_4) — The quantity H_4 estimates the presence of geometrical connections. Internal and external connections can take many different forms: connecting lines or columns; intermediate transition regions; a wide surrounding border, etc. Piecewise connections raise H_4 to 1 or 2. Edges that touch but fail to join through an intermediate region or frame, jutting overhangs without obvious supports, and breaks in lines all lower H_4 to 0. The main connection of any building is to the ground (earth); if this is not strongly expressed by means of structural elements, then we assign a 0 for H_4 .

(H_5) — A building of a single color or without any color at all has color harmony, so assign a 2 for H_5 . If different colors are used, one has to estimate how well the various hues blend to create an overall color harmony. Even with bright colors, a harmonious ensemble is possible, which assigns a 2 for H_5 . Look at paintings, which can have thousands of different colors that harmonize: nothing really jumps out at the viewer (unless that was the artist's intention). The departure from a unified color effect — an unbalanced, clashing, or garish combination — lowers H_5 to zero. Statistical correlation of color effects finds that people agree about which color combinations appear "harmonious".

Together, these quantities give a numerical measure for the architectural harmony H , the sum in equation (2). A form's architectural harmony H increases as the form becomes more coherent (see Figure 5.2). In Table 5.2, estimates of H are provided for twenty-five famous buildings using the method outlined in this section. Since the architectural harmony can be measured in this way, a subjective judgment differing with each viewer is statistically ruled out.

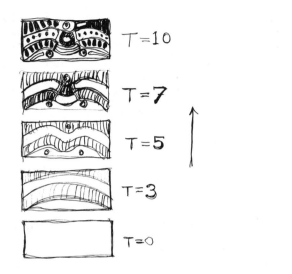

Figure (5.1)
Architectural temperature increases towards top.

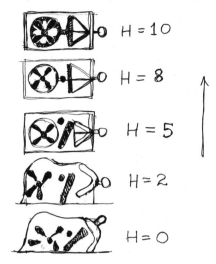

Figure (5.2)
Architectural harmony increases towards top.

3.2. Architectural Harmony and Pattern Recognition.

There is a deep connection between architectural harmony (as negative entropy or lack of disorder) and information in thermodynamics, and this carries over to architecture. Any symmetry in a design reduces the amount of information necessary to specify shapes. A form with bilateral symmetry needs to be specified only on one side, which is then reflected. A design with translational or rotational symmetry is defined by the information contained in a single unit that is repeated. Recognition of an unfamiliar object is greatly simplified if it has as many internal symmetries as possible (see Chapter 4).

Juxtaposing different materials can lower the architectural harmony H by breaking the continuity of a surface. Disconnected forms positioned near each other across an interface or gap create ambiguity, thus lowering the architectural harmony. We cannot comprehend such forms, or what they combine into. When a form's basic attachments to other forms are missing, the brain continues to seek visual information that would establish the necessary connections (Fischler & Firschein, 1987). If these attachments are not obvious, then the ensemble is perceived as incoherent. Recognition is frustrated whenever structural information is missing, or in the opposite case when it is overwhelming. Since pattern recognition is a low-level brain activity, we may be intrigued intellectually by a low H form, but our visceral reaction is negative (see Chapter 4). A low H form can create interesting and powerful images that play with our emotions, as I explain later in Section 5.

The architectural harmony of multiple structures that are unrelated by either symmetry or scaling could be raised through piecewise connections. A geometrical connection relates two separated forms, and becomes a boundary for both of them. Each form then connects individually to a third, intermediate region, which itself must be large enough for this to occur, leading to wide boundaries. (Mathematically, the two original forms A and C relate by establishing a minimal transitive relation via an additional connecting region B; i.e., if A connects to B, and B connects to C, then A connects to C). The linking is successful only when the two principal forms and the connecting region together define a coherent larger unit (see Figure 5.3).

Figure (5.3)
Two forms connect to each other
via an intermediate region.

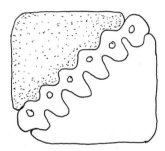

3.3. Raising the Architectural Harmony.

Adding some of the same color to areas of different color connects them harmoniously, raising H_5 (but it also lowers T_5, the contrast among colors, because it makes both regions more muddy). This is delicate to achieve if we wish to preserve any existing contrasts in color. In successful examples, areas are brought together by relating their colors so that the overall result is intense rather than muddy. Attempts at further harmonization, however, will eliminate color contrasts that contribute to the architectural temperature. This shows how H and T are related.

Two very different techniques raise the architectural harmony in what is initially a random design. The first method re-arranges existing details to create a maximum number of symmetries, starting from the smallest scales and working up to the larger scales. This maximizes the architectural harmony with the constraint that the architectural temperature remain constant. The second method eliminates all details, curves, and colors, which lowers T. The mostly plain surfaces that are left can be made totally symmetric, which raises the architectural harmony H. This alternative method can raise the architectural harmony the most by eliminating all randomness, but in so doing, it effectively loses all the architectural temperature as well.

3.4. Lowering the Architectural Harmony.

The architect Lucien Kroll lowers the architectural harmony by randomly arranging small and intermediate-scale components in a building (Kroll, 1987) (the Brussels Medical Faculty, building No. 23 in Table 5.2). Design decisions that use random numbers as a method of composition escape from the monotony of a strict bilateral or translational symmetry. A rigid symmetry may in most cases be arbitrarily imposed, since any lack of architectural symmetries in historical buildings is usually the result of accommodating functional or structural needs. Thus, valid departures from symmetry should not be deliberately random. Functionality is inextricably linked to the form, as first stated by Louis Sullivan, and demonstrated conclusively by Alexander (2004).

Some architects strive to create random arrays of elements in an effort to be different and unique. This practice is not random in a true sense, since each component of the "random" design has to be very carefully and deliberately considered and built so that it looks random.

Adding small-scale structure that doesn't relate to the ensemble lowers the architectural harmony of a design. This could be either a random pattern, or even a regular pattern that fails to connect to existing patterns. Excessive, uncoordinated decoration lowers the architectural harmony, and makes an overall coherence difficult or impossible to comprehend. Many architectural styles evolve historically to reach an overly-decorated style, which is invariably followed by an anti-decorative reaction in a later generation (Fletcher, 1987). By going through a plainer phase that sheds extraneous decoration, this cycle eventually re-establishes high architectural harmony.

4. THE ARCHITECTURAL "LIFE" OF A BUILDING.

Whereas the quantities T and H must be measured and consciously estimated in every structure, their product TH is perceivable without any direct measurements. For reasons that will be explained later, I call this combination of architectural temperature and architectural harmony the *architectural life L* in a structure. Amazingly, the product TH connects emotionally to an observer. A building with a high value of "life" is perceived in similar terms as a living organism, establishing a structural kinship with the viewer. Section 8 below discusses the connection between L and biological forms.

Architectural Life:

$$L = TH, 0 \leq L < 100 \qquad (3)$$

Before the twentieth century, builders unconsciously achieved higher degrees of architectural harmony consistent with the highest architectural temperature so as to maximize the product $L = TH$ (see Figure 5.4). They didn't measure this: they knew it instinctively. The greatest historical buildings of all time consistently embody high *architectural life L* , as can be verified by performing a survey of the world's architecture (Fletcher, 1987) (see Table 5.2 and Section 6). As its two components T and H

take values from 0 to 10, the *architectural life L* takes values from 0 to 100, which is a useful percentage scale for comparison. A low value for the *architectural life* means that people may not connect to that building on the same emotional level that they would with a living organism (i.e., a tree, an animal, or a human being).

Figure (5.4)
Life equals temperature times harmony.

A separate point is that the greatest buildings do not eliminate randomness entirely. The optimal value for the architectural harmony is below its theoretical maximum. Every great building has some degree of randomness, which can manifest itself on different scales. Randomness is usually required to define new scales, or to create new couplings. By working strictly with formal symmetries, a point is reached when the *architectural life L* cannot be raised any further without breaking some of those symmetries. Large-scale randomness may contrast and couple with highly-ordered symmetries down to the smallest detail (the Grande Place in Brussels, building No. 12). Often, a portion of the building material itself can be re-arranged by injecting a small amount of randomness so as to accommodate elements that would otherwise be forbidden by the severity of a strict overall symmetry.

I will now discuss some guidelines for how to design a building with an elevated degree of *architectural life L* . This is the basis for the theory of architecture proposed by Alexander (2004). Achieving *architectural life* is not a simple task, because the measures we have to work with, T and H , can actually depend on each other. Raising the architectural harmony H by lessening the degree of small-scale differentiations and straightening out curves can eliminate the architectural temperature T if one is not careful. This lowers the *architectural life* of a design instead of raising it. Visually, the link between T and H is expressed as contrast between regions of different H . I can summarize these ideas in the following list.

Table 5.4. Techniques for Raising the Architectural Life L .

(a) Raise the architectural temperature T and the architectural harmony H together. The method consists of adding T very selectively, while being careful at each step to raise H . Insert color, detail, or curvature in a very controlled and precise manner so as to enhance and not clash with existing patterns and colors. Do not add anything that might lower H . One preserves the existing geometry and adds on to it, thus intensifying it. What is already there (i.e., structure that establishes high T and H) acts as a framework for guiding all additional structure. Any randomness — which would lower H — is shed via the complex symmetries found in traditional design. This method works well during construction, and is also recommended for the transformation of existing buildings. Most buildings today have acceptably high H , but very low T , so this process of raising T to obtain a higher degree of *architectural life* is called for.

(b) Another method is to first raise T considerably, and then raise H afterwards while keeping T high. Add as much T as may be thought necessary to bring life to a design, then come back and rearrange everything (by making things more symmetrical and connected) in order to raise H . This second method is more spontaneous, but requires subsequent adjustments if something doesn't work and has to be removed or changed. Imposed ordering and regularity must be deliberate, and will not happen automatically. It is better applied to the computer-aided design of new buildings, where many changes on the large scale can be tried and evaluated before the physical structure of the building is in place.

(c) A building with a high number of symmetries (high H) can raise its architectural temperature T even further by including a small portion of highly-connected but non-symmetric design, such as sculptures, representational murals, or calligraphy. All of these are characteristic of an enormous density of connections, and thus of a high degree of *architectural life L* . To be effective, this must not simply be applied decoration, but a portion of high L structure inserted coherently to become part of the existing whole. True ornament is incorporated organically into the overall design, and never appears as an afterthought. Carved human figures introduce sophisticated small-scale symmetries in a portion of a building (the Parthenon and Konarak Temple, buildings No. 1 and 6 in Table 5.2). In Islamic buildings, calligraphic script provides small-scale connectivity that contributes to tie together the large-scale forms (the Dome of the Rock, the Alhambra, and the Taj Mahal, buildings No. 3, 9, 11). This is done flawlessly, so that the viewer perceives a coherent whole, and not a lot of pieces.

Many contemporary and earlier twentieth-century buildings have a very low value for the *architectural life L* . It is worthwhile discussing what techniques actually lower L , which is the opposite of what I propose as necessary for an adaptive architecture. Nevertheless, this discussion is valuable because it reveals that the architects of low L buildings must have followed methods antithetical to what I am proposing to achieve their results. A vast number of buildings representing the "International Style" in the 1960s and 1970s could never be included in my list of famous buildings. Lifeless apartment blocks and commercial buildings that employ a minimalist design vocabulary are by far in the majority of built structures today. Contrast this to ordinary buildings from, say, Haussmannian Paris: I believe that those are so much better liked by so many different people, precisely because they share a high value of *architectural life*. People who enjoy minimalist buildings do so more as an idea rather than with their emotions.

Table 5.5. Techniques for Lowering the Architectural Life L .

(a) Reduce the architectural temperature or the architectural harmony as much as possible. Lowering T while keeping H fixed is straightforward: eliminate all detail, color, structural differentiations, and curves (see Section 2). We are then left with a plain, lifeless rectangular grey box, like most office buildings of the past several decades (the Seagram Building and the plaza of the Salk Institute, buildings No. 19 and 21). Removing raw information is trivially easy to achieve in practice, and should not be interpreted as a thoughtful contribution to design. (Removing disorder while retaining the complexity, on the other hand, requires intelligent effort).

(b) The other way to minimize L is to lower H while keeping T fixed. With an already low T achieved after eliminating design details, one can lower H even further by generating randomness on the large scale composition. H is lowered by breaking bilateral and translational symmetries, and severing geometrical connections. Doing this, we obtain a disjoint, unbalanced, and asymmetric large-scale form without details. Large pieces in curved shapes are constructed out of plain (i.e., unpatterned) materials, with abrupt juxtapositions between surfaces and volumes (Ronchamp, building No. 18). If there is any color, it consists of uncorrelated hues. This effectively renders such buildings lifeless, though not without visual interest (see Section 6).

(c) We can also minimize L by lowering H , working this time on the small scale. Introducing randomness that is restricted to the small scale — as in a totally random, unstructured decoration, surface pattern, or fenestration — lowers H but could also raise T , so it is a less sure method of minimizing L than randomizing only the large scale. It is, however, widely employed in contemporary buildings where traditional ornament (which is high L) would be unacceptable for ideological reasons. Abstract applied decoration with little or no internal connectivity or symmetry (i.e., in a random "contemporary" decorative design) is one means of lowering the *architectural life L* of a building.

It is not accurate to conclude that every architect who does not want to deliberately raise L wants to reduce it instead. There are other directions a design can be drawn towards, and those can be understood as either trying to increase or decrease the *architectural complexity C* (which is defined in the following Section). An architect is free to compromise between different elements in order to express a particular concept. A reader who has studied thermodynamics will be struck with the analogies in the above discussion: adjusting one quantity while keeping another fixed, and using combinations of such quantities is exactly what is done in analyzing thermodynamic systems.

5. THE ARCHITECTURAL COMPLEXITY OF A BUILDING.

The *architectural complexity C* of a building or design can be expressed in terms of its architectural temperature and architectural harmony as follows:

Architectural Complexity:

$$C = T\,(10 - H),\ 0 \le C < 100 \qquad (4)$$

The quantity $T\,(10 - H)$ is perceived directly as a building's complexity, as the term is commonly understood (see Figure 5.5). This impression can range from very low C or $C = 0$ (dull), through low to medium C (exciting), to very high C (incoherent). It is the complexity of an object that arouses a viewer's interest: the *architectural complexity* is the inverse measure of how boring a building is. As I discuss later in Section 7, the quantity $10 - H$ in Equation (4) measures the visual disorder, which is why the formula for *architectural complexity* has this particular form. Using intense and contrasting colors, small-scale differentiations, and curves contributes to the *architectural complexity*, as does any randomness and asymmetry. The buildings of Antoni Gaudí (Zerbst, 1993) provide good examples of high *architectural complexity* (Casa Batlló, building No. 15 in Table 5.2). The highest C structure in Table 5.2 is the curious Watts Towers built from pieces of junk by Simon Rodia (building No. 17). Some recent deconstructivist buildings go far beyond that in visual disorder. Contemporary critics award architects for a high degree of complexity, which extends beyond excitement into anxiety, thus subverting emotional connectedness. For this reason, too much complexity ultimately detracts from a building's adaptivity to humans.

Figure (5.5)
Complexity equals temperature
times randomness (disorder).

I have chosen the word "life" for the quantity L in this model, believing it more immediately accessible to architects. An alternative terminology more appropriate to complexity theory is to call the *architectural life L* the "degree of organized complexity"; and the *architectural complexity C* the "degree of disorganized complexity". Most people understand complexity as being of the disorganized variety, whereas in fact there are two distinct types of complexity: organized versus disorganized. Biological forms are highly complex, and at the same time marvelously organized, thus establishing the relationship between "life" and organized complexity.

Independently of any particular theory or architectural movement, the commercial sector recognizes that people do not connect to plain, grey walls, but instead to bright colors, details, and contrasts. Putting this into practice has generated a high T environment defined by a profusion of colored signs and surfaces. Such an environment is usually uncorrelated, however, so it has a very low architectural harmony and at the same time a high architectural temperature: it therefore has very high *architectural complexity C* (from equation (4)). It is thus incoherent, and leads to anxiety. All over the world, this process is a major force driving building practice, with negative consequences because it leads to a visually cluttered environment.

The architecture of the commercial environment (i.e., signs and billboards) was taken seriously by very few architects (Charles, 1989; Venturi *et. al.*, 1977). As long as this phenomenon of visual clutter is not understood as arising from certain very basic forces expressing information, those forces cannot be controlled and directed, and an incoherent environment will continue to proliferate unabated. Simply banning information by imposing an empty, minimalist style only displaces information, and it emerges in a far more random and disturbing manifestation elsewhere. As a result, most of us have to live and work in environments with far higher *architectural complexity* than the Watts Towers, creating unnecessary stress and anxiety in our daily lives.

At the other extreme, minimalist twentieth-century forms have a very low *architectural complexity C*. Architects reacting against earlier low C forms are today creating buildings with higher values of C. Postmodernist architects of the 1970s defined more structure on the small and intermediate scales, and broke some of the strong overall symmetries characteristic of modernist buildings (Venturi, 1977). That increases the architectural temperature and lowers the architectural harmony to varying degrees. Some raise C by introducing a host of uncorrelated forms to lower a building's harmony (the Brussels Medical Faculty and the Centre Pompidou or Beaubourg, buildings No. 23 and 24). Others use bright overall colors to raise T, usually uncorrelated so as to lower H at the same time, and thus raise C.

Another movement today, the neo-classical style, is defined by Classical symmetry and proportion, which means that the architectural harmony is very high. Since the Renaissance and Palladio, applying and developing the Greco-Roman vocabulary has produced countless successful buildings, because their typology was derived from natural ordering (Charles, 1989; Fletcher, 1987) (St. Peter's, building No. 10). Contemporary neo-Classical buildings, however, rarely have the sculptural friezes, nor the degree of detail and the color of original Classical buildings. Consequently, their *architectural complexity* and *architectural life* tend to be measurably lower than that of Classical buildings, or earlier neo-classical buildings.

6. THE EVOLUTION OF LIFE AND COMPLEXITY IN ARCHITECTURE.

Values of the *architectural life L* and the *architectural complexity C* for twenty-five famous buildings are computed in Table 5.2. The *architectural life* as defined in this Chapter corresponds accurately to what people feel as the "life" (i.e., emergent properties) of a given structure, independently of whether they may like it or not. The numbers given for L and C of a particular building are only approximate, yet most people will agree with the relative ordering of the values. Table 5.2 is used to produce Figure 5.6, which permits us to see the *architectural life* of different architectures. It can also be used to follow the evolution of architectural styles.

Figure (5.6)
The Triangle Classification. Numbers corresponding to the buildings in Table 5.2 are plotted on a (C, L) diagram of architectural complexity versus architectural life. Numbers 15 to 25 represent 20th century buildings. Note that these all lie outside the top corner containing earlier buildings (1-14). Every structure in history, and every structure not yet built, fits inside the large triangle.

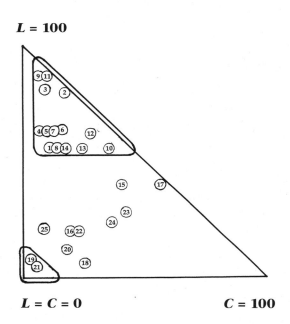

L = 100

L = C = 0   C = 100

6.1. Difficulties of Estimating the Parameters.

I have chosen some of the best-known buildings in history for these examples. Even so, these readings (estimates for T and H) necessarily reflect the existing, and often altered state of many buildings. Sculptures, mosaics, and colors that were an integral part of the original building are now missing; exteriors and interiors have been altered; parts have been extensively re-built; windows are not original. My estimates are based on their present condition, with a partial correction for their conjectured original forms.

The key to estimating meaningful values for T and H is to observe a building's exterior and interior from the human viewpoint. Architecture books favor a view from a great distance that is rarely experienced by a user, but small-scale differentiations are seen only by people close up; in entrances and inside a building, in regions that impact a person immediately. It is essential to determine the impact of a building from up close. It is thus necessary to find close-up photos in color showing sufficient detail of the building's accessible regions — both inside and outside — to determine how far the small-scale patterns are correlated. For the purposes of this evaluation, one doesn't have to be in the actual building to make these judgments.

Another problem is to decide on a particular viewpoint — the values of T and H evolve as one approaches and enters a building, sometimes varying drastically. I have selected a single representative value for T and H in each case. The changing experience as one walks through a building will not be analyzed here. This represents a temporal dimension of architecture, which was carefully controlled by the greatest architects to create the maximum emotional effect on the user (Fletcher, 1987; von Meiss, 1991).

6.2. Analysis of the Carson, Pirie, Scott Department Store.

Louis Sullivan's Schlesinger & Mayer building, now the Carson, Pirie, Scott & Co. store (building No. 14), is a high point of American architecture for its originality and *architectural life* (Frazier, 1991; Frei, 1992; Jordy, 1986). I illustrate the proposed model by going through the measurements of T and H . First, the glorious cast-iron façade has detail down to 1 mm ($T_1 = 2$). Looking up from the street shows the detailed pattern in the extended frame of the upper windows, which cannot be seen in photos taken from a straight-on view (Frei, 1992; Jordy, 1986). Altogether, there is a very high density of differentiations ($T_2 = 2$). The façade is an organic complex of curves ($T_3 = 2$). It is dark green, while the upper stories are faced in white terracotta tiles ($T_4 = 1$). There is no color contrast ($T_5 = 0$). The original interior did have color contrasts, but it is now completely altered.

The building is almost bilaterally symmetric, and its façades and windows are piecewise symmetric ($H_1 = 2$). The windows define rows and columns of translational symmetry ($H_2 = 2$). The cylindrical pavilion on the street corner is similar to the curved corner stories on top of it, while the storefront windows maintain the same scaling as the upper windows ($H_3 = 2$). The façade is connected internally, and the cylindrical corner portion of the building has columns in relief all the way up; but the façade is not connected to the upper stories ($H_4 = 1$). The overall color harmony is pleasing, though the terracotta does not harmonize with the dark metal ($H_5 = 1$). The later removal of the original roof projection and its replacement with a sheer modernist edge has lowered the architectural harmony, as can be verified by looking at older photographs (Frei, 1992; Jordy, 1986).

6.3. Some Comparisons Between Buildings.

To demonstrate the utility of this model for *architectural life* and *architectural complexity*, I compare buildings entirely dissimilar in form, which nevertheless have similar values of L or C . Table 5.2 shows that Charlemagne's Palatine Chapel in Germany (building No. 4) has the same values for L and C as the Phoenix Hall of the Byodo-in Temple in Japan (building No. 5). The former follows an octagonal Byzantine plan, whereas the latter is a development of the classic Buddhist temple tradition. No two buildings could be more different in appearance, yet a viewer responds in a comparable way to both of them.

In the same way, the Romanesque Baptistry at Pisa (building No. 8) compares with the Art Nouveau Carson, Pirie, Scott store (building No. 14). Louis Sullivan's great achievement is that he generated the same degree of *architectural life* without copying anything that had been built before him. By coincidence, the Parthenon (building No. 1) also shares the same values of L or C as these two buildings, but this is not a fair comparison in its existing condition, since it has lost most of its sculptures, walls, and original coloration, which would have raised L. Though well-known to archaeologists and historians, the brightly painted quality of Classical and Medieval architecture is not mentioned very often by architects.

Two buildings that share similar values of L and C are Frank Lloyd Wright's Kaufmann house "Fallingwater", in Bear Run, Pennsylvania (building No. 16), and Jørn Utzon's Sydney Opera House (building No. 22). Both are free, innovative, interesting, and generate feelings of similar positive intensity, despite having entirely different characteristics.

A case of contrast occurs between two religious buildings: the Hagia Sophia (building No. 2), and the Pilgrimage Chapel of Notre Dame du Haut at Ronchamp, France, by Le Corbusier (building No. 18). They have about the same value for the *architectural complexity* — i.e., the same level of raw visual interest — but the former has more than thirteen times the *architectural life* of the latter (see Table 5.2). The comparison belies the statement, common in architecture books, that this particular building by Le Corbusier is not susceptible to systematic analysis with respect either to his other work, or to other religious buildings.

6.4. The Universal Drive to Raise the Architectural Life.

Human beings worked very hard to raise the *architectural life* of their surroundings, up until the twentieth century. People with entirely distinct conceptions of beauty, using very different materials, but driven by similar motivations, managed to build structures that cluster together in the top corner of the triangle classification (Figure 5.6). Surprisingly, these buildings do not resemble each other in form. Furthermore, my choice of buildings is only a representative sample: hundreds of buildings from before the twentieth century might equally lie in the top corner of the triangle classification. Architecture has gone through cycles of styles throughout its history, with either more or less ornamentation, sculptures, frescoes, etc., yet all those buildings up to the twentieth century are situated in the "traditional" corner of the triangle classification.

Like animals with the instinct for complicated courtship and nest-building, we have an instinct to build things that embody certain qualities. For thousands of years, structures were built that do not meet any obvious utilitarian need; and yet they occupy a central role in our cultures, requiring vast commitments in manpower and time. A simple shelter does not require the incredible sophistication that people have invested in buildings. Historically, buildings have reflected humankind's drive to transcend material limits and produce something to which we can relate directly on a deep emotional level.

For millennia, human beings (as well as birds and fish) have used techniques for raising their perceived *architectural life* in order to attract a mate. Whereas animals rely on slow biological evolution to create bright stripes on a fish or patterns in a peacock's feathers, human beings do this instantly through the fashion and cosmetics industries.

What about houses and ordinary buildings? This model applies to all structures, and not just to important historical buildings. Vernacular architecture has reflected the values of L and C of "official" (i.e., major and state-sponsored) buildings throughout history. For instance, Classical Greek and Roman houses were sufficiently detailed and coherent to give high values for L similar to those of contemporary temples, despite having an entirely different form. Although houses and commercial buildings in our time are strongly influenced by architectural fashion to have low L, their inhabitants instinctively raise L by decorating interior surfaces.

In vernacular architecture, L is raised while working with great economy: shapes arise from what is comfortable and practical, and what can be built from locally-available materials. Visually intense buildings are the products of an ornamental, polychromic design culture. People without money will paint the inside and outside of their houses in bright colors, and put up inexpensive, sometimes garish, but often effective decorations. Wealthier people surround themselves with expensive antiques and folk art.

6.5. The Limits of Architectural Life and Architectural Complexity.

The triangle classification includes all buildings within a large triangle, whereas the older traditional and minimalist buildings are each restricted to within their own much smaller triangles (Figure 5.6). This is a mathematical consequence of the definitions of L and C. Adding equations (3) and (4), above, we obtain the identity:

Interdependence of Life and Complexity:

$$L + C = 10T \qquad (5)$$

Since the maximum possible value for T is 10, equation (5) defines an upper limit for the *architectural life* in terms of the *architectural complexity* as $L = 100 - C$. That is, while the value of C does not determine the value of L, there is a maximum possible L that a building with a given C can have. Too much *architectural complexity* keeps down the *architectural life*. If C is any higher than, say 20, then it is impossible for that building to have *architectural life L* comparable to the great buildings of the past. This relationship is represented by the diagonal side of the triangle classification (Figure 5.6). All structures in history, and all structures yet to be built, can therefore be represented inside the triangle classification (Figure 5.6).

Measurements establish the fact that traditional buildings strive for a high value of *architectural life L*. These inhabit the top corner of the triangle classification (Figure 5.6), shown as the upper small triangle. It was already explained in Section 4, above, why the *architectural complexity C* of high L buildings does not vanish, and for this reason the triangle enclosing them is displaced slightly from the L axis.

$$L = C = 0$$

Figure (5.7)
Minimalist forms have no life or complexity.

A similar but distinct relationship holds for minimalist buildings (see Figure 5.7). Their architectural temperature is very low, and this provides an upper bound for both their *architectural life* and *architectural complexity*. The purest modernist buildings included here are numbers 19 and 21 (the Seagram Building and the Salk Institute), which occupy the triangle $L < 10$, $C < 10$ with the diagonal bound $L = 10 - C$. The purest typology arising in the modernist idiom, whether defined by aesthetic principles, or by pioneering buildings that are used as models by succeeding architects, is restricted to a very narrow range of parameters represented by the lower small triangle inside the triangle classification (Figure 5.6).

6.6. The Evolution of Architectural Styles.

For millennia, architects followed their physiological urges and constructed buildings with a high value of L. All of these cluster in the "traditional" corner of the triangle classification (see Figure 5.8). Once architects felt that they could break the traditional — though unstated — principle of always raising L in the built environment, the rest of the large triangle in the classification could be systematically explored with innovative structures. Early modernists took off, moving in all directions and inventing many new styles, but eventually got fixated by the minimalist corner of the triangle, coming back to it again and again. In mathematical terms, the minimalist corner of the triangle has become an "attractor" for twentieth-century architects, just as the traditional corner was an attractor for architects prior to that. Recent decades have seen excursions towards the third corner of the large triangle, which represents the region containing high C deconstructivist buildings.

Traditional L=100

*Figure (5.8)
Historical trajectory of styles
around attractors.*

Minimalist L=C=0

Deconstructivist C=100

7. THE THERMODYNAMIC BASIS OF THE ARCHITECTURAL MODEL.

This model is inspired by thermodynamics, which provides insight into the fundamental processes of architecture. I have taken concepts such as symmetries and coherence that are well known in architecture, and combined them into a sort of thermodynamic potential. Whereas in the past these visual properties have always been considered separately and qualitatively, I made the relevant qualities measurable, and then synthesized the values obtained into a consistent and robust model that has predictive value.

The model depends critically on the degree of randomness, which is measured by some sort of architectural entropy S . (S is the usual symbol for entropy in physics). The word entropy is used in a very particular sense, and its meaning is analogous to but not the same as the thermodynamic entropy in physics. The entropy of a design is defined as the degree of randomness or disorder in the patterns. This is the opposite of the architectural harmony H that I introduced. I used the architectural harmony H in order to measure S indirectly as $S = 10 - H$ on a scale of 0 to 10. Since the architectural entropy S represents the absence of symmetries, connections, and harmony, it is more difficult to measure than the presence of those qualities, which is what H measures. That is why I chose to use H for this model.

The architectural entropy is, like the thermodynamic entropy, an extensive or bulk function. What I define here as the architectural entropy is the average measure of visual and structural disorder over the entire form. This is not the entropy directly, but it permits us to compare the architectural entropy of two buildings of different sizes. Without averaging, the architectural entropy of the sum of two buildings would be the sum of the entropies. Since the architectural entropy is averaged, the entropy of the sum is the entropy of the ensemble, which is more useful for architectural purposes.

The thermodynamic temperature is an intensive or point function that measures quantities locally. The temperatures of two separated points are not additive. The architectural temperature T as defined here, however, takes into account both local and average qualities. Each component T_i of T measures the maximum point value anywhere in the design, as well as the average of that quantity over the entire form. This combined method is the best way to measure local differentiations (details and contrasts) as departures from equilibrium (uniformity), and at the same time, as a value on a quantitative scale.

In physics, T and S have different units. Here in the architectural model, T and S are dimensionless numbers, and are combined to get other dimensionless numbers such as H, L, and C. In physics, it is the thermodynamic potentials that characterize a system, so, by analogy, I defined the *architectural complexity C* as the product TS. This makes C look like the internal energy or the enthalpy (which are thermodynamic quantities in physics). The *architectural life L* $= 10T - TS$ would then correspond to something like the Gibbs potential or the Helmholtz free energy (other thermodynamic quantities). Combinations such as these also characterize the state of an architectural system, which is the key to the present model. The idea is that fundamentally similar laws that govern organization in thermodynamics might be equally applied in architecture.

8. THE LINK TO BIOLOGICAL LIFE.

The notion of "life" in architecture is defined by Alexander (2004), who has worked very hard to achieve it in his own buildings (Alexander, 1984; Alexander *et. al.*, 1991; Fiksdahl-King, 1993). My formulation attempts to codify some of Alexander's results. More than just creating a utilitarian structure, humankind strives to approach the intrinsic qualities of biological forms in its traditional and vernacular architectures. This result is not obvious, because very few buildings actually copy living forms: the resemblance is obtained by raising L via the architectural temperature and architectural harmony.

Starting initially from a traditionalist point of view, Charles, the Prince of Wales has also discovered the value of style-independent rules that raise the *architectural life*. By relying upon his intuition and highly-developed sensitivity, he has put forward several useful ideas, including what he calls his *ten principles* (Charles, 1989). Although the approach and details are different, these developments are supported both by Alexander's results, and by the model of this Chapter. The links between biological life and *architectural life* are now being recognized formally, chiefly by researchers outside architectural academia. We are witnessing a convergence of ideas coming from several different directions, and outlining an entirely new approach to architecture.

One class of examples of artificial objects that mimic living forms is beautiful self-similar fractal patterns. The architectural temperature T of fractals is very high; the architectural harmony H is also very high because they are self-similar (that is, any portion, when magnified by a fixed factor, looks exactly like the original form) (Mandelbrot, 1983). Therefore, they have a high degree of *architectural life L* . As is well-known, fractal graphics resembling natural objects provide excellent representations (Mandelbrot, 1983), and this property serves to support the present model.

The connection between biological life and *architectural life* (as an organization of matter and the energy of human actions) arises from the thermodynamics of living forms. Life is the result of an enormous amount of purposeful complication. Biological organisms are marvelously connected on all different levels of scale, and they are characterized by very high architectural temperature and architectural harmony. It is becoming more and more obvious that biological life works by organizing, processing, and storing information encoded as biochemical structures. Raw information corresponds to T, whereas its degree of organization corresponds to H. My model thus captures something of the essence of living processes and forms. What we are able to observe as the physiology of organisms, moreover, is only the framework for an incredibly detailed and coherent series of life mechanisms that we normally don't see. Biological systems exhibit far more organized complexity in the temporal dimension. The connective thought processes underlying cognition themselves mimic the thermodynamic and connective structures that are characteristic of living forms. We crave information, but we want it organized so we can understand it and use it. This helps to explain our instinct to relate to forms having a high degree of *architectural life*.

It should not be surprising that living beings (both animals and humans) instinctively copy the intrinsic qualities of living systems in their own creations. How can human beings put an image of life into a building? Life processes are highly organized and structured. Apart from figurative icons and statues, we work with emotions: in traditional architecture, structures were carefully tailored to generate positive psychological and physiological responses. Far from merely being a plausible hypothesis, this model suggests that human beings have a basic need to raise the *architectural life* of their environment.

9. CONCLUSION.

A model for architectural forms was inspired by thermodynamics. By measuring the architectural temperature T and the architectural harmony H, I estimate the *architectural life L* of a building by analogy to a thermodynamic potential. The value computed for L in this way corresponds directly to the emotional perception of a building's "life". A different potential, the *architectural complexity C*, is a distinct combination of T and H. Again, the computed value for C in any building corresponds directly with what is emotionally perceived as its "complexity". This establishes a link between intrinsic and measurable qualities of architectural forms, and the subconscious connection they establish with people.

The proposed model represents an analysis of architecture with a quantitative method. While the results depend on the detailed definition of the variables, the basic principles are fairly robust. One of the results is to critically distinguish older historical buildings from those of the twentieth century. This was illustrated dramatically in a plot of the *architectural complexity C* versus the *architectural life L* of twenty-five famous buildings. I interpreted this in terms of the historical attempt of human beings to mimic fundamental processes in nature. Traditional buildings derive their structure from physical and biological processes, whereas contemporary and earlier modernist forms seek innovation through features that do not occur in nature.

This quantitative description of architecture was based on the buildings themselves. I looked at buildings in isolation and gave them a quantitative place on a scale. The model, which follows ideas of Christopher Alexander, also applies to the impact of a building on its environment. Alexander's approach is holistic, and considers a building and its environment to be a whole unit. The measure of architectural harmony applies especially to the juxtaposition of a building with adjoining buildings, natural scenery, the sky, and the ground. Even if a building is internally harmonious, it creates the opposite effect when its edges clash with the environment. A built environment with high *architectural life* therefore connects all structures to each other and to their surroundings.

Chapter Six

ARCHITECTURE, PATTERNS, AND MATHEMATICS

1. INTRODUCTION.

Mathematics is a science of patterns, and the presence or absence of patterns in our surroundings influences how easily one is able to grasp concepts that rely on patterns. The traditionally intimate relationship between architecture and mathematics changed in the twentieth century. The modernist movement stopped using certain expressions of pattern in architecture, which has profound implications for society as a whole. Those architects promoted the repetition of units (which create a very rudimentary pattern), but as I show here, such repetitions are part of a typology that tends to be poor in mathematical content. Eliminating complex patterns from twentieth-century architecture has affected our capacity to process and interpret patterns in thought. Mathematics, and the intellectual patterns it embodies, then lies outside our contemporary architectural world-view's explicitly anti-pattern bias.

Mathematics teachers are bemoaning the fact that there is less and less interest in mathematics, which has resulted in a declining mathematical capacity among students. Architecture students are required to have at best a limited mathematical background. This stands in sharp contrast — indeed a contradiction — with the increasing technological advances we are witnessing in our times. Paradoxically, as architectural education becomes more specialized, it limits the student's contact with knowledge that helps to understand the world via mathematics. While a problem in itself, a far more serious possibility is that contemporary architecture and design may be promoting an anti-mathematical mind-set.

I propose that the contemporary built environmental might be contributing to the overall decline of mathematics in our society. The idea arose from my interest in the theoretical basis behind architectural styles from different periods and regions. Chapters 1, 2, and 3 of this book argue how traditional architectures obey rules that are intrinsically mathematical. Those rules lead to buildings that, whatever their form, embody to a greater or lesser extent multiple mathematical qualities based on the organization of information. The architecture of the twentieth century has achieved novelty, and a break with the past, precisely by eliminating some of those qualities. I will argue this thesis by describing how complex patterns are no longer being used in design.

Figure (6.1)
Pattern created by linear translation
and reflection.

Figure (6.2)
Pattern created by rotational repetition.

The word "pattern" is used here in a very broad sense to denote a regularity in some dimension. The simplest examples are repeated visual units ordered with translational (linear) symmetry or rotational symmetry (see Figures 6.1 and 6.2). Patterns also exist in a scaling dimension, where similar forms occur at different magnification. When geometric self-similarity is defined on a scaling hierarchy, a self-similar fractal is created (see Figure 6.3). The concept of a pattern also extends to solution space, in that solutions to similar problems are themselves related and define a single template that repeats — with some variation — every time such a problem is solved. The underlying idea is to reuse information; whether in repeating a visual unit to generate a two-dimensional tiling design, or in reusing the general solution to an architectural problem, or, in mathematics, reusing the general solution to a class of differential equations.

Figure (6.3)
Pattern created by repetition at different scales.

Environmental psychologists know that our surroundings influence not only the way we think, but also our intellectual development. Trees and plants are not random growth as was once thought, but are instead examples of fractal patterns. Ordered mathematical information in the environment generates positive emotional responses (which is the message of Chapters 4 and 5). If we are raised in an environment that adversely affects our interest in mathematics; possibly even our ability to grasp mathematical concepts, our ability to understand the world is diminished. Does spending a whole life in a pattern-less world weaken or even lose one's capacity to form patterns? Even though the definitive answer to this question is not yet known, its implications are alarming. While there is very strong criticism of contemporary architecture for its lack of qualities that adapt it to human needs and sensibilities (Alexander, 1979; Charles, 1989), the present criticism goes far deeper. This is not an argument about design preferences or styles; it concerns the trained functionality of the human mind.

2. A SCIENCE OF PATTERNS.

Mathematics defines relationships and patterns (Steen, 1988). The mind perceives connections and interrelations between concepts and ideas, then links them together. The ability to create patterns is a consequence of our neural development in responding to our environment. Mathematical theories explain the relations among patterns that arise within ordered, logical structures. Patterns in the mind mimic patterns in nature as well as man-made patterns, which is probably how human beings evolved so as to be able to do mathematics. Only intelligences above a certain threshold are able to recognize patterns. Humankind generates patterns out of some basic inner need: patterns externalize connective structures generated in the mind via the process of thinking, which explains the ubiquitousness of visual patterns in traditional art and architecture.

Patterns in time are also essential to human intellectual development. Daily activity is organized around natural rhythms. Annual events become a society's fixed points. Moreover, these often link society to an emerging scientific understanding of periodic natural phenomena such as seasons and their effects. Mathematics itself arose out of the need to chronicle observed patterns in space and time. All known myths explaining the world's origin rely heavily on patterns, pointing to the birth of the world as the formation of pattern out of randomness. On smaller scales, repeating gestures and motions become theater and dance, and are incorporated into myth, ritual, and religion. The development of voice and music responds to the need to organize and encode rhythmic patterns and messages. All of these activities occur as patterns on the human temporal range (see Figure 6.4).

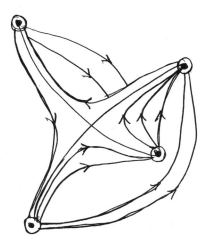

Figure (6.4)
Spatial pattern created by movement.

Complex physical and chemical systems are known to generate patterns in space or time as a result of self-organization. The system's organized complexity is manifested on a macroscopic scale as perceivable patterns. This is not only true for the innumerable static patterns found in nature; patterns also represent collective motions or other forms of organized behavior (examples include convection cells, ocean currents, and whirlpools in rivers). The observation of steady-state patterns in dynamic systems is often indicative of the dissipative system assuming an optimal state for energy transfer (i.e., it is more efficient to get rid of excess energy in a whirlpool than in random motion, which is the reason hurricanes develop). By contrast, there is very little that is ordered going on in a homogeneous state.

Before the era of mass education, and for a great many people still today, architectural patterns represent one of the few primary contacts with mathematics. Tilings and visual patterns are a "visible tip" of mathematics, which otherwise requires learning a special language to understand and appreciate. Geometrical patterns in the built environment were, for millennia, the only source of mathematical learning for a great percentage of the world's population. All these are now mostly gone. I believe that such subconscious assimilation of mathematical information helped people to better cope with the complexities of life and their environment. Patterns manifest the innate creative ability and talent that all human beings have for mathematics. The necessity for patterns in the visual environment of a developing child is acknowledged by child psychologists as being highly instrumental.

As one specific instance of traditional material culture, oriental carpets represent a several-millennia-old discipline of creating and reproducing visual patterns (see Figure 6.5). Carpets were a microcosm of one's world view and identity, recorded in the medium of textiles and natural dyes, and transmitted across generations via a tradition of weaving. A close link exists between carpet designs and mathematical rules for organizing complexity (Alexander, 1993; Salingaros, 1999a). A second example, floor pavements in Western architecture, is now appreciated as being a repository — hence, a type of textbook for its time — of mathematical information (Chapter 7 in this book; Williams, 1998).

Figure (6.5)
Spatial patterns encode mathematical information.

3. ALEXANDRINE PATTERNS AS INHERITED ARCHITECTURAL SOLUTIONS.

An effort to define patterns in solution space was made by Christopher Alexander and his associates, by collecting recurring architectural and urban solutions into the *Pattern Language* (Alexander *et. al.*, 1977). When similar solutions arise independently at different times and in different cultures, they obviously embody one or more invariants. These Alexandrine "patterns" distill timeless archetypes such as: the need for light from two sides of a room, a well-defined entrance, interaction of footpaths and vehicular roads, hierarchy of privacy in the different rooms of a house, etc. The value of Alexander's *Pattern Language* is that it is not about specific building types, but about archetypal building blocks. Each building block represents a proven solution (i.e., a pattern), and the solutions can be combined in an infinite number of ways. This implies a more mathematical, combinatoric approach to design in general (Salingaros, 2000).

Alexandrine patterns represent solutions repeated in time and space, and are thus akin to visual patterns transposed into other, abstract dimensions. Every serious discipline collects discovered regularities into a corpus of solutions that forms its foundation. Science (and as a result, humankind) has advanced by cataloging regularities observed in natural processes, to create different subjects of ordered knowledge.

Alexandrine patterns should not be confused with strictly visual patterns, however (Salingaros, 2000). A pattern/solution links both social and geometrical components, uses and practices. A purely visual pattern may be attractive but irrelevant to particular human needs and activities. Those who design from a purely visual mindset cannot appreciate the full importance of Alexandrine patterns. Nevertheless, visual and Alexandrine patterns do have a common conceptual basis. The elimination of visual patterns from the environment as discussed later creates a mind set that values only unique, irreproducible cases; that has the consequence of eliminating *all* patterns, visual ones as well as those occurring in solution space. Fortunately, the specific structural solutions (which are also patterns) that architects depend upon remain part of engineering, which, unlike architecture itself, preserves its accumulated knowledge for reuse.

Basic laws for generating coherent buildings follow Alexander's more recent work (Alexander, 2004). Successful buildings — those that adapt to human uses and sensibilities — obey the same system laws as a complex organism and an efficient computer program (see Chapter 3). Such theoretical results will eventually become part of a core body of architectural knowledge. One may ignore but cannot circumvent the need for re-usable architectural solutions. If the architectural discipline doesn't provide them (giving us visual patterns rather than adaptive solutions), someone else will come up with possibly inferior substitutes. The design of common buildings is already being taken over by the users themselves in the case of residential buildings, or by the contractors of commercial buildings. Builders have developed their own repertoire of (usually very poorly-adapted) architectural patterns, motivated by the desire to minimize cost and standardize components rather than to optimize human adaptation and connection. Architects increasingly design only "showcase" buildings, which are featured in the architectural magazines, but represent a vanishing percentage of what is actually built today.

Architectural education tends to focus on trying to develop "creativity". Classical patterns of symmetry and ordering are shunned as outdated, and improper for the advancement of architecture. A student is urged to invent new designs — without being shown how to positively utilize anything from the past — but is not taught how to assess whether they are good or bad solutions. This approach ignores and suppresses recurring patterns that might be found or discovered in the space of all possible design solutions. Contemporary architecture only validates designs by how closely they conform to some subjective notion of innovation. The only way to avoid coming back to traditional architectural patterns — which work so well in practice that they keep being rediscovered — is to block the deductive process that relates an effect with its cause. By deliberately ignoring the consequences (i.e., cause and effect) of design decisions, architectural and urban mistakes are repeated over and over again, with the same disastrous consequences each time.

4. MATHEMATICS AND ARCHITECTURE.

Historically, architecture was part of mathematics, and in many periods of the past, the two disciplines were indistinguishable. In the ancient world, mathematicians were architects, whose constructions — the pyramids, ziggurats, temples, stadia, and irrigation projects — we marvel at today. In Classical Greece and ancient Rome, architects were required to also be mathematicians. When the Byzantine emperor Justinian wanted an architect to build the Hagia Sophia as a building that surpassed everything ever built before, he turned to two professors of mathematics (geometers), Isidoros and Anthemios, to do the job (Mainstone, 1988). This tradition continued into the Islamic civilization. Contributions to the world's mathematics that came from the Islamic world occurred at a time when mathematical thought was helping to create its most memorable buildings. Islamic architects created a wealth of two-dimensional tiling patterns centuries before western mathematicians gave a complete classification (Grünbaum & Shephard, 1987).

Medieval masons had a strong grasp of geometry, which enabled them to construct the great cathedrals according to mathematical principles. They were using the experimental method to develop new types of structures. It is not entirely fair to dismiss the middle ages as being without mathematics: their mathematics is built into structures instead of being written down. The regrettable loss of literacy in the West during those centuries was most emphatically not accompanied by a commensurate loss of visual or architectural patterns, because patterns (as opposed to the abstract representations of a written script) reflect processes that are inherent in the human mind. Every traditional architecture has mathematics in it.

I am interested here in what happened in the twentieth century. The Austrian architect Adolf Loos banned ornament from architecture in 1908 with these preposterous, unsupported statements: "The evolution of culture is synonymous with the removal of ornament from utilitarian objects ... not only is ornament produced by criminals but also a crime is committed through the fact that ornament inflicts serious injury on people's health, on the national budget and hence on cultural evolution ... Freedom from ornament is a sign of spiritual strength." (Loos, 1971).

This hostile, racist sentiment was shared by the Swiss architect Le Corbusier: *"Decoration is of a sensorial and elementary order, as is color, and is suited to simple races, peasants and savages ... The peasant loves ornament and decorates his walls."* (Le Corbusier, 1927: p. 143).

These two architects condemned the material culture of humankind from all around the globe, accumulated over millennia (and other architects believed them unquestioningly). While that may seem an action of merely stylistic interest, it in fact has indirect but serious consequences. The elimination of ornament removes all ordered structural differentiations from the range of scales 5 mm to 2 m or thereabouts. That corresponds to the human scale of structures, i.e., the sizes of the eye, finger, hand, arm, body, etc. In the modernist design canon, patterns cannot be defined on those scales, and that removes mathematical information from the built environment. Looking around at twentieth-century buildings, one is hard-pressed to discover visual patterns on any of several different scales. Indeed, their architects go to great lengths to disguise patterns on human scales that are inevitable because of the activities in a building; and which also arise in the materials and as a consequence of structural stability and weathering.

Visual patterns have the strongest emotional and cognitive impact when they are immediately accessible. It is useful to distinguish between abstract patterns on a building's plan, and perceivable patterns on building façades, walls, ceilings, and pavements. Only the latter influence human beings directly, because they are seen and experienced instantaneously. For the past several decades, architects and urbanists have been obsessed with imposing crude patterns and symmetries on a building's plan. Those are not always observable, even if the structure is an open plaza, because of the perspective, position, and size of a human being. In a normal walled building, the pattern of its plan is largely hidden from view by the built structure. A user has to reconstruct a building's plan in the mind; i.e., it is perceivable intellectually, and only after much effort. This goes hand-in-hand with a formal approach to design, which attempts to replace meaning from our perceptive faculties with meaning from our intellectual faculties.

Proportional ratios may be included with architectural qualities that are perceived only indirectly. The presence of the Golden Mean $\Phi \approx 1.618$, the ratios 5:3, 8:5, and $\sqrt{2}$ proportion are found throughout all of architecture, and this topic provides a rich field of study. Nevertheless, no specific mathematical information is communicated to users of a room or façade having the requisite overall proportions, and the effect remains one of only secondary aesthetic impact. What actually occurs is that the use of proportional ratios within a traditional design canon also subdivides forms so as to define coincident scales (i.e., subunits in a scaling hierarchy), creating a hierarchical coherence which is a strongly positive effect (see Chapter 3).

5. ARCHITECTURAL COUNTER-ARGUMENTS.

Books on architectural history emphasize how twentieth-century architecture is supposedly rational, being founded on mathematical principles (von Meiss, 1991). The writings of the early modernists fail, however, to reveal any true mathematical basis. Proposing pure geometric solids such as cubes and cylinders as "mathematical" is overly simplistic. If one looks hard enough, one comes away with a few unstated principles deduced from the buildings themselves. One of these working rules is hierarchy reversal: "build structures on a large scale that are natural only on the small scale; they then appear out of place at full size, and are therefore experienced as novel". This reasoning produces giant pyramids and rectangular boxes that are pure Platonic solids. Building unnatural forms to impress people goes back to the ancient Egyptians, and is definitely not limited to twentieth-century architects.

Much is made of Le Corbusier's "modulor" system of scales as being a link between modernist architecture and mathematics. This is a somewhat confused dimensional rule that uses multiples of the Golden Mean, $\Phi \approx 1.618$, anchored on the height of the "standard man" at 6 ft (183 cm) (von Meiss, 1991). A careful reading of the "modulor" reveals that it is not, and was never intended to be, a method for generating patterns. Le Corbusier himself did not apply it for surface design, preferring visually empty surfaces of raw, so-called "Brutalist", concrete. When he did use it (with his assistant, the Greek composer Iannis Xenakis) on the Monastery of Sainte-Marie de la Tourette, it produced a random façade, and not a pattern.

City planning from this period also imposed simplistic geometric forms, ignoring inherited urban patterns. It straightened out curved streets, and ordered unevenly-distributed buildings into neat rows of repeated identical forms. The urban scale lost the most in mathematical content. This lack of understanding complex mathematical order had catastrophic long-term consequences. By imposing a simplistic geometry on city form, post-war planning drastically reduces the rich mathematical complexity of the urban environment (Batty & Longley, 1994; Salingaros, 1998). That is analogous, perhaps, to reducing the Spinor group in n dimensions (a mathematical group of related elements) into the trivial Abelian group Z_2 (consisting of only 1 and 0). With hierarchy reversal, the monotonous patterns defined by modernist blocks and streets are visible only from an airplane. Urbanists of the early twentieth century didn't understand complex systems, so they were eager to simplify human interactions as much as possible. They removed the essential patterns (not only the spatial ones, but more importantly, the dynamical patterns of human activity) present in the great historical cities, to create empty suburbia and monstrous office buildings.

Throughout this book, I have argued that contemporary buildings fail to attain the human qualities of older buildings, which arose from a building tradition richer in patterns. This Chapter turns the argument towards essential mathematical qualities. I no longer talk about the loss of traditional architectural and urban typologies, but about the loss of mathematical information. We lost that information because we didn't fully understand the architectural typologies that encoded it.

Architects complain that new buildings are bad because they are cheap and tacky; implying that they could be improved by a more generous budget. One hears that: "the reason beautiful buildings cannot be built today is because of the high cost of materials and workmanship". This statement is belied by the wonderful variety of folk architecture built the world over using inexpensive local materials. Architecture is about creating patterns and spaces; a preoccupation with materials only obscures more important issues. It is perfectly possible to build mathematically-rich structures on any budget by applying timeless rules, such as those derived by Alexander (Alexander, 2004; Alexander *et. al.*, 1977) and those elaborated in this book. When they are generated by a set of rules whose purpose is to avoid spatial coherence, new buildings are usually bad — in particular, those with a big budget.

Natural materials embody organized complexity in the scales below 5 mm, and thereby provide mathematical information to a viewer through their microscopic surface structure. Architects have abused this property. Emotionally uncomfortable buildings, starting with the Austrian architect Joseph Hoffmann's Stoclet house in Brussels (1906-1911), camouflage a design mathematically deficient on the intermediate and higher scales, through the use of expensive materials. Attention is drawn to the richness of detail in the materials, and away from the deliberate breakup of geometrical coherence. This was a principal method used by the German architect Ludwig Mies van der Rohe to enliven his transparent, minimalist boxes. The extreme example was his German Pavilion at the Barcelona Exposition of 1929, where giant slabs of colored and travertine marble distract attention from the removal of all other mathematical information. The Barcelona Pavilion is pleasant to be in, until one realizes that it is not a closed building: it is inadequate for any practical function. Seduced by the visual cues, we do not notice this sleight of hand.

6. CLASSICAL AND MODERN MATHEMATICS: IS THERE AN ARCHITECTURAL ANALOGY?

The core mathematics curriculum consisting of calculus and its prerequisites (trigonometry, algebra and geometry) does not yet include newer topics such as fractals and chaos. As Calculus was derived by Sir Isaac Newton in the 17th Century, today's world is solidly based on a Newtonian foundation (Steen, 1988). At the same time, the newer mathematics such as fractals attract student interest because of the very beautiful graphics they generate, and many educators are trying to find a way to incorporate them into the curriculum. Fractals exist in a hierarchical space that relates distinct levels of scale, and self-similar fractals repeat patterns in the scaling hierarchy. Teaching fractals early in one's formal education would help to reveal many of the inherent deficiencies of contemporary architecture and urbanism, which are non-fractal.

Classical and Neoclassical architecture, which tries to imitate the spirit and style of the Greco-Roman tradition, is ordered in a rectangular geometry, which originally included sophisticated Non-Euclidean corrections due to "entasis", the subtle curvature on Greek temples (Haselberger, 1985). Vernacular (folk) architecture, which represents traditional cultural styles around the world, tends to be either more or less curved, and is sometimes profusely detailed. There have been periods when formal architectural movements have incorporated curvature and ornament into the prevailing style; for example, Islamic and Far-eastern architectures,

16th Century Manueline Portuguese architecture, Baroque architecture, and Art Nouveau architecture (Fletcher, 1987).

Architects took the rectangular geometry of Classical architecture, but eliminated its subdivisions and subsymmetries (i.e., detail originally present on columns, cornices, fluting, and sculptural friezes). Through a self-imposed stylistic dictate to minimize what were taken to be "extraneous" details, architecture developed away from fractal properties, and that is one reason why much of it now appears unnatural (Eilenberger, 1985). Traditional architecture, on the other hand, including that in a Classical style, tends to be explicitly fractal (Crompton, 2002; Goldberger, 1996). Fractal subdivisions and scaling can be found in buildings of all periods and styles, and that crucial characteristic divides contemporary architecture from much of what was built before. The exceptions are those older buildings wishing to disconnect from the pedestrian, usually in order to express power and to intimidate. These include monumental Fascist architecture, and its precursors in deliberately imposing (but stark and forbidding) temples, palaces, and defensive military buildings of the past.

An analogy was recently proposed between modernist architecture and Newtonian mathematics (Halliwell, 1995), which, however, is based upon a misunderstanding. A simplistic vocabulary of empty rectangular forms has very little mathematical content. Of course, certain modernists did build curves, complex substructure, and arches (for example, Erich Mendelsohn and Frank Lloyd Wright), and those buildings are much richer mathematically (and, it would appear, are much better liked). The minimalist movement in modernist architecture does not even represent Newtonian mathematics, but predates ancient Egyptian mathematics, stopping at simple squares and rectangles. (The best that this type of architecture can do is to obey some proportional ratio such as the Golden Mean). Where do mathematical structures such as periodic functions, derivatives, curvature, and Taylor series fit into empty rectangles? They don't. The only clear mathematical analogy between distinct architectural styles is the presence or absence of patterns.

7. THE ANTI-FRACTAL MOVEMENT.

A minimalist architectural style removes fractals from our environment. Pure Platonic solids are incompatible with fractals, because the former exist only on a single level of scale. One definition of a fractal is a structure in which there is ordered substructure (i.e., organized complexity) at every level of magnification. Magnifying a fractal by a fixed scaling factor, say $e \approx 2.7$ (see Chapter 3), will give a set of patterns at magnifications 1, 3, 7, 20, etc., all of which show structure and complexity (see Figure 6.6). A "self-similar" fractal has the additional property that all these patterns are related by geometrical similarities (as long as one uses the scaling factor intrinsic to that fractal). Le Corbusier and Ludwig Mies van der Rohe intentionally ignored this rule in their buildings, in an attempt to distinguish them both from natural forms, and from traditional building styles. Some exceptions are discussed later.

Figure (6.6)
Complex structure is obvious
at every magnification.

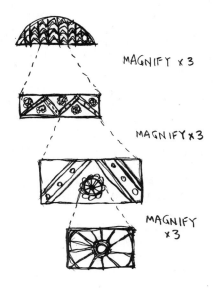

MAGNIFY x 3

MAGNIFY x 3

MAGNIFY x 3

Recently, fractal dimensions have been calculated for Frank Lloyd Wright's and Le Corbusier's buildings, using the method of increasingly smaller rectangular grids (Bovill, 1996). The results show that (at least some of) Wright's buildings display a self-similar characteristic over a wide range of scales, from a distant view to finger-tip size detail, so those buildings are intrinsically fractal (Bovill, 1996). In this, Wright was following the brilliant example of his teacher, Louis Sullivan, both of whom were informed and inspired by nature. Sullivan's buildings engage the viewer on every scale, right down to the details in the materials. By contrast, Le Corbusier's architecture displays a self-similar characteristic over only two or three of the largest scales; namely, those corresponding to a distant view (Bovill, 1996). Up close, Le Corbusier's architecture is flat and straight, and therefore has no fractal qualities. (A fractal dimension between one and two characterizes a fractal design that has an infinite number of self-similar levels of scale, whereas the fractal dimension of Le Corbusier's buildings immediately drops to the number one). In an analysis of the intermediate and small scales, Le Corbusier's buildings have no fractal properties.

8. POST-MODERNIST AND DECONSTRUCTIVIST STYLES.

Architects reacting against "International Style" buildings have reintroduced curvature and subdivisions into their designs. Using curves brings more mathematical information into the environment. With very few exceptions, however, that still does not lead to patterns. The overall form of some famous examples of curved modernist, post-modernist, and contemporary architecture (e.g., the Chapel at Ronchamp, the Sydney opera house, the Denver airport, and the Bilbao art museum) is defined by simple mathematical functions. Mathematics beyond that of a straight line is evident here, but only on the largest level of scale. These buildings are less mathematical than, say, St. Peter's or the Parthenon, precisely because the latter have a linked hierarchy of ordered subsymmetries, right down to the microstructure in the materials. Despite an often sophisticated overall form, the intermediate and smaller scales of the newer buildings tend to be informationally weak, or empty altogether. If they are not empty, then they are disordered and thus lacking informational organization.

Some people relate the deconstructivist architectural style, characterized by unbalanced, chaotic forms, to more modern mathematics such as chaos and fractals (Halliwell, 1995). But they are mistaken, confusing words and superficial appearance for genuine mathematical qualities (Salingaros, 2004). Whereas self-similarity in pure fractals tends to be exact (i.e., mathematical fractals show the same pattern at every magnification), natural and architectural self-similarity is often statistical: the degree of complexity, though not exactly the same pattern, repeats at different scales. Deconstructivist buildings can approach a statistical fractal, but they have no patterns, either on a single scale, or linking across different levels of scale. Innovative architects may wish to generate fractal rhythms in order to explore complexity at the interface between organization and chaos, and to link it to other rhythms (Bovill, 1996). The complexity of such patterns departs from simple repetition, yet the basis for a pattern is that it establishes correlations that are absent from contemporary architectural expressions.

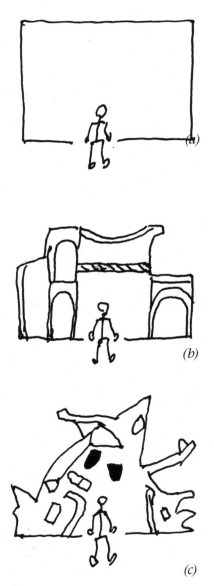

Patterns are essential to architectural form, and deconstructivist buildings deliberately avoid any type of pattern. Architects have taken the mathematical term of chaos to justify the deconstructivist style, but for them, chaos means something else altogether, such as randomness (Salingaros, 2004). Mathematical chaos is the study of hidden patterns in systems that are only apparently chaotic. There is no change in the fundamental aim of mathematics — which is to discover patterns — in going from Newtonian to chaotic models. Despite the enormous possibilities of applying fractals to built forms in an innovative manner, deconstructivist buildings have only led to random configurations. Reacting to empty, minimalist models, deconstructivist examples jump from one extreme to another: from the empty minimalist model straight into random forms, bypassing organized complex forms completely because those look "too traditional" (see Figure 6.7).

As discussed in Chapter 5, coherence is possible only if there exists organized information on many different scales. It is clear, however, that such is not the architects' intent. Any architectural detail appearing on contemporary buildings is either so minimal as to be hardly visible, or the larger scale in which it is embedded is intentionally disarrayed and broken. The detail is thus detached and incoherent. So far, deconstructivist architects have avoided patterns and organized complexity, which are the principal underpinnings of mathematics.

Figure (6.7)
Deconstruction jumps
from (a) to (c), bypassing (b).

9. A MATHEMATICAL TEMPLATE FOR OUR ENVIRONMENT.

The built environment of the last several decades eliminates ordered, fractal structures (trees, rocks, rivers, and older buildings), and replaces them with empty rectangles and planes. Its opposite, consisting of random forms in deconstructivist buildings, urban sprawl, and commercial signs, appear in the landscape; still contradicting and displacing forms with organized complexity (patterns). This provides a strong message that complex patterns do not belong — or are not allowed — as part of our contemporary world. Subconsciously, people learn that objects embodying organized complexity are "not modern", and so there is no reason either to build new ones having those qualities, or to preserve existing ones with those qualities from destruction. Notice with what fervor cities in the developing world eliminate their most beautiful buildings and urban regions, to replace them with a barren emptiness of faceless rectangles; ostensibly in order to imitate the more "developed" world. The latter, in turn, now competes in propagating showcase buildings that exemplify disorder.

Many of us regret the loss of organic forms such as trees from our surroundings, yet the assault is actually far broader: it is against essential mathematical qualities. Our civilization has turned against those structures, animate as well as inanimate, that possess organized complexity. We are taught by our schools and media through examples, which eliminate complex information ordered through mathematics from our environment. We have reversed our mathematical values on the misguided impression that this is necessary for technological advancement. That is both false and dangerous. Emptiness has no content, and randomness can be profoundly disturbing. Human beings evolved by organizing biochemical complexity and signals from our environment. Who we are biologically; how we interact with our world; and how our world is put together is what should be taught and valued above all else. As soon as our priority shifts to understanding and valuing objects with organized complexity, we will again be able to appreciate nature and humankind's greatest achievements.

10. INFORMATION AND COMPLEXITY.

Any effort to quantify the degree of pattern in a structure or design leads us to consider its information content. There are two separate variables here: the actual information and its presentation (Salingaros, 1999b); and how well that information is organized (Chapter 5 in this book; Klinger & Salingaros, 2000). Blank walls convey no information other than their outline. Ordered patterns on the one hand, and chaotic designs on the other, offer a large quantity of information; but it is organized very differently in these two cases. Complex, ordered patterns have a large information content, which is tightly organized and therefore coherent (i.e., it can be grasped and has meaning for a human being) (see Figure 6.8). Chaotic forms have too much internally uncoordinated information, so that they overload the mind's capacity to process information (see Figure 6.9). Random information is incoherent: by failing to correlate, it cannot be encoded (Klinger & Salingaros, 2000).

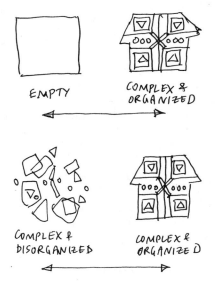

Figure (6.8)
Large amount of information is
organized and coherent.

Figure (6.9)
The same amount of information is
disorganized and incoherent.

Monotonous repetition provides little information, although if it does contain any, it is well organized. Repetition (using translational or other symmetry) of an empty module does not necessarily create patterns with any content; one needs contrast as well (Alexander, 2004). Internal contrast, in turn, can be used to generate symmetries on a larger scale, which is essential for organization. Complex patterns contain more information in their different scales, and also in the interconnections between those scales (Chapter 3 in this book; Klinger & Salingaros, 2000). Monotonous repetition without subsymmetries, however, represents a minimal pattern on a single level of scale.

Even though I have been arguing for the benefits of patterns, it is necessary to explain how simplistic patterns are abused to reduce organized complexity in our environment. Organization depends upon geometrical coherence, which arises when patterns combine and include several distinct scales. If, on the other hand, an empty module is repeated in a way that prevents the emergence of a larger scale, that repetition reduces organized complexity. Very repetitive designs can be used as a way of eliminating complexity and information on many different scales (or conversely, as the means to emphasize a single scale), thereby simplifying the built environment. Repetition applied only to the large scales diminishes its value as an observable pattern. Repetition is more useful on the small (i.e., human) range of scales.

Architectural history suggests that the modernists valued honest structures and rejected "gingerbread"; but they clearly went too far. For example, symmetric patterns on floor tilings were eliminated as not being closely related to the use of the architectural structure. Apparently, the opponents of this type of ornament misunderstood the function of a patterned floor tiling (see Chapter 7, *Pavements as Embodiments of Meaning for a Fractal Mind*). By connecting to the pedestrian through information, the entire space is made more immediate — hence, more useful — and at the same time it supports ancillary functions of the whole building. Incredibly, Le Corbusier totally missed the fundamental role of information in architecture and equated two instances, one with organized complexity index (the *architectural life* of Chapter 5) close to 100, with another close to zero: *"The uniformity of the innumerable windows in this vast wall on the Piazza San Marco gives the same play as would the smooth side of a room."* (Le Corbusier, 1987: p. 69).

11. CONCLUSION.

Does architecture influence our civilization? It most definitely does. To evaluate this effect in earnest, we should once again be investigating the relationship between architecture and mathematics. In the past, the connection was two-way, reinforcing, and mutually beneficial. There are indications that architecture has separated itself from mathematics, first under the influence of an overly simplistic, politically-driven social ideology, and now even further by following the anti-scientific deconstructivist philosophers. This reversal of mathematical values not only applies to buildings and urban regions; it defines a pervasive aesthetic. As architecture is ubiquitous, the ideas it embodies influence our everyday life and way of thinking to a remarkable extent. We have not trained people to recognize the importance of mathematical information in the built environment. We cannot afford to ignore this influence on our culture, especially because of the strong possibility that it may have negative consequences.

Chapter Seven

PAVEMENTS AS EMBODIMENTS OF MEANING FOR A FRACTAL MIND.

By Terry M. Mikiten, Nikos A. Salingaros, and Hing-Sing Yu

1. INTRODUCTION.

This Chapter puts forward a fractal theory of the human mind that explains one aspect of how we interact with our environment. The mind establishes a connection with the environment by processing information, an important process that drove the evolution of the brain. Some interesting analogies are developed here of how we store ideas and information within a fractal scheme. In particular, in this discussion we assert that floor patterns in buildings, and the pavements of sidewalks, streets, and plazas play a role in connecting human beings to surrounding structures, by acting as a vehicle for conveying meaning. Successful pavement design transfers meaning from our surroundings to our awareness. Directional patterning can lead the pedestrian. Such a connection, if done properly, can establish a positive psychological and physiological state. We argue that the success of patterned pavements is due to the fact that they connect hierarchically, which in turn triggers positive emotions.

If we wish to preserve our intelligence in a more permanent form than electrical impulses in biological nerve tissue, we can transfer our thoughts to books; or engrave them on a physical medium such as stone. On a much more fundamental level than written language, however, we could impress (imprint) on open space a geometrical pattern that reflects analogous informational structures in the mind. A patterned pavement has information content and is physical and durable; it is therefore a sign of intelligence encoded in a structure that uses very little energy, hence is relatively permanent. Moreover, since a geometric design doesn't need spoken language to convey meaning, it is universal, i.e., it can be understood in some sense by any mind that can detect it. One may say that geometric design is a universal visual language.

Some of these ideas grow out of an earlier discussion on how human beings interact with their surroundings (Padrón & Salingaros, 2000). The perception of public space is linked with the design of its pavement, and human perception is a natural part of how the mind operates. The mind establishes connections automatically. This process occurs in any physical space, and it is either helped or hindered by design patterns and texture. The floor helps or hinders our perception of the surrounding space. We will build a case for a psychological link between an observer and an open space that depends in part on visual patterns. We claim that the environment links directly to our consciousness, which extends to embrace open spaces via patterns in the pavement. Finally, we provide some very broad guidelines of how pavements should be designed in order to achieve this linking.

2. FRACTALS AND HIERARCHICAL LINKING.

A fractal structure shows non-trivial geometrical substructure at every level of magnification (Lauwerier, 1991). Fractals define a scaling hierarchy that is complex at every level of magnification. The special case of "self-similar fractals" has the additional property that structure revealed at each level of magnification is related by scaling (Lauwerier, 1991). That is, the substructures when magnified by the appropriate factor are all similar to each other. Self-similar fractals are mathematically simple; since their structure is repeated at different magnifications to create the whole, they require only one basic algorithm (design) to generate. A basic design is repeated at different magnifications, and this links all the scales in a self-similar fractal together (see Figure 7.1).

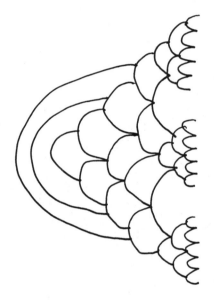

Figure (7.1)
Fractal links different scales in a hierarchy.

Biological forms are always fractal (Weibel, 1994). Many are obviously self-similar, but organisms also include complex structures that are not. For example, the mammalian lung is a self-similar fractal in several of its larger levels (Weibel, 1994; West & Deering, 1995; West & Goldberger, 1987). There is a clear dendritic (tree-like) structure that optimizes — and is a consequence of — the subdivision of the airducts forming the lung (Figure 2.2). As one gets down to the smaller level of the alveoli, exact self-similarity is lost, because different complex substructures arise as the physical needs for gas exchange and blood circulation take over. The lung is a fractal all the way down to the molecular level according to the broader definition of "statistical self-similarity". In a "statistically self-similar fractal" the degree of structural complexity (though not the form) is similar at each scale, still linking the different levels of scale.

A fractal connects several different levels of scale. Whether established via similarity of form on each scale, or through some other common qualities such as texture or symmetries, the scale-connectivity property of fractals creates a hierarchi-

145

cal linking. Hierarchical linking in the environment attaches forms and textures to geometry at different levels of scale, and so to an observer. In such a system, it is very easy to go from the very small to the very large. It is impossible to link forms hierarchically if they are empty, since in that case the absence of substructure leaves too few subscales to link together.

A hierarchically-linked system can encode complexity in a simple manner. We can relate complexity to the length of an algorithm (i.e., a mathematical rule) required to generate a pattern or visual piece of information. If the algorithm is short, then the pattern is termed simple. For example, if one wishes to draw a fern leaf or cauliflower (normally considered complex structures) using a fractal algorithm, the algorithm is very short, because those designs embody hierarchical scaling. The algorithm draws all scales, down to the microscopic level. Fractal encoding is described by many authors (see Section 4 of Chapter 3; Lauwerier, 1991). We utilize this concept to propose that what appear to be complex processes in the human mind and its interactions with the environment could in fact be very simple in a fractal sense. Fractal processes and designs can provide the basis for connecting ideas, memories, architecture, and urban elements (Padrón & Salingaros, 2000).

3. THE CONCEPT OF MIND.

The brain is known to be a structured system of hierarchically-organized anatomic modules. These interacting modules communicate with one another. In turn, the modules contain within them other sub-modules that communicate among themselves (within the larger module). This pattern is repeated at several different levels of scale, culminating in what is a molecular and biochemical fractal of interacting and communicating systems (Alexander & Globus, 1996). Although it doesn't look tree-like, the functioning of the brain resembles the lung in having a linked hierarchy of scales.

In a similar way, we can conceive of the mind (our thoughts and feelings) as consisting of self-similar complexes of hierarchically-arranged modules all linked together in a way that can be continuously changing according to various stimuli and thoughts. The relationship of mind to brain can be characterized as a problem of figuring out in which way the mind (i.e., the processes of perception, consciousness, and understanding) and the brain (a physical complex of neurons) map onto each other.

In this conception of the mind, the brain can be regarded as a relatively isolated system that communicates with the world via nerve impulses generated by sensory receptors in the periphery. Our five senses provide the input, and are thus linked to all these images and memories. The main discourse among the different elements of the brain accomplishes a synthesis of the information coming in, resulting in the internal generation of what we call "conscious reality". Drawing on the analogy of hierarchically-organized anatomic modules in the brain, we assume that the systems of organization that also characterize the mind are at least partially fractal in nature. That is, each contains a hierarchically-arranged system characterized by an algorithmic continuity between the successive functional levels of activity. Our mind appears to deal with hierarchies of thoughts rather than with single thoughts as isolated units.

Must the linking between successive levels of the hierarchy always be the same; i.e., does the mind represent a self-similar fractal? Not necessarily. It is possible to imagine a hierarchical system in which some clusters of levels may be connected according to one algorithm and others according to another algorithm. One of the most interesting aspects of the human brain is that it is capable of generating new hierarchical systems as needed. A synthesis of ideas can result in a new collection of ideas. In this setting, we have one hierarchical arrangement of concepts giving rise to another hierarchical arrangement of concepts. For example, a scientific discovery occurs when we notice a relationship between two or more phenomena: the result is a new idea.

Our essential thesis is that when a fractal system generates a new system, it has the same attributes and characteristics as the generator — especially hierarchical linking. Thus, mental associations that would appear at first to require enormous lengths of descriptive code (and consequently be termed complex) may in fact be handled by very short codes. If that is indeed the case, then the human mind could be using fractal encoding as a standard way of coding enormous chains of related thoughts into a single fractal entity. That fractal entity would then be easy to deal with as a unit. We draw the analogy to a computer program used for outlining text: one writes headings that enclose subheadings, which enclose notes, etc. All of these collapse into the outline. The evidence for this claim is revealed when we see how thoughts are naturally linked to each other internally. A design pattern may well be a representation of an architect's natural expression of these chains of thought in a tangible form.

4. MEMORY AND THE FRACTAL MIND.

Striking parallel properties exist in neuronal and thinking processes. The mind is synonymous with mental activity and is a subset of neuronal processes (Alexander & Globus, 1996). Since the brain consists of neurons for both involuntary and voluntary activities of the individual, the mind is also aware of both types of processes. Cognition depends on how well information is stored, retrieved, modified, and translated into commands. The memory process is central to neural function and is an example of the basic mapping that links the brain and the mind. Information that comes from memory helps to support perception and meaning.

The nervous system has a "massively parallel architecture" in the way this term is used in computer science. Different linked circuits on multiple scales of organization all working simultaneously are based on neurons (which are extremely numerous simple processors). Memory depends on the network formed among neurons. Artificial neural networks have been able to simulate primitive forms of memory function, thus proving that this is the way biological memory works (Rolls & Treves, 1998). Neuronal pathways linking regions of the cerebral cortex correlate with the construction of long-term memories (Rolls & Treves, 1998). It is evident in a diagrammatic representation of connections within the brain that there are layers of structures with projections from one to the other (Alexander & Globus, 1996). The presence of these prominent recurrent linkages has been correlated with the associative memory operated by neural networks (Rolls & Treves, 1998).

Associative memory is very important to architectural design. It can be responsible for powerful emotional experiences when we identify with what we already know, or which reminds us of something stored in our memory. In response to a small cue, which can be as trivial as a particular ornament, a color, or a fleeting odor, we selectively retrieve a specific set of linked memories quickly. A certain smell triggers recall of a past situation, and we remember a whole complex of memories linking emotions of the past moment with details of that event's physical environment, spaces, colors, sounds, etc. (see Figure 7.2). All of this information might have been dormant, i.e., much like a compressed file on a computer disk, and it is suddenly expanded as a result of a trigger. Evidently, the system architecture of our neuronal network is designed in favor of fast information retrieval from multiple locations of our stored memory.

In addition, there must be a flexible mechanism that allows new information to be added without losing old memories completely. The brain's multilayered structure has previously been suggested as providing a framework for associative memory (Marr, 1982). We suggest that a fractal-like neuronal system architecture provides a filter for selected memories to be stored in a stable layered configuration. Thus, associative memories that make us feel at ease would be manifested through this fractal mechanism.

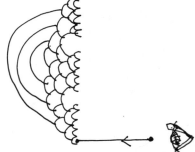

Figure (7.2)
Associative memory recalls a system from one detail.

5. FRACTAL TUNING AND COMMUNICATION.

Fractal systems give rise to fractal-based communications signals. These, in turn, travel through fractally-organized channels. A simple illustration of this would be communications within a biological system. The entire system is fractal-based: the organs that generate the communication signals, the signals, and the receiving devices (the recipient organs) are all fractal in character. A key idea behind this is the concept that the body contains "receptor sites" which are, in effect, "tuned" to recognize certain chemical signals as opposed to others. For example, when the pituitary gland releases thyroid-stimulating hormone, the thyroid gland responds to this hormone but other organs of the body have no discernible response. We have hormones being generated by glands, the glands in turn impacting upon the organs at a distant site via the bloodstream, and finally arriving at the target organ where they manifest their actions in a biological way. All these require fine tuning of signal generation and reception at different levels, so as to provide a balanced control of all physiological processes in harmony with the nervous system (Yu, 1996).

Systems in the body are "tuned" to generically recognize different kinds of fractal hierarchies. We contend that the brain has special systems that are tuned in exactly this way. The brain's neural patterns are responsible for recognizing structured complex systems that have a hierarchical organization in which the levels in the hierarchy are defined in a systematic, algorithmic way. Such recognition has an emotive value for the person (or higher animal) in question. In general, when a system recognizes a structured entity in the environment, it attributes "meaning" to it. Organisms create communication signals that have a special structure, which is to say that they share a common language. Languages are characterized by collections of rules defining syntax and semantics. In a system of fractal-based communications, those rules are tantamount to the algorithmic connectivity among the hierarchies in the fractal structures used for communication.

Following an analogy with radio transmission, where tuning the receiver depends on matching a single frequency, fractal tuning represents a more sophisticated process that matches complex signals having a similar hierarchical structure. Brain mechanisms are especially receptive to such signals, and would screen other signals that have a different algorithmic structure — i.e., any signal that shows no hierarchical linking among its components. This represents a "filter", allowing us to connect selectively and preferentially to fractal forms (see Figures 7.3 and 7.4). It also explains instantaneous cognition as a kind of resonance between an external structure (i.e., the familiar forms and details of traditional architecture) and the internal structure of our cognitive system. Such a mechanism has already been suggested by Gibson (Gibson, 1979; Michaels & Carello, 1981) in his psychological model of "direct perception". The present theory of fractal encoding is thus consistent with Gibson's work.

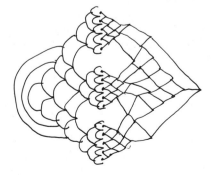

Figure (7.3)
Fractal receptor recognizes another
fractal structure.

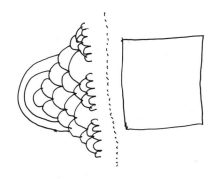

Figure (7.4)
There is no connection between
a fractal and a non-fractal.

6. PROBLEMS OF MISCOMMUNICATION.

Evidence for structuredness in communications is seen in the use of metaphor as a tool for communicating among people. Metaphorical structures impact the way that people communicate complex ideas (Lakoff & Johnson, 1999). A metaphor is the use of words that trigger a complex system of connections and associations, generating new ideas and meaning in the process. We may interpret the effect of a metaphor as the transference of one hierarchical meaning system onto another, very different one.

In the model outlined here, which defines linked hierarchies as the central element in communication, a metaphor represents the act of completion of a partial structure of meaning, which is offered by way of explanation. We grasp the part we know, and then complete the rest in the most obvious manner (to us), which might not be the most obvious manner to someone else, however. Confronted with a complex concept, an individual might use only the easy component of the structure (consisting of a set of communicating elements) to make a point. Unfortunately, the listener in this dialogue then attaches to the entire construct, which was not explicitly given, whether or not this is appropriate in the particular setting. Thus, metaphors give the illusion of meaning and "truth" because they also give the illusion of completeness of structure. When communications channels utilize fractal structures, it is possible that a mixture of rules is being applied at different levels in the hierarchy. Such structures can give rise to ambiguity in communication.

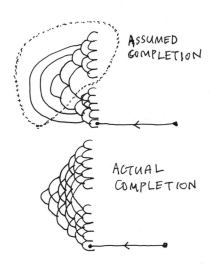

Figure (7.5)
Reconstruction may not be
the intended fractal.

A frequent cause of miscommunication is the certainty of one party that what the other party said is completely understood. A piece of information provided by one individual triggers recall of a fractal construction in the other's mind (see Figure 7.5). Because different fractal encodings have common cross-over points, however, it frequently turns out that the completed fractal is not the one intended. This results in miscommunication. The problem lies in the completion process itself, which gives a feeling of satisfaction, hence the illusion that one has understood what was said. The emotion associated with the fractal encoding of a complete thought (complete in the sense of linking a hierarchy of different levels) could be the same thing as the feeling of understanding. This idea is consistent with the observation of a definite physiological (emotional) state correlated with a mental state such as "understanding" (Lakoff & Johnson, 1999). As thinking processes evolved from sensory and motor systems, the brain still uses those networks for higher functions such as thinking, so thinking is also "feeling".

A short-circuiting of fractal encoding (by crossing different hierarchies or meaning structures) is responsible for making us accept harmful ideas and notions as perfectly natural. This is deliberately practiced by those promoting such ideas, for example in advertising and political and religious indoctrination. The method consists of finding the possible cross-over points of a fractal string of knowledge and associations. A self-serving idea (which profits someone at the expense of others) is then attached to one of those cross-over points. From then on, the individuals whose brains carry this modified circuit will experience an emotional satisfaction that normally characterizes truth, even though they are being manipulated by a message. This is the basis for both the advertising industry, and of political and psychological indoctrination (see Chapter 10, *Darwinian Processes and Memes in Architecture: A Memetic Theory of Modernism*).

7. SHAPING THE BUILT ENVIRONMENT.

The built environment reflects structures in human thought, in that it is created by human minds. Thought works by establishing connections between concepts, creating conceptual structures and ideas. We assume that fractal structures in nature influenced the development of neuronal mechanisms in evolution that could encode and decode these structures automatically. If true, it is reasonable to suppose that the mind, which uses these mental mechanisms, seeks to shape its environment according to the same rules for structural connectivity that inherently make up cognition. Internal patterns of neural nets that form our sensory and thinking processes are organized in a way that reflects similar patterns of organization in the external universe.

People have a basic need to extend their consciousness to their environment, something that occurs effortlessly when surrounded by nature. We normally try to shape the artificial environment in a way that we can connect to it (or at least we did unselfconsciously throughout pre-industrial times). This explains the reason why we built cathedrals as examples of organized complexity: because we cannot connect to objects or environments that are either too random, or too simple. We instinctively use the ordered complexity of our own mind as a template to extend our consciousness outside our own body. Human consciousness is linked, through a hierarchy of structures on different scales, to what we build. Such visual connections extend the mind fractally to the physical environment.

Having put forward a theoretical model of how the mind might operate, we now apply the model to evaluate different visual structures within architecture and urban design. Passive input creates meaning in the brain, which then generates emotion. In principle, we have no control over input except movement; one can approach a source that generates positive emotions, and avoid a source of negative emotions. We can control the sources in the man-made environment through design if we choose to. Traditionally, architects built structures that generated an optimal emotional response, using their experience of what was the most beneficial input. Paradoxically, our intelligence allows us to override negative emotional cues, and to build structures that repel us.

8. PAVEMENTS AND HIERARCHY.

Architecture has in the past felt a need for pavements that are either patterned, or that embody figurative art. Our perception of space is founded on a connection with the ground via design. In creating an artificial built environment to house themselves and their activities, human beings have always been careful to connect with the ground visually. Methods that connect a pedestrian to the floor, whether inside a building or in an open space outside include pavements, tilings, textures, mosaics, etc. Kim Williams (1998) has undertaken a pioneering study of interior pavements. The detailed pavement in Medieval churches makes a major contribution to a user's experience of the architectural ensemble, independently of the structure itself. We are in complete agreement with Williams that pavements are central to mankind's architectural — and intellectual — development. Most twentieth-century pavements are plain and empty, having been built on the belief that there is no functional need for either representation or pattern in a pavement. We will argue the contrary: that pavements can serve a primary function of connecting observers to all visible surrounding structures. The connection becomes all the more necessary for larger spaces, so this effect is most dramatic in external pavements.

Everyday experience — which calls upon visual scales between 1 mm and 1 m contained in the human body — serves as the foundation for any fractal design hierarchy. If we are near enough, then visual and tactile information from a wall is responsible for the necessary connection, because the wall at eye level is closer to the eye than the floor is, and we can easily touch the wall. In a very large room or open space we connect visually and psychologically to an area surrounding our feet. This region defines the first fractal scales in a pavement design, and these external scales become linked to internal scales within our consciousness. Without a deliberate design around our feet, there is a chance that no connection will be experienced with the environment of a large space. Regardless of the smallest unit employed, whether it be a piece of mosaic, a brick, or a tile, contrast should be used to render the smallest scale unambiguously. Nevertheless, most urban plazas, and indeed, brick and stone walls of all types built in the twentieth century, deliberately disguise the smallest scale by repeating a single unit monotonously (e.g., so-called bonded brickwork, which creates a uniform surface), as opposed to defining patterns on different scales.

Spatial coherence requires internal definition on successively larger scales, going up to the size of the entire visual region. A patterned expanse needs to define several distinct scales to create hierarchical linking (see discussion in Chapter 4). Therefore, while a detailed pattern might connect to the user at the smallest scale, simply repeating the design indefinitely without using intermediate scales will fail to connect the user to the larger space (see Figure 7.6). Successful pavement designs contain similar but not identical regions. An urban space lacking such a hierarchical linking can never connect to surrounding buildings at a distance because the jump in scale is simply too large. For this connection to happen, the buildings must define an additional, largest scale in the *same* hierarchy. It is therefore necessary for the pavement texture, color, and design to harmonize with the surrounding structures. Similarity between the pavement and buildings relates the scales.

Figure (7.6)
A design should be used to define a higher scale.

9. THE IMPORTANCE OF MEANING STRUCTURES IN THE PAVED SURFACES OF URBAN SPACE.

The properties of urban space, and how patterned flooring helps to define it are discussed in (Salingaros, 1999b). Commenting on contemporary examples, I said:

*"**Sidewalks, city streets, and street corners.** An incredible opportunity to connect the pedestrian to the pavement has been missed all around the world, by using plain, featureless surfaces (even with expensive materials). The standard concrete sidewalk contains no visual information ... Even when brick is used for paving, perceivable patterns are usually avoided. Yet, patterns on the surface of pedestrian paths can make a great difference. Recall, for instance, all the wonderful mosaic and tiled pavements of the Roman world. Among notable later historical examples are the pavement of the Piazza San Marco, and the Portuguese architectural tradition of lively sidewalk designs. Some of the most famous modern patterned sidewalks are in Brazil, a former Portuguese colony."* (Salingaros, 1999b: page 44).

The design of flooring, as in an open plaza, has to obey the same principles as other time-honored designs such as oriental carpets. Methods for connecting different scales are outlined in the model of complexity presented in Chapter 5 of this book. The basic mechanism for linking among units separated either by distance or by scale is similarity in texture, color, and form. Similarity works via translational, rotational, reflectional, and scaling symmetries in the plane (Washburn & Crowe, 1988). This is understood by artists and architects who seek to establish visual and emotional harmony. The coordination responsible for the visual coherence of the whole requires complex ordering, but not simplistic alignment. Symmetric arrangements on a plan do not connect elements across scales.

Great urban spaces were built before the twentieth century by following traditional design criteria. Discarding such techniques for connecting human beings to the built environment as developed over the previous several millennia, architects now design in a way that disconnects people from surrounding surfaces (Salingaros, 1999b). The focus is on formality and a particular visual style, which neglects more human needs. It is therefore a welcome surprise to see successful contemporary plazas built by the British artist and urban designer Tess Jaray (Williams, 2001). Jaray's pavements provide a satisfactory experience on a number of different scales. Her designs show a well-defined smallest scale; distinct yet connected designs on different scales; and careful harmonization with the surrounding buildings (Williams, 2001). One can see why her designs are so successful, using the fractal model for thinking and memory outlined in this Chapter.

From the informational point of view, an open plaza offers vastly decreased input from surrounding walls compared with a totally enclosed, roofed space. And yet, the greatest urban spaces give the strong impression of containing and embracing the user. It is therefore critical to connect to the ground via geometry, since it is with the floor that we can establish the strongest and most immediate connection in an open space. Thus, the most expressive pavements are to be found in traditional public open spaces around the world. When successful, pavements connect the pedestrian to the ground, and thereby permit the psychological sense of well-being that allows one to feel alive and move around. This is what determines the success of an open space independently of other factors such as exposure, surrounding façades, and density of cross-paths.

10. CONNECTION ESTABLISHES A PHYSIOLOGICAL STATE.

We postulate that the intensity of fractal connection corresponds directly to the degree that human beings intuitively feel a space or design to be meaningful or "alive". This model therefore identifies the visual connection of designs and structures with a viewer's emotional state. It is becoming increasingly clear from neurophysiological research that the human conceptual system and the possible forms of reasoning are very strongly shaped by the wiring of our brains (Lakoff & Johnson, 1999). Moreover, mental activity turns out to be emotionally engaged; i.e., it is likely that we actually *feel* our thoughts (Lakoff & Johnson, 1999).

Subconscious processes exist in our brains, which we believe encompass the fractal connections discussed above. This model of fractal encoding helps explain why we feel emotionally elated standing in a great historical plaza that is paved with some design which harmonizes with surrounding buildings (guidelines for achieving this harmony are given in Section 12, below). If all components work to connect and harmonize, we ourselves become an integral component of an enormous space because we link hierarchically with it. Just as we recall a hierarchy of associative memories from a single detail, we also connect to a large, complex space through a single detail. This represents one of the greatest possible architectural-aesthetic experiences for an observer.

The corollary is also of interest. Urban spaces that conform to the contemporary design canon (of visually hard and minimalist spaces) tend to be dead, because they fail to establish a positive emotional connection with the user. One can argue that this effect is not unintentional. A person feels ill-at-ease in such places, and consequently avoids them. If a space looks cold and austere because it lacks organized visual complexity, then we feel it as the absence of comfort and security. This is not simply a matter of choice; as proposed in this Chapter, non-fractal structures clash with our perceptive process. Not only is our environment thereby impoverished by a reduction of information, but the design rules that generate such environments deny and suppress fractal connections. A widely-embraced design culture ignores the need to create structures that elicit a sense that we are in a meaningful place, thereby severely narrowing the range of our emotional experience.

The environment is not separate from us, offering only objects and external sensations that we encounter: it is part of our being (Lakoff & Johnson, 1999). A balanced, healthy mental state requires an understanding of nature that is linked to our human emotions. The mind is much more than a computer; it is also able to process and engage emotional content. How are we to understand our sense of belonging to a larger whole? In this Chapter, we have discussed the experience of meaning from the environment, yet our explanation is very limited compared to what is described more accurately (more emotionally) in mystical and spiritual literature. Connecting to a larger, all-encompassing whole can lead to ecstatic participation, or a spiritual experience. Such a state has frequently been described as transcendence.

11. THE NATURE OF MEANING.

We wish to concentrate on the perception of meaning coming out of visual complexity in the environment. Visual information presented as a coherent image or coded pattern is cognitively accessible in a direct manner. There is a mapping function between structures in the world and structures in the mind. When the mapping is faithful to the hierarchical linking (i.e., it preserves the information and its interconnections rather than any overall shape), it creates an experience of meaning. Neural structures use information on connectivity to create meaning as an internal state: in our model, meaning is not *assigned* to external forms. The degree of conformal fit or coherence determines the strength of the sense of meaning and also the strength of the emotional experience. In its simplest aspect, meaning corresponds to either positive or negative emotion. When two or more meaningful structures are linked together in a meaningful way, we begin to build a system of beliefs.

If an image is incoherent, then the information it contains cannot be perceived easily as a whole. There is less meaning because, even though there may be considerable information there, the information is difficult to synthesize. This in turn generates a negative emotion. Viewers are more receptive to information that is presented in a pattern which is strongly connected to them. Information structured in this way is typically called "natural" or "intuitive". It has been argued previously that intuition is actually a process involving structured reasoning (Mikiten, 1995). By contrast, a viewer will not be receptive to information that is presented via a visual pattern (or lack thereof) which fails to establish a strong connection with the viewer. We believe that environmental structures need to be fractal to satisfy the deeper connective processes within the human brain.

Our sense of understanding arises from the way we form conceptual structures in the mind. When a collection of ideas has coherence and a sense of relatedness among its elements, we perceive its structure. When we perceive the structure of thoughts and ideas as a coherent whole, we conclude that they are correct and that the construct is valid (Mikiten, 1995). We remember it as a guide for further thought. We also use it to guide our behavior. Ideas that are neatly linked and have a coherent structure are judged to be valid or "true". The nature of intuition may be understood as the ability to match the structure of a present situation with the structures of problems that have been experienced before. Intuition represents the general ability to reach a conclusion on the basis of less explicit information than is ordinarily required to reach that conclusion (Mikiten, 1995).

12. CONCLUSION:
SOME GUIDELINES FOR PAVEMENT DESIGNS.

Rules for creating a memorable open space can be abstracted from studying historical examples (Salingaros, 1999b). The lesson from the fractal encoding model is that there exists a fundamental similarity between complex structures in the environment and structures in the mind. Designing an open space can be successful if one follows one's basic instinct towards ornament and detail, connecting and harmonizing different levels of design. In principle, therefore, there is really no need for rules if one is guided by one's deepest feelings. The closer the match between the architect's felt intuition about a space and the structure that is finally created as an expression of that intuition, the greater the meaning that space should have for the observer. In a sense, the built place becomes the vehicle for the mental structure of the architect to be manifested as a mental structure in the observer.

Nevertheless, some pointers are necessary because of the plethora of negative examples of flooring structures and urban spaces in existence. As discussed in the remaining five chapters of this book, architects' intuitions about space have become corrupted by non-adaptive mental images (in the sense we cannot connect to them as humans), and so those intuitions can no longer be trusted. Even though instinct about pattern and surface is inborn, it can be replaced by a set of arbitrary preferences. Those people then desire an artificial version of reality: they have to be taught how to design in a manner that adapts to human sensibilities. We need to re-learn how to connect with our environment so that the process becomes automatic once again. Even though the best pavements depend on engineering principles, they have to balance and synthesize so many factors that the result should be considered a "work of art". A successful pavement will have the following characteristics, which satisfy hierarchical linking.

Table 7.1. Guidelines for Pavement Designs.

1. Human-scale design that connects immediately with a user.

2. The smallest units defined by contrast and symmetries.

3. A smallest design scale compatible with human dimensions.

4. A sequence of design scales reaching up to the full extent of the open space.

5. Intermediate levels of design that are distinct yet strongly linked via similarity.

6. Larger design scales formed from ordered combinations of elements on smaller scales.

7. Balance among all regions and scales: every element acts as a connector for the other elements.

8. Harmonization via patterns and colors at a distance, which links all scales with the surrounding buildings.

If these conditions are satisfied, then a user, on entering the environment, will experience a sense of meaningfulness as all of the scales in the view are seen as a unified whole. There is a fractal (i.e., hierarchical) connection to the entire space. The strength of each of the individual connections determines the coherence of the whole. In a poor design, the smallest elements are not symmetric, but appear to be amorphous or indistinct so that we cannot connect to them. The connection process starts from the smallest scales and proceeds through the larger scales up to the largest scale, which is defined by the surrounding structures. While our description of the connection process was sequential, the actual connection through perception is sudden. This experience is frequently dramatic, and creates a definite and sometimes intensely positive psychological and physiological state.

In conclusion, we have proposed a theory of pattern perception that can explain how patterns generate meaning in the environment. Although this theory is general, it was applied here to discuss pavements: i.e., floor patterns, and paving patterns for streets, sidewalks, and plazas. A strictly utilitarian approach to pavements requires no promise of destination or completion that attaches meaning to built forms and spaces. We believe that this impoverishes human physical and emotional experience. When the environment becomes more complex, the pavement should become the guarantee that the environment is planned to embody destinations and connections (see Figure 7.7). A pavement that is designed to have meaning will comply with the eight rules given above. Pavements as a definition of space represent the highest order of mapping between an architectural structure and a theme that the human mind can understand. Meaning in the pavement thus allows one to "know" the place without seeing all of it.

Figure (7.7)
The pavement design embodies
meaning and destination.

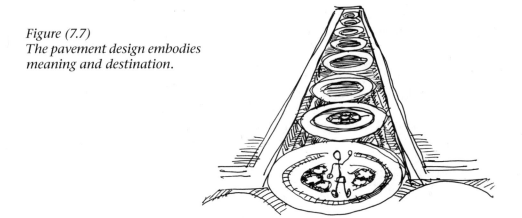

Chapter Eight

MODULARITY AND THE NUMBER OF DESIGN CHOICES.

By Nikos A. Salingaros and Débora M. Tejada

1. INTRODUCTION.

This Chapter compares the number of choices available in different design systems. A simple model allows us to estimate the relative number of design choices in a free, non-modular design system compared to a rigid design system of modules. We show that there are infinitely more choices in a non-modular system than in a modular system.

We also compare the accuracy of approximating a given free (non-modular) design such as a curve. This serves as an easily-grasped metaphor for design in general, where the ability to represent a complex curve depends critically upon having many different scales of geometrical structure (which is the opposite condition of a fixed module). While architects as a rule want to have available a large number of possible solutions, so as to enhance their ability to generate an infinite number of different forms (i.e., novel designs), they acquiesce to industry and aesthetic standards of modular use. Working within a modular system of design (with or without supplementary conditions such as internal structure in a module) restricts the number of possible results in a drastic manner. The restriction imposed by using empty modules (i.e., those containing little or no structural information) eliminates possible designs that relate visually and functionally to human beings. We will argue that using empty modules reverses ancient practices that lie at the basis of human connection with nature.

A "module" could be a semi-autonomous component of design; a piece that can be repeated; or a component produced in a standard size. What is commonly understood as "modularity" in the architectural literature refers to the use of modules and modular systems in design and construction. We are going to analyze one aspect of modularity, referring to any building style that uses large components such as plain rectangular panels, units, or surfaces of the same size and shape. Whether this idea is applied to define a building's elevation, a structure's layout on the ground (its plan), or for the plan of an urban region, each modular unit conforms to previously fixed dimensions, usually in a rectangular grid. At the heart of this approach lie two practices: first, building materials are pre-fabricated in a limited number of sizes and shapes; and second, one adopts a philosophy that subjugates design to empty rectangular modules.

The alternative to modular design creates a form through subdivision or differentiation of the geometry. A structure and its components can in this way have any dimension or shape, and at the same time, the structure can utilize materials in a variety of sizes and shapes. Design can be freed up by subdividing the building's components to achieve a spatial coherence as determined by human functions, movement, the psychological perception of space, connectivity, etc. This is the opposite from rigidly fitting human functions into a geometrical frame that is determined primarily by the size of pre-fabricated construction panels or units. Today we are forced to fit ourselves into some arbitrary geometry fixed by an architect without any regard for the complexity of our spatial and emotional needs.

Modular arrangements in building forms or building materials (using complex modules containing a high degree of visual information) often define the aesthetics of a "style". Reasons for adopting a modular design system in architecture include economy of production: it is easy to repeat a design unit that is readily available. It is true in almost all architectures, including various vernacular traditions, that a style is defined after a successful modular system has been developed, which is then formalized into a design canon such as the Classical orders. For example, the transition from wooden to marble construction in early Greek architecture occurred after the former material was developed into a successful system for building temples. The resulting style re-makes what were originally sensible wooden modules out of marble, which is not all that practical, even though the results are wonderful.

2. GOOD AND BAD APPLICATIONS OF MODULARITY.

Classical, Romanesque, and Gothic Architectures are characterized by the repetition of large geometric modules such as bays, columns, windows, etc. These elements possess internal substructure: architectural detail such as decoration, fluting, borders. Even though some of the smallest modules used in Classical and traditional buildings — such as the ordinary brick and smoothed stones — could be described as undecorated, there exists decoration on those and smaller scales elsewhere in the building. The result is a visual balance between substructure on many different scales, which follows from the fundamental "multiplicity rule" on the relative number of subelements in a structure — the distribution of sizes (Salingaros & West, 1999).

Qualitatively, the "multiplicity rule" of (Salingaros & West, 1999) may be stated as follows: substructure exists in a hierarchy that follows an inverse proportionality; many smaller subelements, fewer intermediate ones, and only very few larger ones. This "multiplicity rule", derived for general complex structures in the physical world (such as biological, geographic, physical, and electronic systems), explains why contemporary applications of modular design are perceived to be deficient. Most often, the entire spectrum of smaller scales is missing.

This criticism does not apply solely to modernist buildings, however. For example, contemporary Neoclassical buildings don't always achieve the visual impact of the original Classical buildings. Their forms clearly refer to Classical forms, but the distribution of sizes is skewed towards the large scale, often closer to the preferences of the early modernists such as Ludwig Mies van der Rohe and Le Corbusier. That is because substructure is missing at the smaller sizes; or even when smaller elements are present, they are not numerous enough for visual balance consistent with original Classical architecture. Despite an obvious attempt to mimic Classical prototypes, some recent Neoclassical buildings tend to resemble in spirit the modernist buildings they are trying to contrast and compete with.

Looking at the architectural and urban failures of the twentieth century, modularity is one candidate for critical scrutiny. Many buildings built within this period look the same, since many of them are composed of large empty rectangular panels or exposed untreated concrete, lacking ornament and color. The distribution of sizes is cut off at the size of the empty module (i.e. at a large size), and so the scaling does not continue downwards into any smaller scales. Thus, the hierarchical connection of the structural scales (which are large) to the scales of human perception and movement is missing, all the way down to the minute scales present in natural materials. The worst urban mistakes are again characterized by homogeneous rectangular blocks arranged in precise modular alignment on a city's plan. The more such buildings or modules repeat, the more they create an inhuman habitat whose negative effect is proportional to the area covered by the modules.

The deficiencies of uniformity become dramatic on the urban scale. The requirements of accommodating several totally different functions would normally generate mixed-use building groups that share the same module, yet the industrial production of homogeneous modules encourages architects and planners to create similar buildings and monotonous urban zones. The alternative is to abandon a pointless strict modularity that leads to homogeneity on such a large scale. Instead of doing that, however, we have eliminated mixed use and variety, partly in order to preserve a visual geometrical modularity on the urban plan. Modularity applied in this simplistic manner thus concentrates and separates functions. This, in turn, eliminates the smaller scales of each urban component, so that, for example, factories exist only on the largest possible scale, which negates any coupling with the residential component. Our cities now assume their form based on visual templates that are totally alien to the complexity of human perception, functions, and movement.

Systems theory has developed as a scientific discipline, yet its results are not known to most architects and urbanists (Salingaros, 2005). Genuine modules observed in functioning biological and artificial systems are very different from modularity as currently understood by architects. Studying the decomposition of complex systems into modules forces one to understand what it is that defines a semiautonomous module. A true module encloses complexity (structure and interactions) as a subset or component within a larger complex system. A true module should minimize its external interactions with other modules; that is, it should contain as much of the local complex substructure as possible. Any module of a complex system will itself have a large degree of internal complexity. A module's boundary is placed around an irreducible/indecomposable subsystem, which cannot be subdivided (partitioned) any further. This means that internal complexity determines a module's boundary (i.e., its physical limit), and not vice-versa.

Furthermore, and most important, there is no unique decomposition of a complex system into modules, which invalidates the idea of building up a structure out of only one kind of piece. Obviously, this concept of module is totally different from the architect's image of an empty building component that is fixed at some standard size.

A free design process — one not restricted by modularity — that allows for numerous subdivisions permits geometrical substructure on many different scales. Leaving aside an empty modularity, one has access to solutions based on a far richer approach to design that creates visually satisfying buildings. Art Nouveau architects like Antoni Gaudí used small modular elements (such as standard bricks) to create curved large-scale structures. This freedom of form contrasts with those instances where a building reproduces the shape of an empty rectangular module. Ordinarily, the small scale can link to the large scale mathematically, because scaling similarity in design is a connective mechanism of our perception (see Chapters 4 and 7). Therefore, the materials can and do influence the conception of the large-scale form, and the larger a module, the stronger its influence. When one chooses to use large, empty rectangular panels, these will necessarily influence the overall building; often implying a monotonous, empty rectangular façade.

3. CHRISTOPHER ALEXANDER'S OFFICE DESIGN SYSTEM.

In 1959, Christopher Alexander wrote one of the most perceptive articles on modularity and proportional ratios in architecture (Alexander, 1959). Much later, he introduced a more human-oriented design system for office furniture and layout (Alexander *et. al.*, 1987). These ideas were developed further in a project for the furniture maker Herman Miller (as described by Alexander (2004)). After thinking about the general problem of accommodating personal needs in an office environment in terms of the built components, Alexander concluded that the modular system of standard-size furniture and office units is far too restrictive. He realized that such a system can never hope to satisfy the personal needs of an individual in an office (or any other) environment. The solution was a more flexible system that broke out of modularity, and which enabled each person to choose their own dimensions for furniture, and especially for spaces.

In describing the user-layout design process he developed, Alexander says:

"It is essential to stress that this process is entirely different from the layout process available in computerized systems using modular components. These systems allow the user to arrange and rearrange the modules. Our research shows that any process of arranging and rearranging modules is fundamentally limited, and cannot produce the kind of comfort — the deep and simple feelings — that we are seeking ... Profound adaptation in which things are comfortably related to one another can only occur when the elements involved are all capable of very fine dimensional variation ... The aspect of the layout process itself which is necessary to make this non-modularity work is that it is a process of differentiation (similar to the process of embryonic development) in which the parts are gradually differentiated from the whole — instead of the whole being made up from modular parts". (Alexander *et. al.*, 1987).

Realizing that this result is fundamental for all design (and is not just restricted to office layout and furniture), Alexander has developed it at length in his book (Alexander, 2004), which details a comprehensive theory of architectural order. We include a few of Alexander's comments describing his office design system in more detail:

"The arrangements that people created in this way were genuinely personal, genuinely well-adapted to the rooms ... They were altogether different in character from the stiff, and usually unworkable arrangements that could be created by arranging the standard components in a few rigid arrays ... My program worked by differentiating space, and allowing different objects to crystallize out from the space, in the shape and size they needed, for their particular role ... Why was I convinced that the infinity of configurations created by differentiation in my system, was a richer and larger infinity than the infinity of geometrical arrangements that could be made by arranging and re-arranging standard components?" (Alexander, 2004).

The derivation presented in the following sections answers Alexander's question, and proves his intuition correct. Of course, the whole point of this Chapter is to discuss modularity using certain simple models to understand more general results. This concept will apply equally to common building materials and units that come in standardized sizes (components), and not just to office furniture.

A person can indeed experience a responsive design when compared to other designs that are deficient in some way. It may be difficult to put one's finger on what is lacking in a particular building, yet the fact that one undergoes a visceral, positive emotional experience in a great historical building is incontrovertible. The point we are trying to make is that placing restrictions on design, as a modular system certainly does, might well eliminate the few optimal design solutions (in human adaptive terms) for that project. In particular, the vast majority of the world's favorite buildings — representative of all periods of architecture, and coming from different stylistic traditions and geographic regions — could not have been built, because of our dependency on a modular system that is restricted to empty units.

4. THE NUMBER OF DESIGN CHOICES IN A MODULAR DESIGN SYSTEM AS COMPARED TO A NON-MODULAR DESIGN SYSTEM.

The number of design possibilities obtainable from a free, non-modular system is infinitely more than the number of all design possibilities obtainable from a comparable modular system. This is obvious. However, this remains true even as the size of the module becomes infinitesimally small — a counterintuitive result. People have always assumed that the freedom of a non-modular system of design is recovered in the limit of vanishing small modules, which we show to be false. Moreover, what follows is the first proof of this counterintuitive result that we are aware of. Those who wish to just accept and apply this result might skip Sections 4, 5, and 6 that contain the details of the proof.

While the eye and mind cannot actually perceive the difference between a very large number and an infinite number of different objects, a design method depends upon the number of solutions it can generate. We are arguing for including all possible design solutions to choose from. For this reason, it makes sense to have a more precise idea of how many solutions can be reached by each separate design system.

Counting the possible arrangements of modular units in a design is a straightforward exercise. Without any loss of generality, we construct a one-dimensional model where the proof is much easier to follow. Consider a line of length equal to one in some system of units. The length of the line is going to correspond to the size of a building or urban ensemble. We are going to imagine n design units or components that can be laid in a row and entirely fill up the line (with no gaps). Each unit labeled i has length x_i, and the sum of all the component lengths x_i equals one (the length of the line). This arrangement can be thought of as a particular subdivision or partition of the line (see Figure 8.1).

How many possible re-arrangements of these n elements are there? That is, in how many distinct ways can we shuffle these n elements, not necessarily all of the same length, along the line? The answer comes from combinatorics, and equals $n!$, where the factorial notation means $n! = 1 \cdot 2 \cdot 3 \cdot \ldots \cdot (n-1) \cdot n$. (For example, $3! = 1 \cdot 2 \cdot 3 = 6$). If there are 5 distinct elements that make up the line, then the number of possible re-arrangements is $5! = 120$. Clearly, as the number of discernible units making up the line increases, the number of possible combinations becomes larger.

We will use the analogy that each re-arrangement of the units making up the line corresponds to a particular design solution. It follows that the total number of possible re-arrangements equals the number of design possibilities inherent in this design system. In practice, however, architects working with modular design usually define only *one* basic unit, which is the single empty module, so that all the units are indistinguishable and of the same size, $x_i = 1/n$. If we have n copies of the same unit, then the number of possible re-arrangements equals exactly *one* — since all re-arrangements lead to the same result — so there is only one solution (see Figure 8.2).

Figure (8.1)
A one-dimensional model. Each distinct modular design corresponds to one particular arrangement of n numbers along a line.

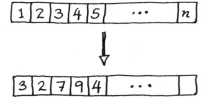

Figure (8.2)
Design based on a single empty module labeled 1 restricts the possibilities to one unique case, because all rearrangements lead to the same result.

5. THE NUMBER OF NON-MODULAR POSSIBILITIES.

When not constrained to work with pre-defined units, then there is complete freedom to make up elements as the design progresses. (We will prove that there are infinitely more possibilities with such a design system than with a modular one). The components can be made any desired size, by subdividing or fitting within the already decided larger dimensions. To show this in a one-dimensional model, start with a line of length one and subdivide it to define n elements, as follows. With a clean line, make one mark that divides it into two segments. A second mark divides the line into three segments, and proceed in this manner until after $n - 1$ marks we have n segments. These $n - 1$ marks generate an n-element partition of the line, which is analogous to the partition defined in the preceding section. To create a different partition in the free design scheme, one merely subdivides at (some) new points (see Figure 8.3).

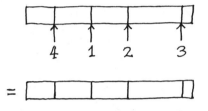

Figure (8.3)
Free, non-modular design corresponds to subdividing a line into an n-element partition. The numbers show the order in which the partitions are made, and it takes n – 1 cuts to separate the line into n elements.

We now count the number of possible ways to affect such a partition. There exists an infinite number of possibilities of where to place the first mark, since it can be made anywhere on the line. Once we start, the positions of the second and all subsequent marks also have an infinite number of possibilities. Altogether, therefore, each partition of the line into n segments has possibility equal to infinity to the power $n - 1$, which equals infinity. This counts the number of ways in which a line can be partitioned into n segments. In a non-modular design system where shapes are defined freely, we have a genuinely infinite number of solutions.

6. THE LIMIT AS *n* BECOMES INFINITE.

Practical constraints of using components in pre-formed industrial sizes strongly influence the design of the building. An architect may be drawn to use as large a module as possible in order to obtain the presumed economical advantages of a modular design system. This is not conducive of design freedom, yet the idea of modularity is still enthusiastically defended. When justifying such a system, however, proponents of modularity turn instead to the opposite case of theoretically small modules, where the number of modules n increases. In supporting modular design, they argue that the limitations of using a modular design system disappear as the module becomes smaller. This is misleading for two reasons. First, economic forces push towards using a large module, not a small one. Second, even a small module severely limits design freedom, although a proof has been lacking up until now.

Shrinking the size of the basic units increases the number of different units, hence the number of design possibilities. Nevertheless, there will always be infinitely more choices in a non-modular system of design, regardless of the size of the modules. The re-arrangements in our one-dimensional model become more numerous as n increases, but one never recovers the design freedom of a non-modular system. We can compute the ratio expressing the number of possible modular design choices over the number of possible non-modular design choices. A common error is to assume that as something becomes infinite, you can cancel with another infinity to get a result of one ($\infty/\infty \neq 1$, but in this case equals zero). In fact, the ratio of modular to non-modular choices equals $n!/\infty = 0$ for all n, so the limit as n goes to infinity is the limit of the sequence { $1/\infty$, $2/\infty$, $6/\infty$, ... }, which is equal to { 0, 0, 0, ... }. The terms of this sequence never change from zero, thus the ratio we are computing equals zero.

From the theory of transfinite numbers in Mathematics, the ideal case of a modular system with an infinite number of distinct infinitesimal units does allow an infinite number of choices, but a non-modular system allows a higher-order infinity of choices. This second, larger infinity is the exponential of the first, smaller infinity. In the case of a single modular unit, as in a minimalist design style carried to its extreme, one still has only a single solution compared to an infinite number of solutions.

7. FRACTALITY VERSUS MODULARITY.

Empty modules define a particular scale, and there are no scales smaller than the module. This practice of defining a single scale contradicts fractal structures having substructure on all scales. People are used to seeing multicolored pictures of mathematical fractals such as the Mandelbrot set generated by a computer. This popular conception overlooks the fact that fractals are overwhelmingly the model used by nature for constructing forms, both living and inanimate (Mandelbrot, 1983). Fractal designs are everywhere: they include trees, animals, snowflakes, folk art, vernacular buildings, great religious buildings of the past, traditional cities, and human artifacts. Far from fractals being exceptional, the vast majority of natural structures is fractal (Ball, 1999). Fractals encompass everything that is alive, and much of inorganic matter. It is principally man-made objects from the twentieth century that have deliberately non-fractal qualities.

Figure (8.4)
A simple self-similar triangular fractal composed of triangles on five different scales.

A fractal's substructure is evident at every magnification, so that at no scale is the structure empty (see Figure 8.4). This represents the opposite of a simplistic geometry of rectangular blocks, where structure is defined on only two scales, usually those of the module itself and the overall size of the building. An important feature of all fractals is that they satisfy the "multiplicity rule" for the distribution of sizes (i.e., there are very few large sizes, several medium sizes, and very many small sizes) (Salingaros & West, 1999). Natural processes generate a number of subelements in inverse proportion to their size. Material stresses create fractures that show as regular or irregular patterns, which prevent a continuous ordering throughout the form. Smooth materials will acquire a fractal structure over time due to stresses and weathering (Ball, 1999). Smooth and empty non-fractal objects don't remain smooth and empty under weathering, which is precisely the reason they are not often found in nature.

Modularity in design is related to the use of non-weathering materials in the following way. As explained above, natural forces and weathering generate substructure, thus destroying scale dominance (Ball, 1999). If we create an artificial non-fractal structure by emphasizing one particular scale — say, the scale (size) of a plain, empty module — then we are ignoring natural processes. To be visually effective in its original intent (i.e., to retain the purity that such modularity seeks), those structures must resist weathering, which is impossible. It is for this reason that the topics of modularity, geometrical purity, and non-weathering materials are inextricably bound together. A preoccupation with shiny, smooth, or transparent materials follows the desire to avoid fractal substructure. It is well known that early modernist architects founded their new style of building in their search for "new" materials that they hoped would not weather at all.

Going upwards from the microscopic scale, similar-size elements in nature tend to join in higher-order groupings. Forces within a higher-order grouping are distributed among many different scales, thus ensuring a more efficient linking of all the elements making up the whole. The emergence of higher scales corresponds to a process that guides morphogenesis and creates complex order while minimizing randomness. The separateness of repeated units existing on one scale is sacrificed to the coherent grouped structure of a higher scale. This generative process is reversed by empty modularity, which uses empty modules to begin with, then tries to maintain the emptiness of its original module. Architectural modules of this empty type are often used to build an empty scaled-up version of the empty module (i.e. a plain façade), resulting in a building with little visual substructure.

An inanimate object can have different degrees of organized complexity. There is a process by which this complexity is developed and maintained. We repair buildings and the urban fabric from wear and tear and physical decay, which is analogous to the feeding and maintenance of organisms or machines. The difference between artificial systems as opposed to biological systems, is that repair is done by human beings rather than by the entities themselves. A structure that doesn't weather at all appears alien to a human being. For buildings to weather well, they have to allow for the development of a fractal structure: they must be designed from the beginning with a fractal hierarchy of scales, otherwise the inevitable patterns that develop as a result of weathering will cut across the original design intentions. The only way to prevent this inconsistency is to anticipate a fractal form in the original design.

8. APPROXIMATING CURVES AS A METAPHOR FOR DESIGN FREEDOM.

This Section presents an entirely different illustration of the limitations of modular design. Whereas in the beginning of this Chapter we set up a model based on subdivisions of a line, here we will try to approximate a freely-drawn curve with different types of modules. Our discussion illustrates graphically the inherent limitations of modular approximation. Once again, we will interpret these results as providing lessons for design in general.

Ordered complexity as characterized by levels of substructure is linked to design freedom. This can be seen in the simplest design problem: creating a curved surface to accommodate human movement, psychological space, or other factor optimizing people's physical and emotional interactions with a building. We will show that a non-trivial curve cannot be constructed without abandoning the type of simplistic modularity discussed earlier. With an increase in the number of system of design components, there is a corresponding increase in the number of intermediate levels of structure. Structural complexity arises from the process of adding components on different scales, with linking and coupling between all those components, and on all scales. This is the opposite of emptiness and plainness, which is achieved by eliminating all substructure.

Any curve can be obtained as an approximation of straight segments of connected lines. Nevertheless, a good approximation depends on the length of the basic segments that are utilized. In a modular system consisting of several distinct elements, one of them is going to have the smallest fixed length. The size of the smallest element limits the curvature of curves that can be approximated. Consider the case of a single module. Comparing the three approximations to a semi-circle shown here (see Figure 8.5), we observe that the possibility of creating an accurate representation of a smooth circle of given radius gets better as the length of the modular segment becomes smaller.

Figure (8.5)
A curve can best be approximated by having as
small a straight module as possible.

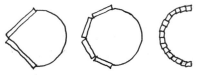

One might think that approximating curves can be improved by introducing modules with curvature. We could then have arcs of different length and curvature. In contrast to the case of the straight segments, however, the curves with greater curvature will not necessarily be better approximated by the smallest modules of arc. The approximation is still limited by the length and shape of the modular segment. Neither approximation shown here for comparison (see Figure 8.6) is particularly satisfying, which reveals the inadequacies of any modular design system. This can be remedied by combining small and large units of different curvature together. Different units will fit different sections of the curve, and clearly establish the opposite mechanism from using a single module. This results in by far the most accurate representation of a continuous figure by means of an encoding scheme. We are thus led away from strict modularity, and into fractal approximation that works on many different scales simultaneously. These visual illustrations are a trivial way of saying what every mathematician knows: a good approximation such as a Fourier or Taylor Series requires the contribution of terms on several different scales.

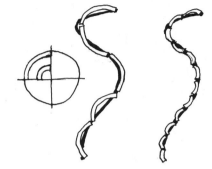

Figure (8.6)
Approximating a curve (shown in solid black) with a curved module is inadequate regardless of the size of the module. Here, two quarter-circle modules with different radii are used.

Our conclusion has direct and far-reaching implications. Adaptive design necessitates the availability of units on a variety of different scales. This was demonstrated by our model of fitting a curve, though the idea applies to design in general, and is not limited to curves. At the same time, modular design was shown to be inherently restrictive.

After this simple analysis, we can see why modular architecture abandons curved designs on the smaller scales: the reason is that realizing a curve using relatively large modules is mathematically impossible. Complex designs require components on different scales — they have to be "made-to-order". Empty modularity restricts the freedom of design, and is incompatible with mathematically-rich designs. Thus, the architecture of rectangular modules eliminates one of the principal components of natural forms. We identify this exclusion as a major reason for the lifeless uniformity of rectangular boxes. Recent buildings such as the Denver airport and the Bilbao Art museum take advantage of stronger materials and computer-aided design and fabrication to break out of the rigidity of form inherent in the limited mechanical reproduction of identical components. Nevertheless, the aesthetic of modular production, this time attached to curved surface modules, remains in effect.

The metaphor of approximating a complex curve shows the need to allow for different structural units at different scales. A building need not be curved necessarily, yet it should ideally follow a similar design freedom in terms of scales. Just as if a user's needs require a curved form, the building's geometry has to bend to accommodate those needs, so in general the geometry must arise from subdivision rather than from modular juxtaposition. We thus propose a metaphor for design that responds better to human physical and psychological needs. The freedom necessary to achieve those aims requires the ability to adjust the built form during design according to complex inputs. This is severely restricted within the confines of a modular aesthetic. If we follow a rigid visual image too faithfully, we cannot create a design that serves unanticipated but important human needs. The reason for this contradiction is the impossibility of predicting in advance the immeasurable effects and interactions between human beings and the built form.

9. MODULARITY AND MASS PRODUCTION.

Modularity in design was spurred by mass-production techniques in manufacturing, in an attempt to simplify production and reduce building costs. American mass production began first in the small arms industry, then spread to domestic machines. Henry Ford introduced the production line in 1913 to mass-produce cars. Buildings were being modularized and industrialized from the beginning of the nineteenth century, with cast iron warehouse construction, balloon frame houses, etc. Architects, beginning in the 1920s, examined the possibility of emulating Ford's methods in the building industry. Nevertheless, with the exception of a few housing systems, mobile homes, and caravans, there has never been a successful production line in architecture. Large-scale experiments in prefabricated housing after World War II mostly ended in failure.

The *idea* of modularity was never abandoned, however, and it has strongly influenced the design of twentieth-century buildings around the world. Even if whole buildings could not be successfully mass-produced, architects felt that the traditional way of tailoring each piece of a building to fit individual uses and shapes was no longer permissible. There developed a confluence between a practical matter (savings through standard sizes) and a concern for social issues (affordable housing for all). This ideology led to the standardization of many building measures and components: i.e. drywall and plywood sizes; low ceiling heights for apartments; fixed sizes of doors and windows; plumbing and lighting fixtures; wall panels; etc. In commercial buildings, modularity went as far as it could go without actually mass-producing complete units such as bathrooms.

Modular construction was accepted by the post-war architectural community as a necessary component of building for the future. Le Corbusier wanted to use his patented "Domino" system to construct buildings cheaply and quickly. We have inherited the idea of modular design in a watered-down version that leads to the most boring and minimally-satisfying results. Today, both apartments and tract houses tend to be built throughout a region according to standardized plans; not an optimized plan for patterns of family life and climate as in vernacular architecture, but simply a dimly-remembered floor plan from the heady days of early modernism. Housing "developments" usually repeat a single poorly-adapted house plan with only minor variations, which moreover offers few of the advantages of modular construction. Ironically, such houses are still built by hand, but using the cheapest possible materials.

A rectangular grid exists in countless examples of post-war buildings and construction. We mention here the 3 ft 4 in x 8 ft 3 in planning grid used in England by the Hertfordshire school system, and the 3 m x 3 m grid used by Constantine Doxiades in building several new villages in the Arab world. Ludwig Mies van der Rohe employed an empty module of 24 in x 33 in for the 1950 Farnsworth house. People continue to think that there is something fundamentally advantageous to such a restriction, which is questionable. It might look more efficient on paper, but it does not lead to life in the built environment. Le Corbusier wrote at length on the presumed advantages of a Cartesian grid in his own journal, *L'Esprit Nouveau*, giving colorful arguments. The visual force of his crisp drawings was enough to establish the modular orthogonal grid in the minds of architects and planners.

Among the few modernist architects who refused to adopt modular design in buildings as a matter of principle was Alvar Aalto, who is reported to have said: "my module is the millimeter". Even the organic post-modernist architecture of Lucien Kroll was praised for using a 10 cm module previously developed by the Dutch group *Stichting Architectural Research* (SAR). Kroll says, however, that: "... even 10 cm is too large; 2.5 cm or 1 cm would be more ideal" (Kroll, 1987: p. 59). Empty rectangular modules should not be confused with complex modules which are organized through translational symmetry in older buildings, because the design intents are the opposite. Joseph Paxton's 1851 Crystal Palace uses a structural frame of 24 ft x 24 ft with good effect. It is misleading to claim that the 13C Amiens Cathedral is modular in this contemporary definition because it has a clearly-defined frame at 23.5 ft x 23.5 ft. This is obviously not an *empty* module, but contains an extraordinary wealth of further structure on smaller scales.

10. CONCLUSION.

There are arguments to be made in favor of modularity, but not for the way it is used in many buildings. If we have a large quantity of visual and geometrical information, then modular design can organize this information to prevent randomness and sensory overload. In that case, the module is not an empty module, but a rich, complex module containing a considerable amount of substructure. Such a module organizes its internal information; it does not eliminate it. Empty modules, on the other hand, eliminate internal information, and their repetition eliminates information from the entire region that they cover. Modularity works in a positive sense only when there is substructure to organize. One aim of this Chapter was to correct certain misconceptions in architectural design, which give the impression that using rectangular modules is somehow more technologically advanced. That is not true. We argued against empty modularity, using mathematics in a scientific proof.

Chapter Nine

GEOMETRICAL FUNDAMENTALISM.

By Michael W. Mehaffy and Nikos A. Salingaros

1. INTRODUCTION.

Twentieth-century architecture and planning professionals have adopted a design philosophy about geometrical shapes that can be viewed as dogmatic. Post-industrial designers purposely applied geometrical abstractions to the built environment, which have effectively erased the design and building traditions of the past, and with them the vital web of urban culture in society. Introducing such abstractions at the beginning of the twentieth century had catastrophic consequences for our cities' urban fabrics, and for the human qualities of individual buildings. By identifying the mathematical core of those beliefs, it is possible to understand the full extent of the damage done, and lay the groundwork for a richer architecture of the future.

Geometrical fundamentalism is defined as the misappropriation of geometrically simple forms as an essential typology for the built environment. It influences not just the large scale (as for example the urban plan and overall building volumes), but determines the details of our everyday environment to an incredible degree. Huge skyscrapers, irrespective of their form, are expressions of *geometrical fundamentalism* because of their inhuman scale. This is most problematic because it usually eliminates the smallest scales.

We argue that the order and beauty attached to geometrical oversimplification is of an artificial and isolating nature, and generates a form of environmental alienation for our communities. Everyday people intuitively perceive contemporary architecture and urbanism to be disconnected from and opposed to traditional human values that they hold sacred. In the Industrialized World, inner-city degradation provided an opportunity to replace traditional urban fabric with abstract geometric (i.e. modernist) blocks. The reaction to despoiling the urban fabric leads to introversion, asocial lifestyles, and further retreat to the suburbs. In the Developing World, it leads to a seething resentment (whose root cause is not necessarily recognized) against the countries that are seen as champions of this destructive process, and which may be perceived as an assault by the industrialized nations against traditional cultures.

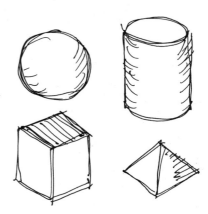

Figure (9.1)
Elementary solids are neither sculptural nor architectural models.

The simplest volumes are the sphere, cylinder, cone, pyramid, cube, while the rectangular slab or square column is preferred for skyscrapers (see Figure 9.1). One often hears such structures described as "sculptural", but that is misleading. Turn-of-the-century designers, in their pursuit of a "machine-age" form, copied sleek, smooth machines, which were themselves an expression of a sleek, smooth aesthetic popular in some art circles of that time. This in turn influenced more industrial forms, which then fed back into architectural design, and so on. A self-referential feedback between industrial design, architecture, and art ties the "machine aesthetic" of the 1920s to modernist forms. This has little to do with sculpture as a source of positive, human emotions, applying only to those sculptures that already satisfy this aesthetic. Buildings that mimic simple solids can be considered as "sculpture" only within the narrow aesthetic that they themselves define.

Moreover, sculptures are fine art structures that are created to engage a viewer. This conception of viewed or "apprehended" form is only one aspect of architecture, but it is an aspect that has come to have a stranglehold on the creation of buildings. Largely lost in the aesthetization of utilitarian ideas is the primacy of architecture as a vessel of life, accommodating the needs of human beings to connect with one another and with nature in a complex pattern. Philosophers and psychologists point out that our experience of the built environment depends upon interacting with deeper aspects of life than conscious experience alone. Yet architecture in our time is reduced to a kind of giant minimalist sculpture in which human beings must unwittingly live.

Surface quality makes a profound impact in the way people perceive and interact with buildings and the urban environment. A fascination with smooth and sleek geometries cuts us off from our surroundings by making it impossible for us to connect to them with our senses. Meaning is removed from the built environment by eliminating information encoded in surface design, which historically served to connect an individual to a structure through mental associations. One of the principal means by which human beings relate to their world is undone (see Figure 9.2).

Figure (9.2)
Empty abstractions replace complex structure.

2. RELIGIOUS COMPETITION.

Such practices present an affront to many religions, by denying their architectural expression (not only on religious buildings, but by denying organized complexity from the entire built environment). They oppose the basic principle of connecting an individual to the universe — hence to God — through color, design, sculpture, and calligraphy. *Geometrical fundamentalism* denies sensory connections. With its insistence on homogeneous surfaces showing minimal information, it questions the continued validity of architectural masterpieces that are also powerful symbols of faith. For example, temples, mosques, and churches conveying meaning via polychrome sculptures, tile work, reliefs, frescoes, and mosaics are all rejected. In Le Corbusier's words: "Decoration is of a sensorial and elementary order, as is color, and is suited to simple races, peasants and savages" (Le Corbusier, 1927: page 143). He appears not to know that the buildings on the Athenian Acropolis, which he professed to admire so much, were originally painted with bright contrasting colors.

Geometrical fundamentalism also forbids the word of God (and God's name) from being used in an architectural setting. Classical Islamic calligraphy constitutes a major art form that has always played a central role in architecture. Arabic script, with rich variation in each stroke, lends itself even more than Latin or Greek letters to visual connectivity using internal scaling. The informational meaning of ornamental Islamic calligraphy on architectural surfaces escapes most non-Muslims. People who understand the language and respect its content connect instantly with a building through the message of the text, which establishes a deeply emotional link to an individual. Those who cannot read the script can only imagine the powerful meaning it endows on a built structure. All of us can observe the incredible degree to which the calligraphy achieves meaning just in design terms. This is also true for Chinese and Japanese calligraphy.

As *geometrical fundamentalism* competes head-on with religious expression through built structures and the informational content of surfaces, it qualifies as a substitute religious movement on those terms alone. It certainly possesses its own moral precepts, admitting freely that Brutalism (the use of raw concrete surfaces) is founded on *ethical* rather than aesthetic concepts. Its dogma insists that "honest" architecture should not hide its structure: architectural "honesty", however, is never defined, nor are any reasons given for why Brutalism has any value. Instead, we are offered arguments only in terms of other parts of the dogma. Even those of the early modernists who were sincere in their attempts to better society through a new architecture didn't notice the negative consequences.

Traditional cultures have a far stronger religious sense than the industrialized western nations do today, and they are frightened by the idolatry implicit in *geometrical fundamentalism*. Contemporary architects worship their geometrical abstractions, and are ready to defend them with their professional lives (in their attempts to share their vision, they impose these ideals on those buildings' occupants). Although this topic is hardly ever discussed, architects' near-fanatical support of geometrical abstractions represents a belief in something far beyond architectural style. Non-architects might think that this is simply a question of efficient building methods, the pressures of the new economy, or the manifestation of new tastes in a global population; the truth is closer to a competition for survival among basic beliefs (see Figure 9.3). Religion is expressed in the form of the built environment through organized complexity, but *geometrical fundamentalism* does not allow any expression other than its own.

Figure (9.3)
More a symbol for cult worship than anything else.

The British architectural historian James M. Richards betrays the religious aspirations of the early modernists through his choice of words: "The gospel the Nazis had tried to suppress now had prophets on both sides of the Atlantic, and the United States suddenly became a place of remarkable architectural energy." (Norwich, 1987: page 233). In unjustly criticizing postwar Italian architects, he juxtaposes the social concern that all religions (genuine or phony) rely upon for their appeal, with an intolerance for apostasy that characterizes fanatical cults and the worst eras of organized religion: "Then, as in recent times, however, Italian architecture suffered, when compared with that in other European countries, from Italy's failure to give building programs much relationship to social priorities. There was also a tendency towards willful departures from orthodoxy." (Norwich, 1987: page 242).

Many architects believe that a simplified geometric form has the power to improve the population's social and moral well-being. They believe this precept so deeply that they will tolerate no questioning of it. Architectural students are often not taught to explore the hypotheses at the basis of any design theory. Nor can they test their hypotheses about the world and design on the real scale. A simple set of beliefs, founded in media-driven architectural authority, drives design. Since the final user's reactions cannot even be anticipated, they consequently assume only minor importance in contemporary design. Based upon strict geometrical dictates, this methodology is akin to religious fiction, whose criterion is its own existential validity. A fiction is an invented principle that is justified solely by its effects. Society is held together by such fictions, which try to counter the human realities of selfishness, greed, violence, etc. It is a mistake, however, to think that geometry — and, in particular, a geometry of disconnectedness — could provide this cohesion (see Figure 9.4).

Figure (9.4)
Another architectural totem for
worshipping the geometrical cult.

One indication of how close *geometrical fundamentalism* is to religious fundamentalism is how it reacts to its observed mistakes. Perpetrators of *geometrical fundamentalism* cannot avoid seeing the disastrous effects that its imposition has on human society, in the way people are alienated from the built environment and are cut off from their traditions. Nevertheless, the programmed reaction is for architects to lament that: "we have not been pure enough; our architectural failures come about because we strayed from the true path". Indoctrination has implanted the only possible direction in thought as always towards the core fundamentalist belief of pure geometrical forms and surfaces.

3. ASSAULT ON TRADITIONAL CULTURES.

The western industrial nations held out to the world a postwar vision of modernity, combining industrial prosperity with a supposedly rational utopia of art and science. In some cases, their influence was so strong as to force modernity onto more traditional cultures, destroying the traditions of centuries. We now know that this vision of modernity was deeply flawed. As a result, we have to deal with an emotional backlash around the world. Though the reaction is a valid one, it often becomes a misguided retreat into various forms of fundamentalism and tribalism. It remains for us to rescue and renew the most precious accomplishments of our civilization: the spirit of pluralism and democracy, and the open and self-correcting institutions of science and learning.

Geometrical fundamentalism is perceived as destructive by many humanist architects and urbanists. No amount of theorizing by architectural gurus can camouflage its implications. The USA, Europe, and Japan identified with the *Bauhaus* style after the Second World War, as did so many other countries wishing to project a "progressive" image to the rest of the world. Their idea of progress was to mimic the sleek and smooth forms of "Tomorrowland" from Disney World. Russia chose its own models of a vastly overscaled and dehumanizing architecture. People in the industrialized world who realized that their heritage was being destroyed were placated by the (erroneous) justification that they were paying the price for technological progress and economic prosperity. The only exception is our youth — before they are numbed by their environment. People in the developing world, however, do not accept the official propaganda: they see themselves losing their age-old attachments without getting any benefits.

Just as religious fundamentalism is perceived by the West as a threat to our democratic way of government, open society, and the respect for human rights, so *geometrical fundamentalism* is perceived by the developing world as a threat to traditional civilization. Ordinary persons the world over don't see *geometrical fundamentalism* as an abstract philosophical idea — an intellectual game played among academic architects and the media — but interpret it according to its direct consequences on their society. People perceive it as being synonymous with enormous economic and military power, so that contemporary architecture and planning is seen as a mechanized assault on the fabric of their cities, their network of human connections, and the tightly-knit social network defining their way of life.

Corporate America — and its extension into the global business-industrial complex — has identified itself with *geometrical fundamentalism*. We do not intend to critique economic globalization, but to focus instead on the perceived effects of tying global business to a philosophy of intolerance towards more traditional forms. People around the world have seen their architectural and socio-urban traditions classified as abstractions (i.e., non-essential practices), then dismissed as primitive, backward, unmodern, and as impediments to progress. Many of those who welcome progress are thus turned against their own civilization, whereas others learn to hate the countries which promote this philosophy. The assault is not only directed on the urban fabric and built surroundings, but more alarmingly, on the fabric of culture itself.

Ways of thought that evolved along with humanity, inseparable from the network of socio-urban interactions defining a particular culture, are erased by *geometrical fundamentalism*. This is painfully obvious in the wholescale destruction of traditional housing patterns as "urban renewal". Residents of the developing world are severed from their cultural roots and forced into high-rise buildings. At the same time, their governments are seduced into building (and paying for) the latest architectural extravaganza — often but not always belonging to *geometrical fundamentalism* — in order to "catch up" with the industrialized nations. People see alien forms imposed on their cities, often to replace beloved architectural landmarks. Building without regard has desecrated sites of incalculable cultural and archaeological value. Western education has succeeded in turning a country's governing and architectural elite against its native artistic and architectural traditions.

Architecture today has lost a sense of accountability. The completion of a megalomaniac highly-publicized contemporary building in the developing world is celebrated as a victory by architectural academics. It is featured in the glossy architectural magazines, where erudite commentators heap praise upon its architect (often a Westerner). The "star architects" gloat after placing yet another symbol of their omnipotence into the world. The other side is far darker: for many, it represents a call to arms against a symbolic invasion of traditional culture. Groups of sensitive persons most likely resent this affront to their sensibilities, and prepare themselves to fight against even worse things to come. Architects, complacent in their dream world, simply have no conception of the consequences of their actions on others whose values and beliefs are culturally situated. They fail to see a Western expression of dominance encoded in contemporary architectural forms, and would not even consider the reality of this effect.

4. GEOMETRICAL SIMPLIFICATION VERSUS CONNECTIVITY.

Science can throw a bright spotlight on what is going on, providing some critical insights that will help to hasten the inevitable crisis of the current paradigm, and point the way to a new and more advanced one. The crisis is certainly well under way, as cultures around the world instinctively recoil from modernism in all its forms. Not understanding how to effectively counter the dehumanizing nature of *geometrical fundamentalism*, people turn to reactions which are focused in many different, random directions. Fortunately, there is a rich alternative to this, combining the best of science with the best of traditional art. We have no choice but to build a new kind of society — a society that is postmodern, yes, but one that articulates new "connectivist" principles, combining the wisdom of history and of traditional cultures with the latest insights of science and mathematics.

The central idea of connectivity — which opposes geometrical oversimplification — is a defining trait of good structure and good architecture. This ties in to the idea of a network, a connective structure that is the antithesis of simple abstractions. Connectivity is the result of new geometrical insights into fractal structure, iterative processes, emergent properties, etc. Natural and biological structures arise from the complex interaction of many elements on different scales (both smaller and larger). Organisms, the unselfconscious creations of human beings, and our past's greatest architectural achievements are all fractal, complex, and internally connected to an incredible degree (see Chapters 5 and 6 in this book).

Such structures exhibit many of the connective properties of natural structure that have only recently been described by mathematical analysis. These include: the iterative generation of complex form using simple rule-based processes and patterns, the fractal repetition of forms and textures at distinct yet related scales, the varied adaptation of many elements to a complex biological pattern, the emergence of an overall pattern of coherence, and beauty from relatively autonomous elements operating in simple and direct response to their environment.

Look at the geometry of a building or a city analytically, as pure mathematical structure. The connective relationships, the possible number of pathways between units and to the public realm define the "life" in the built structure. Living environments — those we experience with our senses and on a deeply emotional level to "be alive", and in which we ourselves feel more "alive" — exhibit the classic structural characteristics of a network (Salingaros, 2005). Surfaces connect directly to the user, and to each other via innumerable mathematical symmetries and similarities. Buildings are physically connected in the visual sense through an iterative process that produces intense variety with a remarkably limited palette of materials and forms. The entire structure is richly connective on many levels of scale.

The difference with what we build nowadays is striking. Images tend to be generated by a grand abstraction imposed on the site — the ultimate act of *geometrical fundamentalism*. Each building's exterior geometry is similarly stiff and absolute — conforming rigidly to relatively simple concepts of line, grid, and plane. The connective relationships are again severely constrained by the simple, fundamental (and quite alien) geometries that are imposed, left over from early modernism. The driving assumption of the twentieth century was its belief that geometrically simplistic structure is actually more sophisticated and "modern" than anything built previously. We now know that the converse is true. Technological prodigy is not to be confused with cultural advancement. It remains for us to use these insights to create (or recreate for our own time) a more connective architecture.

5. ARCHITECTURE FOR THE NEW MILLENNIUM.

The death of modernism has been loudly proclaimed by many leading architects and urbanists in recent years. Yet today most of the "star architects" do not seem to have progressed beyond early twentieth-century primitivism, even in their supposedly avant-garde fashions. While they claim to eschew simplicity by dabbling in complexity theory, they are still playing the same disconnected abstract sculptural game, using only a superficial and flawed understanding of complexity. In the end, this process doesn't concern itself with human life. It is a game that uses the egos of developers and the fashion whims of the public as so much art supply. The new designers still live by geometrical disconnectedness. There is no real concern for nourishing human sensory experience, for making connections to daily life, for any kind of profound daily interactions of users in these places. If there were, it would of course be revealed in an appropriate complexity in the geometry.

Why, then, do so many architects still have such a powerful affection for the antiquated principles and aesthetics of emptiness? Why do they perceive geometrically lifeless buildings as beautiful? We suggest an explanation from cognitive science. The order sought by architects is determined by images in their own minds, and has nothing to do with mathematical symmetries of real, complex, connected places. Such internal references can be quite compelling and beautiful — in the abstract realm. Designers manipulate geometries in their own minds, and become quite taken by them. Since mental images are de-contextualized, designers don't have to deal with the multiple effects that actually influence the human experience of forms. When such images are executed in reality, the designers still see only the simple, pure mental forms. The rest of us see something else altogether: a natural context that has been imposed upon, often severed and damaged.

The heavy dominance of primitive geometries in design is a product of what the philosopher Alfred North Whitehead called "the fallacy of misplaced concreteness". These include not only such simple abstract shapes as straight lines, grids, boxes, cones, pyramids and cylinders, but also an underlying geometry that depends upon its elements existing in isolation. The history of twentieth-century mathematics and science, by contrast, is a series of revelations that the structure of nature is characterized by patterns of network, overlapping connections, complex interaction of many elements, and fractal repetition at many levels of scale.

Geometrical fundamentalism is a philosophy operating under the firm belief that the ideas themselves are total and complete. This is a seductive thought. We may think that our ideas are quite perfect as long as they are inside our own minds; but they utterly fail the test of what makes a good human environment. Once built, they sever delicate relationships, destroying the vitality of place. And yet, many have come to believe that purity is all that matters. There is no place for adaptation, no linking of scales. Architects lost the distinction between an abstract idea and physical structure. They believed that the idea *is* the thing, and the thing *is* the idea. This is the essence of what might best be described as modernist conceit — the ignorance of organized complexity, coming from the dangerous idolatry of abstractions — which survives in all subsequent architectural trends that are derived from modernism.

The legacy of *geometrical fundamentalism* is part of a broader legacy, a historic trend toward greater levels of abstract manipulation, manifesting itself variously as disconnected economic process, meaningless fashion, and the increasing superficiality and "dumbing down" of culture. As Whitehead said: "Mankind is distinguished from animal life by its use of abstractions ... The degeneracy of Mankind is distinguished from its uprise by the dominance of chill abstractions, divorced from aesthetic content." Or, we would add for emphasis — divorced from natural aesthetic content, and increasingly bewitched by the detached aesthetic qualities of the abstractions themselves. The task of bringing to an end a fundamental misuse of geometry must take place within the broader framework of ending an era of mistaken design philosophy.

6. ABSTRACTION AND THE LOSS OF THE SMALLER SCALES.

A complex hierarchical system is composed of components and processes occurring on many different scales. All of the scales interact to create a whole from interdependent parts. From the theory of complex systems, all the higher scales are dependent upon the lower scales. Hierarchical coherence is the result of connecting different scales to create a complex system (see Chapters 3 and 7). As with pathologies in a biological system, all the higher scales in the hierarchy depend on the smallest scales working well. A microbe kills a plant or animal by attacking its cells, which are the smaller scales of the organism. Using *geometrical fundamentalism* to remove connectivity on the smaller scales in the environment works in a similarly destructive manner (see Figure 9.5). This guarantees that we will never connect to this type of built environment, regardless of what the larger scale looks like.

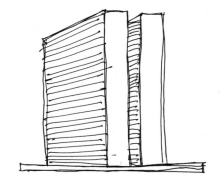

Figure (9.5)
Geometrical fundamentalism
erases the human scales.

In opposing complex systems, *geometrical fundamentalism* loses the hierarchy of interconnected scales, eliminating all but the largest scale. Abstractions focus on a single scale — usually the largest one — and eliminate from consideration all the other scales that would normally cooperate to create a complex interacting system. This is the danger of reductive abstractions: the loss of system coherence through a failure to understand that living systems cannot exist on one level alone. This mathematical result invalidates assertions to the contrary, and contradicts practices implemented by disciplines such as architecture and urbanism.

In a social system, geometrical oversimplification focuses on a group of people as a (non-interacting) unit, ignoring their differences, needs, and uniqueness. It eliminates the individual from consideration, which we will explain later is an extremely dangerous form of abstraction. In an architectural system, the same mathematical error eliminates the smaller scales of structure, and concentrates only on the largest scale. Abstraction of this type is driven by a need for "purity" of structure, which leads to oversimplification and destroys a complex system, whether it is a society, a building, or a living city.

The negative consequences of "urban renewal" programs have been well-documented. At the height of modernist dominance in the post-World-War-II years, it was standard practice to bulldoze poor neighborhoods and to build a concrete utopia of high-rise apartment blocks on the site. An alternative was to move the poor people far away and use the vacated land for more commercially lucrative ends. This process presupposes a series of abstractions. The first is that people are a "class" whose dwellings can be destroyed without any consideration, and who can be relocated, again as a "class", to another location chosen by the planner. In order to do this without pangs of conscience, the class of people must be treated as an abstract set — individual human beings cease to exist in this abstraction; people become a class and thus lose their identity. Nothing has changed today.

How can we justify forcing a class of people into a high-rise tower? Because *it is good for them*, according to architectural beliefs (i.e., residents would benefit from the geometric idea we impose on them). Never mind that environmental psychologists have discredited this assumption with extensive experimental data. This urban typology reflects the use of another abstraction (buildings) to justify the uprooting and displacement of the first abstraction (people). Planners considered high-rise buildings as ideal residences or workplaces for people who can be treated as abstract classes: the poor and the blue-collar working class should inhabit towers of apartments, while the middle and upper classes should work in towers of offices. Despite the usual justification of economic efficiency, this flawed idea follows simple geometrical abstractions that ignore the principles of urban form (Salingaros, 2005).

We have identified and will focus on the mindset that invents and supports such abstractions. This thinking is part of fundamentalism in its most narrow application, and is not restricted to either architecture, or urbanism. To explain the most obvious aspects of the built environment in the twentieth century, therefore, we will refer to totalitarian philosophy, religious extremism, and the forces behind the Holocaust. Inevitably, some readers will object to making such comparisons. Nevertheless, we are convinced of the important philosophical connection between these mindsets.

7. LE CORBUSIER'S GEOMETRICAL FUNDAMENTALISM.

In the history of architectural theory, one text stands out as a polemic advocating *geometrical fundamentalism*: Le Corbusier's 1923 work *Towards a New Architecture* (Le Corbusier, 1927). This is where the geometry of modernism was best articulated, and where the plan to create sprawl, implemented so obligingly in the postwar years, originated. Here, in detailed drawings and impassioned arguments, are the wide freeways, sprawling office "parks", concrete shoebox towers, and boxy retail centers set far back from the street.

Towards a New Architecture is undeniably a landmark document of twentieth-century architecture and planning. While this book is used in almost every university as a textbook on architectural theory, we propose reading it not as a serious text, but rather as a propaganda manual for destroying architectural and urban coherence. In the same way, Adolf Hitler's book *Mein Kampf* is widely read at universities, not as a rational reference on politics and government, but (putting aside one's reaction of disgust) in order to understand how its author was able to manipulate a nation so as to destroy Europe and implement the Holocaust.

Le Corbusier's *Plan Voisin* (labeled *A City of Towers* in his book) shows the center of Paris destroyed and replaced with enormous high-rise buildings. The imposition of a simple, powerful, almost authoritarian abstract idea (towers, ostensibly to remove one from noise, smells, and dust) severs the urban relationships, the web of interconnections that weave the urban fabric of a city and make it part of human life. While the intention of cleaning up dark and unhealthy alleys was good, these radical changes were totally untested. Yet a vast experiment was tried (in many other cities) on thousands of lives without any controls. The proposed monolithic geometry, when applied, erased an intricate connective network and replaced it with a grandly simple non-hierarchy. In so doing, it destroyed both complexity and life.

The Swiss architectural anthropologist Nold Egenter aptly summarizes our own assessment: "Imagine Paris today with Le Corbusier's plan realized! A deadly desert. No tourists come to Paris anymore". Coincidentally, Hitler, also a master propagandist with architectural pretensions, wished to destroy Paris in 1944.

This grand abstraction (which precipitates disconnection) is the essential idea of modernism, and its ultimate flaw. It exists at all levels, from the urban plan to a building plan, all the way down in scale to individual ornament and detail. Under this regime, the complex organic relationships of life and the world are totally severed. In 1923 Le Corbusier was a man clearly taken by the simplistic, totalitarian philosophies then taking root in society. He succumbed to simple abstract geometries that he saw in the reductionist machines around him, saying: *"The Engineer's Aesthetic and Architecture are two things that march together and follow one from the other: the one being now at its full height, the other in an unhappy state of retrogression ... The Engineer, inspired by the law of Economy and governed by mathematical calculation, puts us in accord with universal law. He achieves harmony."* (Le Corbusier, 1927: page 11).

Le Corbusier's words at first glance might appear to support the point of view of this book; but what he proposed for architecture and urbanism does the opposite. Following the tactics of all great propagandists, he said things that sound plausible and even attractive in order to promote an agenda. A crude, primitive geometry captured him: certainly not even as sophisticated as mathematics and science were at the beginning of civilization. He confused the superficial appearance of technical solutions with progress. *Geometrical fundamentalism* is not an enlightened advance, as some imagined, but a reactionary embrace of the pure geometrical abstractions of Euclid, Pythagoras, and the ancient Egyptians: *"Gothic architecture is not, fundamentally, based on spheres, cones and cylinders. Only the nave is an expression of a simple form, but of a complex geometry of the second order (intersecting arches). It is for that reason that a cathedral is not very beautiful and that we search in it for compensations of a subjective kind outside plastic art. A cathedral interests us as the ingenious solution of a difficult problem, but a problem of which the postulates have been badly stated because they do not proceed from the great primary forms."* (Le Corbusier, 1927: page 30).

So a cathedral is not very beautiful? Then what is beautiful? Le Corbusier explains: *"Thus we have the American grain elevators and factories, the magnificent FIRST FRUITS of the new age. THE AMERICAN ENGINEERS OVERWHELM WITH THEIR CALCULATIONS OUR EXPIRING ARCHITECTURE."* (Le Corbusier, 1927: page 31).

This is the "Grand Idea" sweeping away all detritus and preparing for the new age: the age of the machine. Of course the detritus happens to encompass all the greatest creations of humankind spanning the entire globe and built over millennia. These were to be replaced by buildings mimicking American grain elevators (see Figure 9.6). It is obvious to us today that the machines of the 1920s Le Corbusier praises and illustrates in his book are quite crude by any later standard. But Le Corbusier is completely, utterly taken by them, so much so that he considers them actually superior to the realities they crudely reflect. This is a striking and rather extreme example of the phenomenon Whitehead called "the fallacy of misplaced concreteness" — an idolatry of abstractions to the point where one loses connection to the richer and more complex concrete reality they represent. The abstractions replace the reality.

Figure (9.6)
Ordered substructure makes building
on the right more alive.

It is easy to be captured by such simple, strong, bewitching abstractions. Let us boldly go forward, Le Corbusier says, into this program of imposing these simple abstractions on the world on a massive scale. His proposal for Paris shows no mercy for the rich nuances and complexities of human life; only contempt. According to him, cities should be bulldozed and rebuilt — this time with enlarged children's blocks on a huge, totalitarian scale. Le Corbusier was a master at providing totally crude abstractions that ignored deeper and subtler relationships. Obsessed and seduced by his own grand abstractions, he either misses or deliberately ignores the richness and subtlety of traditional buildings, the kind of subtle organic relationships that his crystalline mechanical architecture could never create.

In hindsight, it is astonishing the degree to which Le Corbusier's program was so successfully implemented on a vast, global scale. How did this happen? Who was Le Corbusier, anyway? Charles-Edouard Jeanneret-Gris was an unknown Swiss architect working in Paris, making a living mostly by selling commercial advertisements in his journal *L'Esprit Nouveau*. He wrote and published whatever he wanted in it, and later collected these unrefereed articles into his books. After he adopted the pseudonym "Le Corbusier", people began to pay more attention to his architectural and urban ideas. He came along at the precise moment when the western world hungered desperately for a utopian "new world". His ideas served the brutal new industrialism. Le Corbusier and the other modernist pioneers were happy to oblige the revolutionary fervor of the times, encouraging it to sweep away all vestiges of the past.

8. CLASSICAL ARCHITECTURE.

Classicism also incorporates geometrically simple forms, but does so in a carefully adaptive way (making them more accessible to human sensibilities), with archetypes developed over centuries. This crucial distinction is equally true for vernacular design. In any rich traditional design, as in nature, there are connections and reflections at all levels of scale. Geometrically simple abstractions exist in abundance; but they are subordinated to an interlocking hierarchy of structures, and are not masters of the overall design. Many subtle and complex pathways link up the structure within itself and with the surrounding environment. Classical buildings were exquisitely tuned to their site and to surrounding buildings so as to create urban space (and a satisfying urban space is something that modernists were rarely if ever able to achieve).

Le Corbusier scored a clever propaganda coup by filling his book (Le Corbusier, 1927) with photos and sketches of the Parthenon. He was a master propagandist, and a pioneer in applying techniques of visual persuasion to create the paid advertisements published in his journal *L'Esprit Nouveau*. He misleadingly claims to extract his *geometrical fundamentalism* (and even the machine aesthetic) from the buildings on the Acropolis. This is achieved by careful selective cropping of photos. Le Corbusier's hagiographers are fond of showing him pictured against the Acropolis, using publicity photos that he himself had carefully prepared. The forced misappropriation of Classical architecture by Le Corbusier amounts to the old confidence trick of inventing a fictitious relation to figures of authority in order to acquire credibility.

In the end, neither Le Corbusier's architecture nor his urbanism bear any relation to Classical solutions. The buildings Le Corbusier fostered might as well have been razor blades, slicing the world to shreds. Though many critics have attacked them as ugly, their fundamental fault is not an aesthetic poverty so much as a structural poverty: a lack of organized complexity, a toxic disconnectedness. Our civilization's task of replacing its architecture and urbanism of disconnectedness with a newly adaptive architecture of connectivity cannot even begin before Le Corbusier's pervasive influence ceases.

There are those who argue that contemporary architecture and urban planning have since moved on to new — and even more horrific — typologies. In fact, Le Corbusier's legacy, and that of other early modernists, is everywhere still today. Architectural academia deified him, and continues to present him to impressionable architecture students as a supreme role model: an architectural legend. His ideas have spread into our society's collective mind, distorting and confusing the message of Classical architecture. He bears the responsibility of initiating an inhuman approach to the built environment, where adaptation and responsiveness are unnecessary, even contemptible. That provided the fertile ground for present-day architectural and urban insanities.

9. FUNDAMENTALISM AS A DEFINING FORCE IN TWENTIETH-CENTURY ARCHITECTURE.

The distinguishing characteristic of fundamentalism is that it relies too narrowly on a simple set of principles. While there is nothing inherently wrong with that, extremists find it easy to hijack those principles. They turn them into abstractions that promote an insular mind-set condoning destruction of any perceived "impurity". They express intolerance towards competing ideas, and channel the energy of followers against those ideas. A fundamentalist belief that is taken over by fanatics is antithetical to the principles of a plural and democratic open society — or indeed, of any open, evolving and self-correcting system, including the institution of science itself.

Fundamentalism in architecture is no different from religious fundamentalism. One might associate the drive to a fundamentalist belief with the need to establish an identity in the face of complexities of human culture. Those who have difficulty coping with urban complexities — as, for example, Le Corbusier — would prefer to eradicate them. His horror of and hysterical aversion to the hustle and bustle of lively street life are well documented. He was single-mindedly obsessed with erasing the lively Parisian street, which he pathologically despised.

We interpret this abhorrence of complexity as the manifestation of a basic insecurity. It represents a profound lack of confidence in oneself, which would otherwise anchor a normal person's psyche to human society. Without such confidence, one feels lost unless there is something else to which one can attach. Insecure persons need something stable to cope with uncertainties in their own identity. A simplistic ideal — particularly if it is of a utopian nature — offers a readily recognized alternative to the complexity of real life. One identifies a (frequently fictitious) true state, and is supposed to dedicate one's life to the constant search for purity. As has been stated by religious leaders of all denominations, however, that is the opposite of achieving wisdom through personal equilibrium in a constantly changing and complex world.

The danger of adopting an overly simplistic world-view is that, when it is combined with intolerance, it is used to justify destruction. A turning inward, and a ruthless comparison with impossibly pure ideals prevents pluralism and the evolution of new complexities.

Geometrical fundamentalism started with a call to destroy the smallest scale: ornament was identified as a criminal activity, and was banished from architecture in the early years of the twentieth century. It took some time for this interdiction to take affect, but it did so almost universally after the Second World War. As explained by the Austrian artist/architect Friedrich Hundertwasser: "The Austrian Adolf Loos brought this atrocity into the world. In 1908, with his manifesto aptly entitled 'Ornament and Crime'. No doubt he meant well. Adolf Hitler meant well, too. But Adolf Loos was incapable of thinking fifty years ahead. The world will never be rid of the evil he invoked".

This war against ornament and decoration actually hides an ideological failure in modernist architecture: the lack of a cultural basis. That should not be surprising, since those who turned against ornament deliberately sought to destroy all ties (and reminiscences) of historical architectures. More than any other group of architects, those trained in the anti-ornamental school showed no respect for preserving architectural masterpieces of the past. True to their fundamentalist beliefs, traditional buildings held no value for them. Older buildings continue to pose a danger for empty assertions praising architectural abstractions, since ordinary people can maintain their own sense of reality by connecting emotionally to the built surfaces of more traditional buildings. As in other fanatical movements, it is essential to erase any examples that contradict official dogma.

Chapter 5 of this book showed that an infinite variety of non-traditional architectures remain to be explored. Yet, those early modernists who practiced *geometrical fundamentalism* immediately used their newly-acquired status and power to marginalize or discredit other, much more innovative architects. As I argue further in Chapter 10, *Darwinian Processes and Memes in Architecture: A Memetic Theory of Modernism*, the Art Nouveau, Expressionist, and Art Deco form languages were dealt a fatal blow not from more traditional Classical architects, but from their modernist brethren. Those styles were condemned as supposedly "not pure enough".

The German architect Walter Gropius set an example of architectural assassination by supporting the demolition of New York's Pennsylvania Station, built by McKim, Mead, and White in 1911. He is on record as calling it: "a monument to a particularly insignificant period in American architectural history ... a 'slip-cover civilization' ... a case of pseudotradition". The British architectural historian David Watkin, on the other hand considers it: "one of the great masterpieces of twentieth-century New York. Pennsylvania Station has probably never been equaled as a triumph of engineering and organization in which the Classical language was used to ennoble a mundane activity. Its shameful demolition in 1963-1965 marked the nadir in American architectural life."

Architecture has been accompanied by a vast amount of text (misleadingly called "architectural theory") supporting and justifying this architectural dogma. The sheer weight of all those arguments about modularity, functionality, efficiency, technology, the "spirit of the age", the "machine aesthetic", etc. says something very revealing about a basic insecurity. A living culture of building has no need to justify itself to anyone — it is automatically and intuitively perceived as serving human needs. It doesn't need convoluted arguments or propaganda to prove its worth. The problem is that, whenever twentieth-century architecture has been assessed on intuitive grounds, it has invariably been rejected by the general public: hence the need for theoretical posturing and indoctrination.

Players of this abstract game must constantly remind themselves of the rules, which, unlike generative rules, are actually rules for *eliminating* structure. Architecture students are taught what *not* to do: a design must not even remotely look like anything traditional, or pre-modernist. Students remain ignorant about techniques for generating coherence. Learning is based on looking at contemporary buildings and trying to reproduce the same unnatural feeling or similar sensation in one's design. This way of learning internalizes an aesthetic without understanding its basis, training the architect by rote memorization of visual examples, rather than any intellectual explanation. This is a standard technique of psychological conditioning; for getting people to do something without question, often against their natural instincts. It is the method of indoctrination used by fundamentalist sects.

10. MODULARITY AND HOMOGENIZATION.

The most abused material in twentieth-century architecture is concrete. Empty rectangular panels of raw concrete abolish surface richness, losing the texture normally found in natural materials such as stone and wood. Concrete has an unfriendly surface, but great plastic properties. Architects have gone to great lengths to produce large square panels out of concrete that are then used as modules in construction. This practice makes little sense for a material that is quintessentially versatile. Concrete can be cast into any shape and size required, on or off the building site, so why make it first into modules? And why strictly flat, rectangular ones? The reason is that an image of large square panels is imprinted into the collective memory of twentieth-century architects, who appear to reproduce them unthinkingly.

It is here, in the deliberate intent to deny human beings any sensory connection to architectural surfaces, that *geometrical fundamentalism* most clearly reveals its goals. Removing color and texture from the environment by leaving brutal surfaces of raw exposed concrete (following Le Corbusier) denies two of the human senses: color vision, and touch. Two more senses, hearing and smell, are assaulted when concrete is used in interior walls. Since concrete is acoustically "hard", it produces an unpleasant echo compared to the more pleasing echo from acoustically softer materials such as wood and lime plaster. In addition, raw concrete surfaces tend to give off powder with time that not only has a unpleasant smell, but also poses a respiratory health hazard. The Romans, who first used concrete extensively as a building material, never let it show in large exposed surfaces.

This insistence on surfaces without any informational meaning is misleadingly tied into other ideas such as modularity. Modular design coupled with homogenization has become the visual expression of *geometrical fundamentalism* in our times (see Chapter 8). None of this has anything to do with the commercial benefits of modular production, however. Modular construction that employs empty rectangular panels is simply conforming to a visual design template. A profound and far-reaching shift occurred when architects went from using complex modules within a free system of design (i.e., a method not tied to any rigid geometry or specific dimensions), to fitting empty components into a rectangular modular grid. This shift represents the transition from the traditional use of modular components, to an implementation of simplistic geometries.

Beautiful buildings were created in the past using richly complex and detailed architectural modules. A thousand years of Islamic architecture relied on glazed ceramic tiles for its most glorious effects. Modules such as polychrome tiles and wicker-like brick patterns in relief are themselves internally complex, and serve to generate ordered complexity over a large region. The nineteenth century saw the mass-production of intricate decorative panels and architectural elements, such as those used by the French architect Hector Guimard for the components of the Paris Metro station entrances. Louis Sullivan's buildings are unthinkable without the mass-produced and richly-ornamental metal and terracotta panels he employed. The "International Style", however, sought surface purity. Its architects insisted on using large, visually empty modules, which eliminate internal structure and information. To do this, the larger the module is, the better (see Chapter 8).

Homogenization creates a plain, continuous surface perceived as a single unit. It achieves this by disguising a module's edge as much as possible, so as to blend one module into the next. With bricks, this effect is obtained by minimizing the mortar's exposed width, and choosing its color and consistency so as to blend in with the brick material. The result is bonded brickwork preferred throughout the late twentieth century. A brick wall is made to resemble a single sheet of the same material. Erecting an obsessively smooth, homogeneous wall out of bricks denies the creative freedom inherent in using such a small unit. Homogeneity is the opposite of the deliberate contrast in color between bricks and mortar in older, traditional brickwork, where also the thickness of the mortar is in a scaled relationship to the width of the brick itself (Figure 2.8).

In stonework, a homogeneous effect is achieved by having no discernible transition between one stone and another. Smooth rectangular stones are arranged on a plane surface with their edges touching, without any connective material showing. This produces one continuous surface of stone, since the joint is visible only at arm's length. A similar effect is obtained with glass panels. Unlike stone slabs, glass as a building material has to be supported by its edges and not by its inner surface. Even so, we see glass panels made as large as possible according to their freestanding strength, with as minimal a frame support as is practical. The desired fundamentalist effect is a continuous wall of glass. Other materials are treated in the same way to remove information. In more recent buildings, such as the Guggenheim museum in Bilbao, the curved surface was originally conceived as a continuous metal surface.

11. GEOMETRICAL FUNDAMENTALISM VERSUS MONUMENTALITY.

Our colleagues have asked: "does *geometrical fundamentalism* encompass the work of the architects Etienne-Louis Boullée, Karl Friedrich Schinkel, and the ancient Egyptians?" Boullée had visionary schemes for megalomaniac buildings in elementary geometrical shapes, and so would appear to qualify as prefiguring Le Corbusier's fundamentalism. As Boullée's designs were never built, however, the question remains an academic one. Schinkel, on the other hand, built a number of great buildings — well connected on all scales, and paying attention to the user. Yes, they are grand, yet they are also composed of connective elements. They satisfy the criterion of great humane architecture by connecting the individual through a sequence of increasing scales to a very large and coherent overall scale.

The ancient Egyptians created one typology that intentionally disconnects: the pyramid. It was a Royal Tomb, after all, and was not meant to be entered; on the contrary, its form was carefully chosen to send a clear message for mortals to stay away. The ancient Egyptians were also masters at erecting humane monumental architecture, and though much of it was funerary, it is all marvelously connective through a complete hierarchy of scales (with the exception of the pyramid's original austere exterior). Early modernists often confused *geometrical fundamentalism* with monumentality. This is surprising, since those architects studied monumental Greek and Roman civil architecture on the one hand, and ancient defensive installations on the other. There is where one learns the crucial difference between the two typologies.

Other styles crossed the line from monumentality into *geometrical fundamentalism* by making buildings and urban dimensions too large; by removing visual and geometrical structure on the human scale that individuals can relate to; or simply by making the urban environment so sterile that pedestrians cannot enjoy it. The Fascists distorted and stripped ancient Egyptian, Greek, and Roman architectures to create a pompous style that is as fundamentalist as it is monumental (Mussolini's and Marcello Piacentini's EUR — the "Third Rome"; Hitler's and Albert Speer's unrealized "Grand Axis" for Berlin). Contrary to what is frequently but misleadingly asserted, there is nothing particularly "Classical" about this monstrous, oversize architecture other than a very superficial resemblance — it is instead a pure expression of totalitarian power. This power resonates through the authority of simple geometry. Albert Speer's greatest achievement was his "Cathedral of Light" (1934) created for the Nuremberg rallies: a very modern architectural conception based entirely on technology.

For sheer size, however, we have to look to recent times for the most harmful examples: rectangular megatowers; vast, hard, unusable (supposedly "pedestrian") plazas; enormous treeless parking lots; etc. A textbook example of this faceless megalomania is realized in La Défense on the outskirts of Paris, a triumph of the will of French President François Mitterrand.

The problem we face is an assault on the mathematical properties of life, which leads to the elimination of living structure. People confuse organizational principles creating large-scale symmetry on the one hand, with imposed ideal forms on the other, even though the two have an entirely different origin (Salingaros, 2005). Organizational principles connect processes and elements occurring on a smaller scale, in a process that itself generates ordering on the larger scale. By contrast, imposed ideal forms ignore what is happening on the smaller scale, and arbitrarily force a geometrical straitjacket onto the ensemble, commonly disrupting what was occurring there originally (or could possibly take place in the future). Organization connects and coordinates processes; whereas imposition from above may eliminate them (Salingaros, 2005). This is precisely the difference between a monumental architectural or urban statement and *geometrical fundamentalism*.

Postmodernist architects fanatically avoid organization (connectivity on the large scale). This is, of course, the other side of the same coin: if one cannot impose a simplistic form on structure, then at least one can destroy the overall coherence by using disconnected, unrelated components. It's still *geometrical fundamentalism*, valuing simplistic geometrical games above the adaptivity of buildings to their users, and dictating that we should avoid anything reminiscent of living structure. This mindset permeates the profession, and belittles efforts towards a new vernacular or traditional architecture for our time. Its origins are traceable to Le Corbusier's stubborn refusal to align structural elements on some of his buildings, going out of his way to prevent the harmonious matching of articulations. Again, he showed us the way to avoid life by introducing randomness into design (see Figure 9.7).

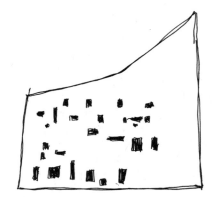

Figure (9.7)
Le Corbusier's randomization of windows
expresses nihilism.

Often, the simplest, most natural organization of individual components generates an overall symmetric form. Especially on the urban scale, linearization results from the organization of movement. When small-scale connective processes are understood and respected, they can be aligned (though not necessarily in a straight line) to reinforce processes occurring on the large scale. Geometrical abstractions are a necessary prerequisite for any design project, yet adaptation requires bending any abstract ideals to serve human needs and satisfy structural constraints. If an abstraction becomes so powerfully embedded in our minds that it takes over, then it turns into fundamentalism. The abstraction of ideals from their realities should never become dogmatic or arbitrary.

12. ABSTRACTIONS IN CREATING AND DESTROYING BUILDINGS.

The abstract conceptions linked to architecture encompass a wide range of ideas. We focus here on three of them: "pure geometry", "giant scale", and "monofunctional use". Although strictly speaking these are separate concepts, they are linked abstractions that are almost invariably applied together. The same mindset that uses a high degree of abstraction is required both to define enormous structures, and to destroy them. Both acts (creation and destruction) presuppose that the buildings' inhabitants are not individuals, but can be identified as an abstract class. Let us first discuss the reductionist acts of conceptualizing and planning the giant building.

Ordinarily, human beings don't like to be isolated in order to do only one thing: we crave variety in actions to be performed, and joy in our visual surroundings. Anyone sitting in his or her office needs to take a break now and then, and the best refreshment is a total change in action and surroundings. That is not possible in a monofunctional environment. People still like to work in cities, despite the high cost in commuting and parking inconveniences, precisely because they can at least spend some fleeting time in a stimulating environment. (Unfortunately, this does nothing for the life of the city after business hours — that depends on the continuous presence of local residents).

Any large monofunctional building is conceived to house a very large number of people doing more or less the same thing. This is a function of an industrial philosophy that reduces tasks to interchangeable elements. Yet there is excellent evidence that the giant monofunctional building goes against basic human needs. Hundreds or even thousands of lives are here subordinated to a geometrical abstraction. Such a building exists only because of its geometry — its function is to house an abstract class of people, and in doing so it disregards the needs of the individual. The shape is most often a formal geometrical statement having nothing to do with the persons inside it. Such a building could just as well be empty. We have to *imagine* it full of people, because there is no geometrical indication that it was intended for people to spend a major part of their lives in it or around it.

Abstraction creates a dangerous dehumanization. This point was previously made by Eric Darton in his prescient book on the World Trade Center (Darton, 2000). Darton raised the frightening prospect that the creation of giant tower buildings is related to the mindset of those who would wish to destroy them (Darton, 2000). His reasoning is as follows. It is impossible to contemplate killing thousands of people in a single building unless those people are viewed simply as an abstract class. They must not be considered as having any separate existence apart from the building's geometry, which is itself defined abstractly. The geometry of huge, monumental, monofunctional office towers makes it difficult to imagine that they are full of people, hence it becomes possible and even rational for someone who thinks only in abstractions to contemplate their destruction (Darton, 2000).

13. POLITICAL ROOTS OF DEHUMANIZING ABSTRACTIONS IN ARCHITECTURE.

A principal root of modernist design lies in Fascist Italy. The Futurist manifestoes declared total war on the architecture (and society) of the past. Sharing the German National Socialist beliefs in a "new society" that subordinates the individual to more lofty political and social goals, Benito Mussolini's regime sponsored some of the most characteristic examples of modernist architecture. Giuseppe Terragni, Luigi Moretti, Adalberto Libera, and many other Italian architects built "pure" modernist buildings. Their blatant association with Fascism makes architectural historians uncomfortable, forcing some into an unprofessional expedient of ignoring those buildings altogether (or, like Sigfried Giedion, intentionally mislabeling Terragni's "House of Fascism" as "House of the People"). Unlike in Germany, modernism was promoted by Fascist Italy, and its architectural aspirations were in harmony with the regime's totalitarian philosophy about the future.

Dehumanizing abstraction was embraced by architects in early twentieth-century Germany. That era in Germany is well-recognized as a time of rejection of the individual, and a belief that a new machine architecture should serve the needs of the worker class. The Nazis later adopted this socialist worker spirit as their own, along with an early modernist style of architecture. Gropius (who served as director of the *Bauhaus* from 1919 to 1928) originated the curtain walls and ribbon windows of the "International Style". Ludwig Mies van der Rohe (who headed the *Bauhaus* from 1930 to 1933), proudly proclaimed that: "the individual is losing significance; his destiny is no longer what interests us". In 1921, he came up with designs for glass skyscrapers. For such structures to be inhabited, the normal wishes of individuals have to be subordinated to the idea of a building as an abstraction.

Although both Gropius and Mies van der Rohe later emigrated to the US and became respected world-famous architects, they first offered their services to Hitler. Having strong architectural preferences himself, Hitler refused because he despised modernism as a style. He also mistrusted the *Bauhaus* architects politically, since they all had some association with the socialist movement in Germany. Gropius had designed the monument to the "March Heroes" who started the 1848 revolution (1921), and Mies van der Rohe had designed a monument (1926) to the communist politicians Rosa Luxemburg and Karl Liebknecht, both of whom had been murdered by the proto-Nazi *Freikorps*. The Swiss architect Hannes Meyer (who headed the *Bauhaus* from 1928 to 1930) had introduced obligatory courses on Marx and Lenin. While the Nazis embraced the same ideals: industrial production tied to dehumanizing architecture and urbanism (preferring a style more Art Deco than Classical), they found the original Bauhaus teachers politically unacceptable.

Neither their damning overtures to the Nazis, nor the real reason why some of the Bauhaus teachers left Germany — because they could get no major commissions — are mentioned in History of Architecture courses. Instead, we are told that those architects were "good" because they fled Hitler. The point is that their architecture, far from being the reaction to National Socialism that it later claimed, was in fact its philosophical sibling. It is only by historical accident that the two were separated. Fritz

Ertl, a Bauhaus graduate, was one of the architects of Auschwitz-Birkenau. According to Jan Maciag: "It is a terrible, modern, rational city as a machine for death".

A few initial works by early modernist architects were either commissioned by wealthy individuals who championed the artistic avant-garde; or by European cities run by politically radical local governments that promoted collectivism. It was these two types of client that bought into the architects' bold promises that their geometrically singular style of architecture was able to transform society. Other governments sincerely wished to provide a better environment for their citizens, but this promise appealed directly to totalitarian regimes either on the right or the left. The possibility of social engineering via geometry was seductive to those in power. Having designed the Centrosoyuz building (1929-1934) and unsuccessfully competed to build the Palace of the Soviets (1931) in Moscow, Le Corbusier urged France's successive governments (including the collaborationist one) to implement his plan for destroying Algiers. It was tragically carried out after the War by a different government.

14. THE NEED FOR ABSTRACTION IN DESTROYING CLASSES OF SOCIETY.

Authors such as Zygmunt Bauman insist that an abstractive process lies at the root of the Holocaust (Bauman, 2000). Human beings can carry out acts of organized mass-murder on a systematic scale only if the victims are dehumanized — redefined as an abstract class dissociated from humanity. Whereas individual murder involves emotion, and is driven by passions and forces, mass murder on an industrial scale has to be carried out dispassionately. For this to take place, the victim class must be identified in the most abstract terms. It is essential to sever any human connection between the victims and the perpetrators of the crime. This cutting of connections was very carefully thought out by the Nazis, who maximized the isolating abstraction of the Jewish people as a class separate from other Germans.

An enormous effort was expended by the Nazis to segregate their victims socially and geographically. People were uprooted and relocated to ghettos, and their legal identity and citizenship was taken away in helping create this abstraction. The desired result was the redefinition of a large segment of the population as an abstract, alien class, defined geometrically by residence in the ghetto, with no legal or social connection to the rest of the German nation. Once that stage (the definition of an abstract class) was achieved, it was only a technical step to physically destroy the class. Note how the other aspects of dehumanization much beloved by architects such as mass-production, mechanization, efficiency, modularity, and functionality played a major role in implementing the "final solution" (Bauman, 2000).

Albert Speer, a practitioner of *geometrical fundamentalism* especially in his urban projects, shows how an architecture of megalomania is related to the Holocaust. Before being appointed Minister of Armaments, from which position he directed industrial production that used slave laborers, Speer was in charge of building the "Grand Axis" in Berlin. This vast urban project required the demolition of existing buildings. Tens of thousands of apartments were evacuated on his orders: their non-Jewish residents were resettled elsewhere, but Jewish owners were deported to the camps. (This was not known at the time of the Nuremberg trials, and became public only after his death). Speer was intelligent enough not to apply *geometrical fundamentalism* to his interior architecture, however. The interior of the New Chancellery (1938) was built in an ostentatiously Neo-Baroque style (not Classical) — imagine a vastly magnified Barcelona Pavilion stuffed with heavy furniture and hanging antique tapestries — to create an opulent working environment for his beloved Führer.

Now that historians of the Holocaust have identified abstraction as a necessary precondition for genocide, the phenomenon is easy to recognize in other atrocities. In almost every case that one cares to study, before and since the Second World War, the prelude to mass slaughter is an abstraction of the victim group as a class stripped of its humanity and declared to be foreign to the perpetrators. If the atrocities are state-directed, as is so often the case, then an official propaganda campaign is aimed at removing any possible traces of individual existence from the class; it is forbidden to mention individual human beings, but only the victim class as a whole. Only via this abstraction can the rest of the perpetrator population be turned into accomplices for the horrible deeds.

From these conclusions, we gain a better insight of the dichotomy between reductive abstractions on the one hand, and a respect for complex systems on the other. The first is the enemy of the second. Any philosophy that eliminates the individual human being from consideration merits an automatic commonality with destructive events such as the Holocaust. This is a mathematical similarity: when the smaller scales of a complex system are eliminated, the system is destroyed. We have argued at great length in this Chapter that *geometrical fundamentalism* in architecture belongs to this type of essentially destructive ideology.

15. CONCLUSION.

A *geometrical fundamentalism* lies at the core of post-industrial planning and design. We are convinced that this has destroyed our cities and has made even ordinary buildings less human. We suggested that *geometrical fundamentalism* plays a role in creating the resentment the rest of the world feels against the industrialized western nations. Such is its commercial success and its continued sway upon the building arts, however, that an understanding of its philosophical basis is needed before any change can be implemented. We must understand the weaknesses of twentieth-century design in the light of new insights into the rich connective structure of nature, a structure also seen in pre-modern design and urbanism around the world. Only then can we do what all great designers throughout history have done: learn from the past, borrow liberally from it, and synthesize those lessons for our own time and place. Today we possess new mathematical tools that can energize us while instilling a new humility about the complexities of nature and of vernacular design. We believe that a new connective architecture for our time is possible. Contrary to the early modernists' quixotic hope, we have not arrived at the end of architecture.

Chapter Ten

DARWINIAN PROCESSES AND MEMES IN ARCHITECTURE: A MEMETIC THEORY OF MODERNISM.

by Nikos A. Salingaros and Terry M. Mikiten

1. INTRODUCTION.

The world of the architect is created in an architect's mind according to physical systems that govern the biology of the brain. According to one theory of the thinking process, an idea arises out of the competition and selection among similar and dissimilar ideas occurring simultaneously in adjacent neural circuits of the brain (Calvin, 1987; 1990). The same principles of competition and selection might be said to apply to the general public in their willingness to accept architectural forms and styles. Things in the built environment originate and endure — not just in the tectonic sense, but in their survival value in a society's common language — because they "make sense" in some way. Competing ideas in a society eventually suppress or reinforce each other to produce one or more dominant themes. In other words, creativity and survival work in ways that are compatible with the cognitive machinery that makes up the mind.

Nevertheless, sometimes the mind works against the body by acting in a harmful manner. An architect's mind has the power to either create designs that adapt to human needs and emotions, or to impose arbitrary forms on the environment. A Darwinian selection process in architecture takes place among competing ideas in the mind of the architect (see Figure 10.1).

A second selection process, also Darwinian, occurs in the society of consumers. This second process acts among styles, where certain styles dominate over others. In both of these selection processes (i.e., in the architect's mind, and in society), the criteria are a mixture of human needs and irrelevant forms. We will set up a model to explain why these two disparate sets of selection criteria can coexist, and how one set can displace the other.

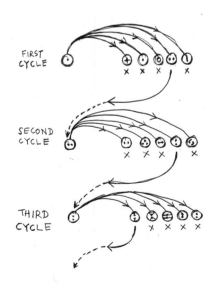

Figure (10.1)
Darwinian cycle generates variants,
then selects from them.

The word "meme" denotes any idea, image, tune, or advertising jingle that endures and propagates (Brodie, 1996; Dawkins, 1989; 1993; Dennett, 1995). Memes — ideas, tunes, or images — are the equivalent of agents that "infect" memory. An image will stick in memory if it is encapsulated in a meaning structure. Memes are conceptual entities that propagate among human minds. An image will be more likely to be transmitted to others if it is easy to remember. What distinguishes a meme from a more complex entity is the meme's low information content. For example, the typical advertising jingle is not a complete song or musical composition; it usually lasts only a few seconds. In the same way, an image meme is not a detailed picture but usually a simplified advertising logo. An idea meme has no intellectual depth, but is usually a simple catchy slogan. In all these cases, the brevity of the meme is what helps it to propagate.

This Chapter applies the theory of memes to the field of architecture. Two main points are argued. First, Darwinian processes (combining variation and selection) are important to architecture. Second, the specific case of minimalist architecture corresponds to a meme, which has spread in spite of its being non-adaptive for the people that make use of such buildings (because of its mode of transmission, it may be termed "parasitic"). These two theses are logically independent, though both are necessary to present a picture of how architectural styles propagate. A reader may feel sympathetic towards the first thesis, yet it has unexplored implications for the design process in general. The second thesis is more controversial, and is discussed in greater depth. Our eventual goal is to explain the unlikely success of modernism by other than subjective criteria.

Contrary to architects' regard of design as a purely creative process, adaptive design is a problem-solving activity. Human intelligence allows both the generation of possible alternative solutions and selection among them to take place mentally. This summarizes our intellectual advantage over other animals: our imagination is a profoundly useful virtual reality simulator. A more intelligent system will have a more efficient mental representation and selection process. The architect's mind is impacted by the problem space — the space of all possible solutions — and various memes from a variety of sources. These could come from one's own memory; from visual templates from the environment; from the influence of other architects; etc. Competing forces such as engineering constraints, a desire for creativity, and the unique need to express oneself drive the design to its final state.

A Darwinian process in the mind of the designer depends on a set of selection criteria. Traditional societies such as pre-industrialized people, and the industrialized nations up to and including the nineteenth century used a wide range of selection criteria that, among other practical constraints, enhanced emotional well-being for the user. Specific architectural styles, however, can replace the selection criteria of traditional adaptive design by a process of matching to visual templates, or memes (see Figure 10.2). Once adaptive design is abandoned, the spread of architectural styles depends strictly on factors governing meme propagation in a society. A minimalist style then possesses an unbeatable advantage over more complex styles, because of its low information content. This is one of the main points of this Chapter.

Figure (10.2)
Selection based on images is not Darwinian.

VISUAL
REFERENCE

SELECTION
AFTER ONE
STEP

It is possible to explain in this way an important event in the evolution of humankind: the drastic change in the visual character of the built environment during the twentieth century. After a design style is introduced and is accepted for whatever reasons by a group of people, then it is subject to Darwinian selection from among the pool of competing styles. This is where consumers, the construction industry, and the architectural establishment come into play by exerting selection forces. A second selection occurs entirely outside the architect's mind, within the arena of human society (de Jong, 1999). Some architectural styles die out, whereas others survive and become popular. Perhaps surprisingly, their success has little to do with their fitness for human habitation. The criteria for success in Darwinian selection of architectural styles have changed to an abstract set that is not based directly on human needs, even though it is human beings that do the selecting.

An architectural meme is a visual component of a particular architectural style. It is a representation of form, geometry, surface, etc. Studying how architectural memes spread in a society, and how competing memes are selected requires a knowledge of the factors affecting meme propagation. The philosopher, physicist, and Computer Scientist Francis Heylighen has identified a list of these. We will discuss seven of his factors: SIMPLICITY, NOVELTY, UTILITY, FORMALITY, AUTHORITY, PUBLICITY, and CONFORMITY in the context of architecture (Heylighen, 1993; 1997). With the exception of UTILITY, none of these factors serves actual human needs. We will argue, therefore, that the spread of a design style occurs in a society more because of the proliferation of images through mass media than for practical reasons. Even UTILITY will be shown to obey memetic transmission, but in a roundabout way. Often, the mere promise of UTILITY is responsible for the success of an architectural style that creates buildings impractical in actual use.

We will propose here an eighth factor that aids meme propagation: ENCAPSULATION describes how memes link with other memes. This process confers an advantage to the encapsulated meme because it increases the meme's virulence by making it appear more attractive, and it protects the meme from external challenges by insulating it inside a complex of other, beneficial memes. For example, in advertising, the image of a product can be encapsulated in a musical meme such as a jingle. From that time on, people recognize the product by way of the jingle. An encapsulated architectural meme also manipulates our emotions in order to propagate. ENCAPSULATION embeds a meme or collection of memes into a meaning structure (i.e., a set of related concepts that we attach meaning to; see Chapter 7 in this book). Through this mechanism, visual memes can acquire an emotional and physical basis. At that point, they cease to be regarded as mere ideas open to debate, but assume the fundamental character of beliefs defining one's ideology.

It is also possible to discredit an architectural style by deliberately encapsulating it within a shell (an encapsulating meme) of negative associations. By using EN-CAPSULATION as a weapon to discredit competing styles, a useful idea can be tainted (whether there is any basis for that association or not). A society's collective unconscious from that point on automatically rejects such an idea or style without question, even though it may offer excellent solutions to urgent problems. In contemporary architecture, destructive encapsulation is used to discredit new buildings in the Classical and Nineteenth-Century styles. This has happened despite the fact that earlier buildings in those styles are among the most comfortable and best adapted to human needs. We will argue that by encapsulating them using pathological memes as a shell, those styles have effectively been placed in a sort of quarantine.

Success in the spread of social memes is measured by how deeply they establish themselves as basic beliefs in a society. A group of memes achieves its greatest success when it becomes part of the establishment; i.e., it is institutionalized. We are first going to deal with those factors that increase the spread of memes, and thereby help in their chances for eventual institutionalization. In the final section of this Chapter, we explain how once memes have been institutionalized they acquire a rigidity that makes them extremely difficult to replace. The institutional perspective offers some strong explanations for the remarkable persistence of some twentieth-century typologies of architecture and urbanism in spite of their inhuman qualities.

2. ARCHITECTURAL STYLE AND MILITARY ARCHITECTURE.

The "International Style" of architecture has been the overriding building design since the 1920s. The style is instantly recognizable by its geometry of cubes and rectangular slabs; flat plain surfaces; the lack of wide frames and thick connective boundaries; the use of steel, glass planes, and concrete panels; and in many cases the elimination of color and visual structure on the human range of scales 1 mm to 1 m (see Chapter 1). Representative buildings and architects include the Bauhaus building (1926) by Walter Gropius; the *Pavillon Suisse, Cité Universitaire* (1932) and Carpenter Center for the Visual Arts (1961) by Le Corbusier; the *Casa del Fascio* (1936) by Giuseppe Terragni; the UN Headquarters (1950) by Wallace Harrison and Max Abramovitz; the Seagram building (1958) and the *Neue Nationalgalerie* (1968) by Ludwig Mies van der Rohe; and the National Theatre (1967) by Denys Lasdun.

Designers claimed their buildings to be "functional", based on a "machine aesthetic". Simply looking like a sleek machine from the 1920s doesn't guarantee functionality in a building, however. Those machines providing the visual inspiration for that style of architecture were either housed in smooth metal shells, or followed cubist aesthetic principles. Surface qualities and appearances substituted for genuine structure, reducing complex forms to simple images. In either case, their "look" had nothing to do with their function: it merely conformed to a passing artistic fad. A culture that substitutes images for the real thing risks losing its accumulated knowledge. Many authors claim that this has already happened, since our generation has lost innumerable adaptive architectural traditions stretching back several millennia.

More recently, "high-tech" has become the fashionable international style of corporate architecture, simply because its superficial appearance of metal pipes, glass, mirrors, and plexiglass links it to modern technology; this goes on despite high-tech's extremely high cost and low user comfort. Representative high-tech buildings and architects include the *Centre Pompidou* (1977) by Richard Rogers and Renzo Piano, and the Hong Kong and Shanghai Bank (1986) by Norman Foster.

Two contradictory movements in twentieth-century architecture work against Darwinian selection that adapts towards the human needs of users. The first is an attitude taught in recent decades by our schools: that an architect has artistic license to look beyond certain practical constraints — indeed, that it is necessary to do so — in the pursuit of a "great work of art". The second is a standardized approach to buildings, behind which is a conviction that shaping design to particular individual needs (i.e., those of the client or user) is simply being self-indulgent and therefore socially irresponsible. Early modernists set up standards for minimal dwellings that had little relation with the living needs of human beings, and incredibly, most of them are still applied today. A central idea in German social housing of the 1920s, the *Existenzminimum* (Broadbent, 1990) codified the minimum space in which a German blue-collar worker and his family could be housed. We inherited those absurd restrictions on living space as part and parcel of twentieth-century architectural typologies. That is where oppressively low ceilings and cramped, tiny kitchens in today's apartments originate.

There are obvious stylistic similarities with military architecture, since many modernist buildings look forbidding, ominous, stark, alien, faceless, and present a generally hostile appearance. The reason for this impression is that they utilize some of the same typology from military and prison architecture. Here we face a paradox: how could society select an architectural style for human use that has a similar typology as a style developed specifically to make people feel uncomfortable? Our explanation is that modernist architecture is a meme group that has memetic advantages (discussed in detail later), which helped it to take over. It is for this reason that modernism won out over competing architectural styles, even though it contains typologies that are non-adaptive to human use and sensibilities.

Although most traditional architecture for human use adapts to human needs and sensibilities, military architecture is the exception. A well-defined typology has been used throughout the ages to construct deliberately uncomfortable environments. These include defense installations and castles (experienced from the outside), and dungeons, prisons, crematoria, etc. (experienced from the inside). Such environments lack texture, color, and decoration, preferring damp, grey surfaces that are usually punishing for human beings. Their forms and surfaces are meant to oppress and frighten us: they communicate danger, anxiety, and evil directly through architecture. Where possible, a grandiose scale dwarfs the role of a human being in the environment. To achieve a forbidding, hostile exterior, a building must reveal a minimum of information. This makes sense when defensive fortifications protect against attack by infantry. One would never have expected this architectural typology to spread to residences, schools, hospitals, and commercial buildings, but that's precisely what happened.

3. DESIGN AS A DARWINIAN PROCESS.

Design ought to begin by understanding a building's particular uses. A designer is aided by recalling built examples that work under similar circumstances; this is the idea behind Alexandrine Patterns, which distill working solutions from widely different cases (Alexander *et. al.*, 1977). Alexander's *A Pattern Language* provides a collection of design constraints extracted from traditional architecture the world over that are meant to anchor and guide an emerging design (Salingaros, 2000). These aim to make the designed structure adaptive to human needs (by guaranteeing that all the pieces relate to each other, and come together in a way to enhance human utility), while leaving the overall form and visual aspect unspecified. It really doesn't matter what triggers one's creativity — the manner of creation — as long as many alternative designs that cover a broad enough range are generated, and the selection process is adaptive. The possibilities of a Darwinian process of design are tied to the system of alternative options within which it operates, and the richer the system is, the broader the field of design possibilities, and the better the architecture.

Each design scheme competes in the mind of the designer with other conceived possibilities, and the fittest ones (those that partially solve the problem as posed) survive to the next generation. More detailed designs generate further alternatives, which are culled by selection in the subsequent round of the selection process (Figure 10.1). The cycle starts with the creation of variants, which then get culled by using a set of selection criteria; the survivors are used to create a new generation of variants, which get culled in turn; and so on. This represents a typical Darwinian process (Calvin, 1987; 1990; 1997).

Visual inspiration can fix the entire gestalt of a project in a single initial image. Often, it is precisely such a conceived image that, through the emotional feedback it generates in the mind of the architect, sustains the design and drives it towards completion. Nevertheless, this initial inspiration must be used for momentum, and not held onto uncompromisingly. An adaptive design must be allowed to evolve, which means that architects should learn to let go of fixed ideas.

When architects turn for inspiration to fixed images from a set vocabulary defining a style, images displace the adaptive component of design by changing the selection criteria. You change the selection from satisfying human uses to how a design looks. Design then becomes a process of comparison with certain visual stereotypes, which radically affects the end product. Matching to currently popular images takes priority over all other design constraints (Figure 10.2). You copy from buildings already in existence. The selection does not aim at adapting a design to human needs.

Also, the process itself ceases to be recursive (i.e., doesn't go through several cycles) because selection occurs only on the first level. An immediate visual matching is derivative of memory and stored images rather than adaptivity. If structural, functional, and practical constraints are abandoned in the interest of maintaining images, however, such a design method acquires advantages of economy over more complex approaches that are adaptive (and which allow it to propagate more easily).

By accepting input from natural objects (e.g., Le Corbusier from a crab shell he found on the beach and later used to model the Pilgrimage Chapel *Notre-Dame-du-Haut* at Ronchamp); man-made artifacts; buildings originally intended for another use (e.g., the fascination of Walter Gropius and Le Corbusier with American grain silos); architects chose not to follow an adaptive process for turning their inspiration into a practical design. Copying an image is very easy to do, and gives a superficial sense of understanding while ignoring the complexities of both the copied structure, and the needs of what is being designed. Grain silos were the end-result of adaptive design for agricultural storage, not for habitations. Copying the "look" of a structure developed for something else, and applying it to a use for which it was never intended, is not adaptive. A crab shell is beautifully adapted to house a crab, but not for its magnified shape to house human beings wishing to worship in a church.

We don't wish to diminish the value of having a "concept" or "vision" of a building that can guide the design process through its multitude of iterations. Frequently, it is precisely such an inspiration that leads to an innovative design. We insist, however, upon a stepwise selection according to human needs, through which the initial vision must necessarily change in adapting, sometimes into an unexpected final state.

4. MEMES AND ARCHITECTURE.

Memes have a theoretical lifetime; they can "die" when they cease to be of interest to the population for whatever reason. If memes die, then in a given collection of them, one can speak of the survival of some, and the death of others. Survival in an environment, coupled to forces that promote mutation and change, leads to Darwinian selection. The concept of memes thus has explanatory value. It also has heuristic value because it forces us to examine how ideas in general persist and propagate.

While our topic is architecture, it is instructive to discuss for a moment a parallel situation in biology where the concepts of memes and Darwinian selection are routinely useful. In considering how microbes attack tissue, as for example those in the oral cavity that cause tooth decay, the scientist studies the tendency of a microbe to adhere to the tooth surface. Microbes that have the greatest stickiness are also likely to have the greatest virulence; i.e., cause the most serious disease. The logic is straightforward: the stickier the microbe, the greater the number that will adhere to the tooth at any one time. Research shows that the surface of tooth enamel has a certain chemical structure, and the virulent microbes have a corresponding chemical structure that binds to it; rather like the two mating surfaces of Velcro.

Similarly, an image has a set of attributes that makes it more or less likely to stick in memory and to be transmitted to others. In the universe of Art and Design this mechanism is readily apparent. The volatility of design themes drives the world of fashion, where the business and sales force creates a strong pressure for selection that is Darwinian at its core. New meme mutations arise with regularity, and these are tested against the environmental forces in which they appear. The life and death cycle can be swift for unsuccessful fashion styles. The same is true in architecture, where there is an undeniable and changing "fashion". Fashion is adaptive, but to artificially-created criteria, which moreover, are constantly changed by the industry. A fashion arrests the adaptive design process as it relates to genuine human needs, in which selection evolves specific solutions to individual problems that are exquisitely suited for their job and surroundings (Salingaros, 2000).

Architectural memes, through their materiality, are more nearly analogous to physical replicating entities such as viruses, than to more general memes representing only ideas that exist only in the space of information. The reason is that the former are encoded as actual structures (other than neuronal circuits). It is only their replication that occurs through memetic transmission; the artifact in this instance has a physical existence outside the human mind. An architectural style thus exists in two very different forms: first, as an ideology codified in books and taught in architecture schools, which perpetuates a group of memes in people's brains; and second, as images represented in the built environment. Each aspect reinforces the other. The built environment serves as a source of continuous re-infection by visual architectural memes. The image/building/image cycle feeds on itself, and can lead to an exponential rate of infection (see Figure 10.3).

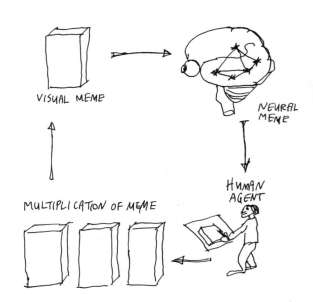

Figure (10.3)
Architectural meme proliferates
using a parasitic cycle.

While architecture is often classed along with music, poetry, and the fine arts as a vehicle for individual artistic expression, it is actually far more than that. Humanity needs to house itself, and architecture represents a world-wide building industry that is forever looking for prototypes to copy. The vast majority of buildings, be they commercial (a non-contextual typology) or vernacular (a contextual, local typology), require a typology of reproducible patterns. Clearly, the process by which architectural styles spread through copying is one that lends itself to a memetic explanation. This is seen in practice, where throughout history, a single example was often sufficient to establish a new style of architecture. Even though the early buildings defining a new style could number only a handful, their true impact lies in their easy repeatability. Conversely, a style that is difficult to reproduce because of its complexity (i.e., Art Nouveau) will die out. A style succeeds not because its original examples are either attractive or useful, but because of its simplicity, which allows it to easily infect the vernacular building tradition.

5. EXPLAINING THE UNLIKELY SUCCESS OF MODERNISM.

In 1922, Le Corbusier exhibited a series of drawings labeled "A Contemporary City" at the *Salon d'Automne* in Paris; he built the *Pavillon de l'Esprit Nouveau* for the International Exposition of Modern Decorative and Industrial Arts, held in Paris in 1925; Walter Gropius built the Bauhaus building in Dessau in 1926 as a visual example; Ludwig Mies van der Rohe organized and contributed to the mass housing projects for the Stuttgart *Weissenhoffsiedlung* in 1927, which consisted of very similar white, rectilinear, flat-roofed temporary and permanent buildings. All of those buildings and drawings provided images for young architects to copy. The reason anyone would even consider such excessively plain prototypes was the promise of inexpensive housing for all made possible by modular design, bolstered by proclamations of links to a "new" society.

The rate of transmission of a visual style among human minds depends on several factors. Considered simply as information, the success of an architectural style is governed by the speed at which the associated memes can propagate. The situation is akin to percolation or diffusion: copies of an object (a piece of information encoding the style) have to pass from one human mind to another. This resembles the mechanism by which infectious agents spread in a population. Individuals in the population have little control over the process. Propagating agents are obviously not selected by the host, since they parasitize their more complex hosts. The process is infection rather than fair competition among similarly endowed entities. An epidemic occurs when a virus has evolved an unbeatable advantage over its hosts.

Francis Heylighen has identified factors contributing to meme propagation (Heylighen, 1993; 1997). The meme could be an image, or a set of rules defining an architectural style. We will start by examining the four factors SIMPLICITY, NOVELTY, UTILITY and FORMALITY, which are relevant for explaining the initial spread of modernism. Three more of Heylighen's factors helped in the institutionalization of modernism, and they are discussed later in this Chapter. One of Heylighen's criteria is SIMPLICITY. A simple idea is easier to reproduce and has a competitive edge over ideas that are more difficult to grasp; it poses a lesser burden on our cognitive system (Heylighen, 1997). Therefore, an architectural style that is simpler to encode will propagate more successfully than one that is difficult to encode (see Figure 10.4). In an analogy with life forms, viruses reproduce much faster than more complex organisms because of a reduced structural investment. Biological and computer viruses take advantage of their host's structural complexity, using it to propagate themselves, and without which they could never replicate at all.

Figure (10.4)
Styles with lower information
content diffuse faster.

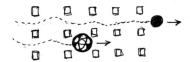

Early modernist buildings provided images of geometrical emptiness with enormous replicative power. An abstract sense of purity leads to SIMPLICITY. The modernist vocabulary of plain, featureless surfaces in a flat geometry of cubes and rectangles eliminates substructure; eliminates borders; eliminates contrast and color in design by using only plain white or gray; and finally, tries to eliminate the building material itself through its replacement by glass panes (see Chapter 1). We see some or all of these features used in a majority of buildings throughout the second half of the twentieth century. Design richness and complexity in the prevailing architectural style were eliminated in the drive to create forms with minimal information content. Other architects of the 1920s working in a traditional style originally dismissed this effort as perverse and not worthy of notice; they didn't realize that it satisfied the SIMPLICITY criterion for memetic propagation.

Another criterion is NOVELTY, where standing out and thereby attracting one's attention facilitates a meme's assimilation. New, unusual, or unexpected ideas arouse one's curiosity (Heylighen, 1997). Twentieth-century architecture used novelty of a deliberately shocking kind. The early prototypes looked strange to people used to Nineteenth-century architecture. Indeed, the modernist style is arrived at by reversing design criteria of previous traditional styles (see Chapter 1). The spread of those novel images occurred primarily through the media before any significant number of examples were actually built. Le Corbusier was remarkably successful at propagating these architectural memes through the journal *L'Esprit Nouveau*, which he controlled (Colomina, 1994). That was the age when picture magazines became a popular medium for visual information, helped by technical advances in photography, printing, and distribution. People were eager to read about new ideas, especially if they were accompanied by never-before-seen and futuristic-looking illustrations.

UTILITY plays a double role here. First, the architectural media declare (without justification) that a minimalist structure is somehow more efficient or is better adapted to the functions it is supposed to house. The opposite is true: many modernist buildings are dysfunctional because their imposed form and impractical materials hinder human activities. Criticisms include the impossibility of effective temperature control in a glass-walled structure; the tremendous energy waste in attempting to do that in a sealed building; the "sick building" syndrome; the social damage of living in skyscrapers (most severe for children and the elderly); the dangerous wind shear created on the ground by smooth-faced skyscrapers; flat roofs that invariably leak; the staining or cracking of large plain surfaces; a general problem of joints when connective interfaces are eliminated in the interests of style; psychological alienation produced by dead gray surfaces and concrete slabs, which give an unpleasant "hard" echo; etc. Still, the mere promise of UTILITY is often enough for propagating spurious ideas (Heylighen, 1997).

Second, the modernist style represents a genuine advantage for the construction industry that can build cheap, minimalist box-like structures without having to worry much about accommodating human physiological and psychological needs. A visually simplistic architectural style thus offers a commercial benefit via UTILITY that counts as a major factor in its propagation (Benedikt, 1999). Modernist memes found a ready environment after the Second World War, when buildings had to be produced in large numbers and at low cost. Never before in history had such building efforts taken place. This was also in the period that the industrialization process was at full speed, penetrating more and more economic sectors of society. The construction industry eagerly embraced the UTILITY offered by modernist memes. Philip Johnson (the American architect who promoted modernism) frankly admitted that: "The "International Style" did sweep the world because it came along at the same time developers wanted to make cheap buildings, and this was cheaper than other architectures" (Kunstler, 1993).

Yet another factor is FORMALITY: the more formally an idea is expressed, the more likely it survives in transmission (Heylighen, 1993; 1997). Adaptation requires selection on the basis of local climate, materials, culture, and relationship to adjoining buildings and specific human needs. Since its inception, however, modernism has been "universal" because it is based on a small set of simple images. Different individuals in different contexts can interpret modernist rules in the same way. A modernist building can be put up anywhere in a city, anywhere in the world, because the style is independent of locality or particular circumstances. The intention of modernist design is to be context-independent. Materials of choice are preformed panels, glass, steel, and reinforced concrete; these are industrial materials that are detached from any region. Modernism imposed an abstract visual language to come up with "one single building for all nations and climates" (Blake, 1974).

Non-adaptivity to human needs helps in memetic propagation. The philosophical origins of modernism in Germany of the 1920s reveal a parallel with totalitarianism (Watkin, 2001). The German art historian Wilhelm Pinder (a supporter of Hitler) and his student Nikolaus Pevsner (an architectural historian who was one of the strongest promoters of modernism as a guide for social and political ideals) argued that great architecture is the product of the *Volk*, during periods when ideology triumphs. Adolf Hitler, Josef Goebbels, Walter Gropius, and Ludwig Mies van der Rohe all shared the conviction that architecture was an expression of the central spirit of an epoch, and thus justified idealism, absolutism, and arrogance (Watkin, 2001). In this view of the world, the individual is insignificant, and the needs of the human user are thus of little consequence (Watkin, 2001). Philip Johnson complained of the futility of trying to discuss the aesthetics of modernism with Walter Gropius: "Talking to Gropius was a dead end because he would still mouth the Giedionesque platitudes of social discipline and revolution" (Colomina, 1994).

6. COMPETITION AMONG EARLY TWENTIETH-CENTURY ARCHITECTURAL STYLES.

We are now ready to use this model to explain historical events. The successful spread of modernist design is interpreted in terms of the replication of memes in a Darwinian process.

The unbiased human mind applies selection criteria that seek the most positive emotional feedback from a built structure. This is something we have evolved to do: we instinctively avoid pain and discomfort, and seek out physical environments that are emotionally nourishing. If a design (and, by extension, the building when finished) is emotionally satisfying to the architect, then one can expect the user to share that experience. The same does not follow, however, when purely intellectual selection criteria replace those based on a local vernacular context, which coincidentally elicits the most positive emotions. What one person believes in ideologically is not necessarily shared by others. Modernism was very successful at convincing people to forgo sensual pleasure from built forms, as minimal surfaces and spaces offer less visual stimulation than human neurophysiology is built to handle (see Chapters 4 and 7). Memes help us to understand why architectural styles that give emotional satisfaction were replaced by those that don't.

Once built, structures survive or not according to Darwinian selection. Here we are no longer talking about Darwinian processes in the mind of the architect, but survival in the outside world. Occasionally buildings get destroyed by natural or human acts; most often conscious decisions are made on whether to repair the inevitable wear in an existing building, or to build a new building altogether in its place. In biology, the survival rule for a species is to procreate before death. Culling of organisms is determined by survival in the environment. In architecture, survival of a particular style depends on whether the buildings representing that style are preserved, or are replaced by those of another style. Architectural survival therefore depends upon decisions that are heavily influenced by stylistic concerns, independently of the buildings' adaptivity to human physical and psychological needs.

Different styles competed with each other at the beginning of the twentieth century. Any architectural style that contained traditional elements was doomed to extinction because people now demanded (or were manipulated to demand) NOVELTY. Neoclassical, Beaux-Arts, Victorian, and Edwardian styles were thus abandoned. Styles that had comparable NOVELTY were further selected on the basis of SIMPLICITY, UTILITY, and FORMALITY.

Art Nouveau is very high in informational content. The convolutions, curves, and complex colors upon which the style depends do not propagate rapidly, and that's exactly what happened. Also, its NOVELTY was short-lived. Even though Art Nouveau buildings were certainly novel at the time, they are reminiscent of organic plant forms. Very soon, the fickle critics led the public to crave styles with even more visual NOVELTY, which could only be satisfied by the opposite of organic forms. Despite an initial flourish, Art Nouveau didn't last for more than about a decade. Its markedly plainer successor, Expressionism, was equally short-lived because of its curvature, which encodes mathematical complexity. Art Deco abandoned the curves of Art Nouveau and Expressionism, adopting a more rectangular geometry, and was somewhat longer-lived. One could surmise that, by lowering its information content, Art Deco acquired greater staying power. Finally, minimalist modernism got rid of the visual richness of Art Deco, reducing its information to an absolute minimum; it won out over its competitors by spreading around the world and surviving until today. These events in architectural history support a memetic theory of architectural styles, with selection on the basis of SIMPLICITY.

Looking at both UTILITY and FORMALITY leads to the same conclusion. Unless there is a strong societal demand for information-rich buildings and environments, the construction industry will select those that are visually plain (since they are often cheaper to build, though not to maintain). This is selection on the basis of UTILITY for the construction industry, but not for the user. Modernism is a highly formal design method, thus possessing the FORMALITY criterion for propagation. A set of context-independent rules was never established for either Art Nouveau or Art Deco, thus both those styles lack FORMALITY. We have no formal set of symbols that can generate an Art Nouveau building. The style depended upon the individual creative genius of say, Louis Sullivan or Victor Horta, who drew their inspiration freshly from each new specific architectural context.

It is worthwhile noting that a highly successful style in architectural history, the Classical Style, also depends on rather precise formal rules that can be applied in any situation regardless of context. Nevertheless, its much higher complexity compared to modernism allows for design that is adaptive to human needs and emotions, as witnessed by the countless locally-adapted Neoclassical buildings built around the world in the last two centuries. Those buildings today are rightly judged to be far more useful and sustainable than the "International Style" buildings that replaced them as the preferred institutional style.

A large number of Art Nouveau and Art Deco buildings were built in the early decades of the twentieth century, before the modernist selection criteria took hold. Many of those buildings did not survive, precisely because the selection criteria used in the 1960s for preserving older buildings were the same as those for designing new buildings. The stereotyped visual template of a glass or concrete box determined which buildings to save from demolition, and those buildings that did not match these images were destroyed. In effect, structures were categorized according to specific images, thus providing a mandate to eliminate those judged to be "misfits". Such decisions were supposedly founded on rational laws as opposed to base emotions, which is true up to a point. Nevertheless, the incredible persistence of modernist architectural memes in the twentieth century is fundamentally emotion-based. This emotional dimension of memetic transmission will be discussed next.

7. ENCAPSULATION OF IMAGES IN THE MIND.

Entities with a finite lifetime will survive in the sense of propagating their information only if they are favored by selection forces. An encapsulating shell that surrounds a meme by an attractive verbal explanation endows it with a meaning structure that helps in transmission. Once inside a mind, a meme will lose its boundaries as it is sacrificed to a larger meaning structure that is expressed as a physical grouping of neurons. The mind shows itself to be a multiply-connected network, where ideas, opinions, factual knowledge, and prejudices are all interlinked into what may be called one's "consciousness" (see Chapter 7; Edelman & Tononi, 2000). In this way, memes influence an individual's thoughts and actions. This is the idea behind advertising: embedding a commercial product into a person's consciousness will guarantee the use or purchase of that particular product as the result of a subconscious decision (Brodie, 1996).

Architecture and advertising act in much the same way. After they are taught in Architecture school, the memes of an approved style become a permanent part of one's thinking patterns. They are encapsulated into meaning structures such as metaphors. The group of neuronal circuits recording images, their encapsulation, and their interconnections defines some domain of one's consciousness. Those regions of the brain provide bases for meaning structures, which are used to interpret the world throughout one's life (see Chapter 7; Edelman & Tononi, 2000). We are thus programmed to automatically replicate memes whether or not they are good or useful; that's because they are part of a person's inner belief system (Brodie, 1996). This also explains why visual icons can rarely be dislodged by scientific arguments. A simple but irrational belief can displace an accurate but more difficult description of the world.

TOXIC MEME

ATTRACTIVE
SLOGAN

Figure (10.5)
A toxic meme appears attractive
from its shell.

ENCAPSULATED
TOXIC
MEME

We propose here another factor affecting meme propagation: ENCAPSULATION. A meme boosts its virulence by linking itself to other attractive memes, which then shield the original meme (see Figure 10.5). (This is related to but distinct from Heylighen's criterion of COHERENCE, wherein the assimilation of new ideas depends on their being consistent with existing knowledge (Heylighen, 1993; 1997)). The advertising industry is founded upon techniques of encapsulation: either physical packaging, or the packaging of products within ideas. A commercial product sells just as much because of an attractive package as for any other factor. An effective marketing strategy encapsulates a product with emotional appeals to self-esteem, sex, status, power, individuality, etc. It is not a coincidence that modern advertising techniques developed alongside modernist design, and early modernist architects showed a keen interest in psychological manipulation as it was then being incorporated into the advertising industry (Colomina, 1994). Le Corbusier actually made a living from mass media and commercial promotion independently of his work as an architect (Colomina, 1994).

This concept applied to architecture reveals an unexpected yet major reason for why architectural design evolves the way it does. A change in encapsulation comes from societal discontinuities, which affect architecture just as much as practical matters such as the introduction of new materials and novel methods of construction. For example, immensely powerful social forces unleashed between the two world wars led people to adopt modernist design memes as a reaction to class oppression. They identified decorated buildings as visual symbols of what was wrong with the past. With all the old values discredited by the horrors of the First World War, people eagerly embraced new ideas and hopes, thus linking desirable social aims to encapsulated memes. They willingly sacrificed immediate and direct pleasure from their surroundings for the promise of a better future. Human beings will adopt almost anything that promises them a better life. The *1918 Manifesto* of the Dutch group of modernist architects (that included Gerrit Rietveld and Christian Küpper alias Theo van Doesburg) known as "De Stijl" states:

"The war is destroying the old world with its content ... The new art has brought to light that which is contained in the new consciousness of the age ... Tradition, dogmas and the predominance of the individual stand in the way of this realization. Therefore the founders of the new culture call upon all who believe in reform of art and culture to destroy those obstacles to development ... The artists of today, all over the world, impelled by one and the same consciousness, have taken part on the spiritual plane in the world war against the domination of individualism, of arbitrariness." (Conrads, 1964).

Bruno Taut, a key member of the German group of modernist architects, had this to say in his *Frühlicht* of 1920:

"Oh, our concepts: space, home, style! Ugh, how these concepts stink! Destroy them, put an end to them! Let nothing remain! Chase away their schools, let the professorial wigs fly, we'll play catch with them. Blast, blast! Let the dusty, matted, gummed-up world of concepts, ideologies and systems feel our cold north wind! Death to the concept-lice! Death to everything stuffy! Death to everything called title, dignity, authority! Down with everything serious!" (Conrads, 1964).

These extracts give an indication of the rage against traditional styles in art and architecture prevalent at that time. They reveal the profound societal discontinuity that was to provide a breeding-ground for any ideology, mixing political as well as artistic memes, which promised radically new solutions to the problems facing humankind.

A biological virus remains infectious against the continuous development of antibodies by host organisms. The way it does this is to change its encapsulation so that it is no longer recognized by the host. This is said to be one of the mechanisms for the resistance of the HIV virus to therapy (Levine, 1992). In exactly this manner, modernism successfully changes the shell in which its memes are packaged (Figure 10.5). Modernist ideologues accomplish this switch with great dexterity: almost a sleight-of-hand. As soon as one of the encapsulations is identified, and it is realized that it does not lead to the promised benefit, the shell is changed to a new one. The central core — containing images that lower information and organized complexity in the built environment — remains the same. We list eight encapsulations for modernist memes, where each encapsulation is itself a meme:

Table 10.1. Encapsulations for Modernist Memes.

(1) "progress and economic prosperity from technology";

(2) "freedom from class oppression through new design";

(3) "social equality and housing opportunities for all";

(4) "moral superiority from using honest materials";

(5) "improved health and hygiene through smooth surfaces";

(6) "the mathematical principles of pure form";

(7) "cost benefits resulting from modular production";

(8) "design that expresses the spirit of the age".

Today, the modernist style predominates in architectural practice, and is taught in our schools to the exclusion of most other styles. The above encapsulations are therefore presented and discussed at length as part of the standard architectural literature: not as misleading packaging, but as "truth". It is not useful to repeat that propagandistic material here. What is of immediate interest is that the eight slogans listed above are very successful at encapsulating modernist memes, thus helping their propagation. These are very powerful promises. Our point is that, in the absence of either a scientific or sensory basis, modernist architecture justifies itself solely by its memetic encapsulations. For detailed criticisms of the claims of modernism and the weakness of the usual arguments trying to justify those encapsulations, see (Alexander *et. al.*, 1977; Blake, 1974; Salingaros, 2000).

It is worthwhile remembering that meme (5) in the above list was created soon after the devastating 1918 influenza pandemic, and thus touched upon questions of life and death. While microbes can stay on any type of building surface, a smooth, non-porous surface appears easier to clean. Shiny polished metal, ceramic, and glass surfaces looked more hygienic, and this "look" caught on. We adopted the hospital aesthetic for our kitchens and homes.

An architectural meme that has become part of our meaning structure (and is thus fixed in our world-view) is protected by its ENCAPSULATION. Attempting to revise the meme pulls at the entire meme complex, which is attached to the rest of the mind's associational network of concepts. Writings by modernism's proponents link the visual images representing the style to other, beneficial memes, so that questioning modernist design appears to question the technological, scientific, economic, and social progress of the twentieth century. This often triggers a strong emotional reaction that is reminiscent of religious intensity (Watkin, 2001). We suspect that certain memes such as these become fixed into our belief systems in places traditionally occupied by a religious credo.

When confronted by criticism based on scientific reasoning, many architects base their arguments on what the modernist "masters" said (i.e., "less is more"), as if that were some sort of revealed truth. This is indicative of religious fundamentalism. An automatic reliance on any dogma as part of one's basic belief system is consistent with a memetic infection; i.e., the justification for a belief is the infecting meme itself. It is pointless to argue against ideas and values that people accept unquestioningly, or have adopted in the struggle to better their lives (Brodie, 1996). The reason is that people are physically, viscerally, and emotionally attached to their beliefs, regardless of how they acquired them, and irrespective of their absolute validity. No-one wants to have to reach back and re-wire their brain into new habits of thinking, because such a process can be traumatic. It is far easier to hold onto one's ideas and values, and when challenged, the natural reaction is to defend them emotionally without thinking about their origin (Brodie, 1996).

8. THE TWO FACES OF ENCAPSULATION.

ENCAPSULATION has also been used to discredit traditional architectural styles and throw them out of favor. The meme here is a negative association, which spreads independently of whether the accusation is true or not. This happened to the Beaux-Arts style, which was tainted by association with pre-World-War-I society in supposedly "decadent" western Europe. The same is true of the Victorian and Edwardian styles in England (Watkin, 2001). The Classical style, after surviving for more than two millennia, was discredited because Neoclassical buildings were erected during the Second World War in Germany, Italy, and in Stalinist Russia (Watkin, 2001). The absurdity of this argument does not however undo the remarkably effective use of ENCAPSULATION to further an agenda. As a result, there exists a violent resentment today against traditional architectural styles; although no-one who feels that way can explain logically why that should be so (see Figure 10.6).

ADAPTIVE
DESIGN
METHOD

Figure (10.6)
An adaptive method of design
is made to appear toxic.

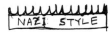

UNATTRACTIVE
SHELL

ENCAPSULATION
BURIES
METHOD

It is very ironic that the superficially Classical style adopted by Hitler and Stalin for their grandiose public buildings is itself an ENCAPSULATION of something sinister. The underlying architectural style is certainly not Classical, but is instead a pure expression of megalomania and the power of a totalitarian state. In order to disguise this obvious but disquieting message, buildings that represented each regime's public face were given a superficial veneer of Classical elements. This was done so that people would naturally associate that regime with the positive qualities of "stability", "wisdom", and "balance" that are the traditional message of Classical architecture. Unfortunately, even eminent architectural historians confuse this misappropriation of Classical architecture.

Destructive ENCAPSULATION is well known in the political arena, where it is used for character assassination. In the world of art, the Iconoclastic movement declared figural representation to be unholy, despite the complete absence of any such restriction within Christianity. This happened around the 9th century, and led to the wanton destruction of religious paintings and mosaics before it was reversed. Early Christian icons dating to before the 11th century are as a consequence extremely hard to find. A brief resurgence of Iconoclasm occurred in Italy in the 15th century, instigated by the deranged monk Savonarola, which prompted the burning of several of Botticelli's paintings. History is unfortunately replete with examples in which individuals, groups of people, races, ideas, or artifacts are eliminated, after being branded by association within a destructive ENCAPSULATION.

One of the twentieth century's most successful memes is: "Ornament is a crime", coined by the Austrian architect Adolf Loos in 1908 (Conrads, 1964). This phrase is impossible to forget; it goes straight to one's memory whether one agrees with its message or not, thus ranking it with the most successful advertising jingles ever (see Figure 10.7). Because of the NOVELTY criterion, the more outrageous social memes are often the most virulent (Brodie, '96). This particular ENCAPSULATION identifies anyone who dares to enjoy architectural ornament with persons who by creating ornament supposedly become criminals, and "inflict serious injury on people's health, on the national budget and hence on cultural evolution" (Conrads, '64). Infection by this meme continues to this day because Loos is presented as a pioneer of the modernist movement, instead of as an eccentric who used frosted window panes in his buildings so that people could not look out (all the photos featured in histories of European architecture have been altered to hide this) (Colomina, '94: pages 234 & 272).

Figure (10.7)
Architects believe propaganda
like they do advertising labels.

Something occurring outside established architecture may eventually prove far more damaging in the long term. For millennia, people have built modest structures such as pieces of wall, a raised flower bed, a veranda, or an addition to someone's house, etc. This vast "architecture without architects" is simple, functional, often ornamented, and made out of available materials. Some of humankind's most endearing artifacts are produced within this tradition. They possess an emotional appeal and mathematical coherence that is lost when such structures are replaced by rigid industrial objects trying to emulate the purity of a crystalline geometry. People infected with modernist memes are eager to erase their heritage, since it reminds them of the past. Because of inner fear and feelings of inadequacy, people are terrified to risk losing what they believe to be progress. In many societies, it has actually become illegal to build anything that doesn't fit within modernist terms. Something wonderful and complex — a tradition of building modest things to please one's emotions — is becoming extinct as a result of this memetic infection.

9. A COMPLEXITY THRESHOLD.

The rapid spread of modernism is reminiscent of the spread of biological and computer viruses. What links them is their reduced complexity overhead (i.e., the minimum structural complexity they have to maintain during transfer from site to site). By sacrificing the structural complexity needed for metabolism, viruses gain an unbeatable advantage over more complex, metabolizing life-forms that they infect (Levine, 1992). There is a parallel here with minimalist design as it competed with more complex architectural styles such as Art Nouveau and the Classical style.

Any style that attempts to adapt itself to human physical and emotional satisfaction, as well as to local materials and climate, will necessarily exceed a certain complexity threshold. In neglecting those needs — indeed, in making it its explicit aim to ignore them — minimalist architecture crossed the complexity threshold going towards total abstraction. This brought it an unprecedented memetic advantage, but removed an essential quality that we associate with "life".

Although "life" has not been rigorously defined as a concept, biological life consists of two components: metabolism, and replication (Dyson, '99; Maynard-Smith & Szathmáry, '99). The apparatus for metabolism represents much of what we observe as biological structure in every organism. The machinery for replication, on the other hand, occupies only a limited portion of an organism's structure. A virus replicates its encoded genetic information without being able to metabolize. It is the simplest possible life form, and by this definition, it is not "alive" in the sense that a more complex metabolizing organism is. In an analogous manner, minimalist structures, though immensely successful at replicating in the built environment, do not possess the same degree of "life" (measured in terms of organized complexity) as do more traditional architectural styles that adapt to human use and emotional needs.

There is a debate going on in evolutionary biology as to whether viruses developed before, concurrently, or after metabolizing life forms (Levine, 1992; Maynard-Smith & Szathmáry, 1999). The third option argues that parasitic replicators have to have a population of more complex organisms to parasitize before evolving. A probable scenario for this third option is that some incomplete pieces from the replicating apparatus of an organism found it possible to lead an independent existence outside the metabolizing structure. Whatever the actual case, this third option is intriguing for its parallel to architecture. With the above analogy, minimalism could not have taken root before society became complex enough to support it. The intuitive perception of minimalist buildings as "alien" forms invading our cities (and minds) makes more sense in a society that is so morally and ideologically confused as to be in no position to stop the invasion.

Evolution relies strongly on the organization of complexity. The metabolizing structure of all life forms exceeds a certain complexity threshold. Natural selection pushes organisms to become more complex. It is true that some species reach a plateau when their structural complexity provides a reasonably good chance for survival and reproduction. Those that do this have no need to change as long as their environment or ecological niche remain stable. Nevertheless, the direction of evolution as defined by the progress from elementary life forms to humans is one of increasing complexity. A sudden decrease in organized complexity thus appears as a catastrophic reversal akin to species extinction. Just as when viruses kill off a population of mammals, or when computer viruses erase a host of hard disks full of organized data, so the organized complexity of the built environment is erased when Nineteenth-century buildings are replaced by ones in a minimalist style.

The low information content of minimalist design distinguishes it from other, more traditional styles of architecture, as well as from more recent stylistic trends. We want to clarify a misunderstanding in discussions of complexity in architecture. Biological forms are characterized by their extraordinarily high degree of organized complexity. A high degree of organized complexity (visual as well as structural) is also found in the great buildings of the past such as mediaeval cathedrals and mosques, and in vernacular architectures. This property is the opposite of the high degree of disorganized complexity that is seen in detailed, busy, but disorganized buildings such as postmodernist and deconstructivist structures. Disorganized complexity is also encoded in the visual cacophony of signs and materials in the suburban commercial strip, and the jumble of neon signs of the Las Vegas casinos. Our age appears incapable of organizing spontaneously-generated complexity.

10. HOW ARCHITECTURE PERPETUATES MODERNIST MEMES.

By a remarkable confluence of historical events and circumstances, selection on the basis of empty images has succeeded in displacing a variety of architectural traditions based on adaptation to human needs. Those who promote minimalist structures agree that the style's lower organizational complexity is meant to deliberately contrast with the higher complexity of traditional architecture. Is it possible now to re-establish traditional adaptive design methods in practice? Additional insight comes from seeing how three more criteria proposed by Heylighen: AUTHORITY, PUBLICITY, and CONFORMITY, contribute to the propagation and eventual institutionalization of memes (Heylighen, 1993; 1997).

AUTHORITY from famous architects and their sponsors legitimizes design memes in people's minds. The backing from a recognized expert or institution boosts the acceptance of a particular idea (Heylighen, 1997). After the Second World War, the United Nations built its headquarters in New York City as a validation of the modernist style. Several progressive governments reinforced this example by building new capital cities in a modernist style: India (Chandigarh); Brazil (Brasilia); Bangladesh (Dacca); and Australia (the post-war buildings in Canberra). The U.S. Government adopted modernism for its international trade missions and exposition spaces, projecting images of prosperity from a superpower, while corporations competed to outdo each other in occupying modernist headquarters. In our times, the administrative buildings of the European Community in Brussels embody modernist memes. People conveniently forgot that modernism was the official architecture of Fascist Italy (see Figure 10.8).

Figure (10.8)
Fascist architecture is modernist
and not Classical.

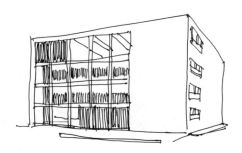

The acceptance of architectural memes by governments and organizations elevated their architects to a position of AUTHORITY. The 1932 exhibition on Modernist Architecture at the Museum of Modern Art in New York was a highly influential event, using the museum's AUTHORITY to promote the so-called "International Style". After New York, the exhibition traveled for seven years around the United States (Colomina, 1994). Two former directors of the German Bauhaus school were subsequently made heads of Architecture schools in the United States when they emigrated from Europe. Those architects then used their positions to promote memes through their teaching, and the media. Their positions of AUTHORITY also guaranteed them more commissions to erect buildings, thus setting up a self-sustaining cycle. The public rarely feels confident enough to challenge the AUTHORITY of individuals presented as the world's experts on the topic, even if what they say runs contrary to people's basic feelings and intuitions.

Professors at prestigious universities such as Sigfried Giedion and Nikolaus Pevsner — the first enormously influential as the Secretary of *CIAM* (*Congrès Internationaux d'Architecture Moderne*) — wrote scholarly "histories" of architecture that twisted facts to promote an ideology (Watkin, 2001). Modernism was falsely presented as the inevitable end result of the continuous evolution of historical architectures, instead of the radical negation of traditional styles that it represents. By claiming that modernism is not a style, and thus not subject to stylistic competition, they extended its AUTHORITY above and beyond architecture. Styles that modernism competed with and displaced (e.g., Neoclassical; Edwardian; Art Deco) were either dismissed as irrelevant, morally reprehensible, and were ignored altogether, or they were misleadingly appropriated as ancestors of modernism (e.g., Art Nouveau; Expressionism). An invented architectural history thus endowed modernism with false historical and moral AUTHORITY. Those treatises, along with others bearing the same misleading message, became the standard textbooks for more than one generation of architecture students.

An essential feature of evolution is that complex organic systems build upon existing complexity: each new development adds something to what already works. New layers of functionality develop on top of older structures, without altering them radically. This summarizes both the advantages and disadvantages of cumulative design by selection (Dennett, 1995). We can trace evolutionary ancestry by looking for features in common with less developed organisms on the evolutionary scale; some of which survive in an inactive or useless form (like our appendix). For an architectural example, the Classical style retains features of its ancestral wooden construction, although they make no structural sense when building with stone. Nineteenth-century styles retained much of what had developed up until then. As modernist architecture was intent on replacing all past and existing styles, however, it cannot be termed an evolution of those styles.

PUBLICITY is the effort to spread an idea; often an ideology includes explicit injunctions that believers should spread the word (Heylighen, 1997). In architecture that is taken care of by a wealth of picture-filled books and architectural magazines, films, television documentaries, and the press; all of which promote memes. These offer a platform from which often confused ideas are endowed with visual legitimacy. The 1932 "International Style" exhibition was conceived as a publicity campaign for modernist architecture, and its catalogue as a propaganda tool for disseminating the new style in the United States (Colomina, 1994). Architectural memes spread though advertising techniques coupled with proselytizing in architecture schools. Since its inception in 1979, the Pritzker architecture prize has been awarded to architects who best embody the latest trend in design; such prestige and accompanying PUBLICITY in turn helps to perpetuate those design trends. The same is true for numerous other architectural prizes of lesser prestige. Those prize-winning built examples are publicized by the media, and influence the design of new buildings.

CONFORMITY guarantees that newcomers into a group will be infected by an accepted meme, even though it might reject sound knowledge and contradict established beliefs. CONFORMITY pressure establishes and maintains an invariant belief over a group of people (Heylighen, 1993; 1997). The constant exposure to a particular architectural style creates a familiarity, which in turn promotes CONFORMITY to what many others have already accepted. Peer pressure from the architectural community maintains approved architectural images, with the threat of ostracism for apostates (Watkin, 2001). Many cases are known of ridicule heaped upon architects who stray from the currently trendy design style. In their efforts to meet their audience's expectations, architectural magazines tend to publish only articles featuring buildings that maintain the party line. Architecture students are naturally under pressure to conform to what is celebrated by these magazines.

The teaching of architecture changed in response to concepts established by the Bauhaus, such as the architectural design studio, creating an environment where design is almost entirely image-driven. It is very difficult even to discuss adaptive design components such as Alexandrine patterns (Alexander *et. al.*, 1977), because those concepts are not images. In avoiding patterns, academic architects still invoke the tired "modern versus traditional" argument based entirely on superficial visual appearance, which ultimately thwarts adaptive endeavors.

11. MODERNISM HAS BECOME AN INSTITUTION.

Thus far, this Chapter described how modernist memes spread in society, to the point where they displaced most other architectural styles. We now wish to discuss how to remove those memes from our society. A group of memes achieves its ultimate success by becoming institutionalized. The rigidity of institutionalized memes then makes it extremely tough to get rid of them. This Section explains the great difficulty in displacing ingrained memes from today's architectural establishment. We don't believe that significant changes can come from within mainstream architecture, because it is itself a product of (and is totally dependent upon) modernist memes. It is more likely that users rather than architects will begin to consider alternatives once they understand the effects of memetic infection.

An institutional system will take actions to protect its political base, which results in a conceptual bias. Decisions are made as to which information is relevant to it (i.e., relevant to architecture strictly as defined by those in power), whereas other conceptual models will be ignored. The political agenda favors specific issues, deciding as well how dialogue with competing issues is to be addressed, if at all (de Jong, 1999). The same rules apply to any other meme group that has become institutionalized, and are not specific to either architecture, or design (de Jong, 1999). The institution defines both the importance and the interpretation of concepts, so that it controls whether a particular idea will be discussed, and whether any action will be taken. Not surprisingly, arguments and actions that do not fit into the conceptual framework of those in power are not pursued.

This analysis is confirmed by how architecture has progressed since the Second World War. The institutionalization of modernism in our society acts as a filter for innovation within architectural design. Despite well-publicized reactions against empty forms, most of the original visual memes have been retained in post-modernist design. The overall forms may vary, yet the basic "look" is still familiar. Architecture today remains at its core non-adaptive to human needs; that basic aspect certainly has not changed. Neither has the proscription against detailed ornamentation and complex color harmonies that the early modernists imposed. Materials tend, on the whole, to be those preferred by the early modernists because of their universality, and even when traditional materials are used, they are used strictly in ways so as to mimic the "pure" surfaces of industrial materials.

Because every institution acts as a memetic filter, innovative concepts may be able to evolve only outside it. In the case of architecture, the evolution of design that is adaptive to human needs is taking place mostly outside the establishment: either spurred by architects who have been evicted from the establishment, or by other professionals who have discovered that the official system is too rigid to deal with societal problems. The establishment is reacting in a predictable manner by ignoring innovations that could threaten its power base. Instead, it underlines its absolute control by allowing limited debate within certain boundaries. The debate is very tightly controlled, however, and is never allowed to endanger the institutional basis. Topics from the present book appear in mainstream architectural publications, but in a primitive guise, and always accompanied by twisted arguments whose aim is to support the establishment fashions rather than to understand architecture. Thus, the declaration of the postmodernists that "modernism is dead" should be interpreted for what it really is: a diversion meant to protect the architectural establishment from any serious attack.

Proponents of modernist design sought to eliminate competing styles by employing two tactics: aggressive attack, and ridicule. The switch from one to the other marks the point when modernism became an institution. In the years up to the 1950s while modernism was peripheral and was trying to gain the upper hand, destructive encapsulation was used with great effect (see Section 8, above). By the time this tactic succeeded, the establishment (now modernist) found it more appropriate to express its strength by ridiculing its competition. The word "pastiche" was henceforth used to make fun of any architects who tried to incorporate traditional elements into their designs. "Pastiche" is the artistic equivalent of "plagiarism" in the sciences, and implies that such an architect is not being original. In fact, those who follow the establishment typology are doing exactly that, since the majority of buildings still copy the same industrial typologies from the 1920s.

Developments in architectural design touch upon the commercial benefits of a particular style in comparison to other factors. Modernist designs, because of their simplicity and context independence, are designs that can be produced industrially for a reasonable price. The institutionalization of modernist architecture has taken place in the entire construction industry, driven by the rise of industrial construction. This institution is separate, and more powerful than architectural education, institutes, and magazines. Some authors have identified this as the dominant factor for modernism's success (Benedikt, 1999). In accepting a Faustian bargain, architects provided ever plainer designs that could be built even more cheaply, until by now the level of design complexity is so low that it is extremely difficult to raise. Any change that threatens to increase construction costs while lowering productivity in the construction industry is going to be fought by a massive establishment.

12. CONCLUSION.

The idea of design as a Darwinian process that relies on selection has interesting ramifications for architecture as a whole. This explanation of how design emerges in the human mind reveals a split between design methods based on stereotyped images, and those based on adaptation to human needs. Both architectural and popular literatures come back to the theme that a majority of twentieth-century buildings provide neither the physical nor the emotional comfort for their users that older buildings — which are built in a freer, more adaptive style — almost invariably do. Nevertheless, despite such strong criticisms, certain visual styles continue to dominate construction and design practice today. An answer to why this is so comes from visual memes: self-sustaining conceptual entities that become fixed in human memory. Originally introduced in discussions of evolutionary biology, memes serve well to explain why architectural fashions survive and propagate. In particular, memes explain why the modernist style has achieved such remarkable success in displacing traditional as well as other innovative architectural styles.

Chapter Eleven

TWO LANGUAGES FOR ARCHITECTURE

1. PATTERN LANGUAGE AND FORM LANGUAGE.

Architectural design is a highly complex undertaking. Heretofore, the processes at its base have not been made clear. There have been many attempts to clarify the design process, yet we still don't have a design method that can be used by students and novices to achieve practical, meaningful, nourishing, human results. In the absence of a design method and accompanying criteria for judging a design, things have become very subjective, and therefore what is built today appears to be influenced largely by fashion, forced tastes, and an individual's desire to garner attention through novel and sometimes shocking expressions.

There exist invariant laws behind design in general, and architecture in particular. This Chapter puts forward a theory of architecture and urbanism based on two distinct languages: the *pattern language*, and the *form language*. The *pattern language* codifies the interaction of human beings with their environment, and determines how and where we naturally prefer to walk, sit, sleep, enter and move through a building, enjoy a room or open space, and feel at ease or not in our garden. The *pattern language* is a set of inherited tried-and-true solutions that optimize how the built environment promotes human life and sense of well-being. It combines geometry and social behavior patterns into a set of useful relationships, summarizing how built form can accommodate human activities. The *form language*, on the other hand, is strictly geometrical. It is defined by the elements of form as constituted by the floors, the walls, the ceiling, the partitions, and all the architectural components or articulations, which together represent a particular form and style of building.

The importance of a *pattern language* for architecture was originally proposed by Christopher Alexander and his associates (Alexander *et. al.*, 1977). A fairly general *pattern language* was discovered and presented by Alexander, who emphasized that, while many if not most of the patterns in his *pattern language* are indeed universal, there actually exist an infinite number of individual patterns that can be included in a *pattern language*. Each *pattern language* reflects different modes of life, customs, and behavior, and is appropriate to specific climates, geographies, cultures, and traditions. It is up to the designer/architect to extract specific non-universal patterns as needed, by examining the ways of life and tradition in a particular setting, and then to apply them to that situation (Salingaros, 2000).

Living architecture is highly dependent on patterns, which shape buildings and spaces accordingly. A pattern is a set of relationships, which can be realized using different materials and geometries. Architects, however, confuse patterns with their representation, i.e., what an arrangement looks like. The pattern is fundamentally human, whereas its physical realization (representation) can occur in myriads of slightly different ways. All those representations, some more and others less successful, are what we experience first-hand as the pattern. Even as structures get rebuilt so they may no longer represent a pattern, the pattern itself persists in human memory because it is independent of any particular representation. Patterns are not material, though we experience them with our senses. It is far more difficult to understand them intellectually, and almost impossible to grasp patterns from within a world-view that focuses exclusively on materials.

One would think that designing an appropriate work environment would take precedence in our civilization, which is driven by commerce and industry. Yet that is hardly the case. A *pattern language* for work environments can be put together by examining the components of successful emotionally-comfortable work environments from different cultures and periods around the world (Alexander, 2004; Alexander *et. al.*, 1977; Alexander *et. al.*, 1987). A software developer today has many requirements in common with one of our distant ancestors looking for a comfortable place to sit and carve a bone or paint a piece of pottery. Being able to work in an emotionally-supportive environment boosts morale and productivity, and cuts down on workplace errors. For several decades, however, architects and interior designers have insisted on applying formal design rules to office environments. Such rules tend to give a standard compromise that satisfies almost none of the fundamental requirements for a good working environment. Their occupants usually characterize them as ranging from sterile to oppressive. Here is a fundamental disconnect between what architects imagine office space should look like, and the characteristics of the kind of space that users actually require to be productive in. This has not gone unnoticed by companies, which have undertaken their own *pattern language* development for office and work environments. A good *pattern language* can generate a personalized work environment at no extra cost. The trillion-dollar information and communications industry has embraced *pattern languages*, even as all of this extensive work remains outside today's architectural paradigm.

Alexander also uses the term *form language* to describe the geometrical basis of an architectural expression (Alexander, 2004). It has been used in this context by other architects, for example Robert Stern (1988). A *form language* is a repertoire of forms and surface elements that can be combined to build any building, and so it represents more than just a superficial style. The *form language* depends on an inherited vocabulary of all the components used in the assembly of a building; rules for how they can be combined; and how different levels of scale can arise from the smaller components. It is a particular and practical conception of tectonic and surface geometry. One extremely successful *form language*, the "Classical Language", relies on a wide range of variations of the Classical style of building based on Greco-Roman ancestry (Stern, 1988).

After centuries of Classical buildings, even with varied and successful adaptations to local climates, conditions, and uses, the Classical *form language* remains intact. Every traditional architecture has its own *form language*. It has evolved from many different influences of lifestyle, traditions, and practical concerns acting together to define the geometry that structures take as the most natural visual expressions of a particular culture. A *form language* is a set of evolved geometries on many different scales (i.e., ornamental, building, urban) that people of a particular culture identify with, and are comfortable with. It is highly dependent on traditional and local materials — at least that was the case before the global introduction of nonspecific industrial materials. Along with many other changes that came along

221

with the industrialization of the building process in the twentieth century, traditional *form languages* around the world have been lost.

2. LINKING PATTERN LANGUAGE
TO FORM LANGUAGE.

Here, a general theory of design is proposed, which supports many of the ideas of Alexander. Its essence is to link one *pattern language* to one *form language* so as to create an adaptive design method. The process may be summarized as follows, with details to be developed later in this Chapter.

Proposition: An adaptive design method arises out of a complementary pair consisting of a pattern language and a form language (see Figure 11.1).

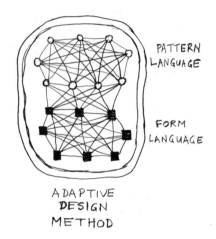

Figure (11.1)
A pattern language links to a form language:
Pattern Language + Form Language = Adaptive Design Method.

I have indicated very briefly what a *pattern language* and a *form language* are; we still need to understand what an *adaptive design method* refers to. Out of many contemporary approaches to design, there are very few that result in structures and environments that are adapted both to physical human use, as well as to human sensibilities. In the past, the opposite was true. Human use is straightforward to understand: the physical dimensions and geometry have to accommodate the human body and its movement. By accommodating human sensibilities, I mean that environments should make human beings feel at ease; make them feel psychologically comfortable so that persons can carry out whatever functions they have to unselfconsciously, without being disturbed by the built environment in any way. This imposes a strong constraint on the design process to adapt to the many factors (both known and unknown) that will influence the user on many levels, including emotion. An adaptive design method should accommodate all these criteria, and this Chapter shows how this may be accomplished.

A major source of confusion is that a design method could adapt to a style, but not to human use and sense of well-being. For example, it might adapt to (conform to) a set of predetermined geometrical prototypes, such as cubes and rectangular slabs. It takes on that particular *form language*. Minimalist modernism has a clearly-defined geometrical goal; i.e., its peculiar crystalline *form language*. It is successful on its own terms while at the same time ignoring, or not trying to accommodate, human patterns of use and the sensory response to built form and surface. This is the reason why minimalist modernism is incompatible with Alexander's *Pattern Language* (Alexander *et. al.*, 1977). In this Chapter, I will use the term "adaptive" to refer strictly to fitting the built environment to human beings, and not to abstract ideas or geometries.

Since there exist an infinite number of patterns that can contribute to a *pattern language*, and an infinite number of *form languages*, there are of course an infinite number of adaptive design methods that combine two languages. Each adaptive design method is unique. The crucial point is that there are also an infinite number of design methods that act against adaptive design by producing structures which are not suitable to human needs. In the absence of an accepted term for design that ignores human needs, I will call such actions "non-adaptive design".

Post-industrial design is not fundamentally adaptive. Its *form language* (or rather, set of related *form languages*) produces structures that are often hostile to human sensibilities. Studies by environmental psychologists have confirmed physiological reactions such as the onset of anxiety and signals of body stress in such environments (see Chapter 4). I want to look for systemic causes of this non-adaptivity. For reasons already discussed in Chapter 6, minimalism effectively precludes the use of patterns, both visual and Alexandrine patterns. That means that patterns of human activity cannot be accommodated within its design canon, thus characterizing it as non-adaptive. To proudly proclaim such a design method as "functional" is a mockery of the term, but it is admittedly a remarkably effective propaganda ploy that helps in its proliferation.

Architectural *form languages* survive because they often acquire non-architectural meaning, after which they can ignore the need to be adaptive to human needs. In that case, a *form language* is no longer part of an adaptive design method; it becomes split from its complementary *pattern language*. Instead of expressing an adaptive tectonic culture, the *form language* becomes a set of visual symbols that operate under the guise of moral principles (and thus become emotionally loaded). Using that *form language* then becomes an end in itself, detached from human life. This architecture has little to do with buildings that accommodate human beings, or with tectonics, but is a statement using a formal visual vocabulary. Such an architecture has its own purpose, disguised with moral precepts that together define a completely different world-view for those who accept them.

3. ANTIPATTERNS DO NOT DEFINE A LANGUAGE.

In the theory of *pattern languages* — actually developed more extensively in computer architecture than in buildings architecture — the concept of "antipattern" plays a central role (Salingaros, 2000). An antipattern shows how to do the opposite of the required solution. An ineffective solution is often repeated because the same forces that gave rise to it in the first place recur in other similar situations.

Assuming that the futility and counterproductive nature of such a solution is evident (which is not always the case), its occurrence can be studied to see what went wrong. Documenting an antipattern can save future designs from the same mistakes by identifying a problematic solution before it is adopted. The problem is that some antipatterns persist out of habit, causing a source of errors to become institutionalized. As discussed in Chapter 10, repeated use makes an error more acceptable, while institutional support from that point on makes it decreasingly likely that an error will ever be identified as such. Sometimes this knowledge can be helpful in order to avoid making the same mistake repeatedly, but only after the mistake has been recognized.

However, knowing the antipattern does not automatically indicate the pattern, since the solution space is not one-dimensional (Salingaros, 2000). If there were only two possible choices, knowing which one is wrong tells you which one is right. That simple situation almost never occurs in practice. More often, there are immeasurably more wrong than correct solutions. Doing the opposite of the antipattern will not give the pattern, precisely because there can be many different "opposites" going out in many different directions in the solution space.

Antipatterns do not comprise a *pattern language*, just as a collection of mistakes do not comprise a coherent body of knowledge. It is therefore not appropriate to talk of a language of antipatterns, but simply a collection of antipatterns. Nevertheless, antipatterns could (and often do) substitute for, and displace a genuine *pattern language*, with very negative consequences. I have given rules for distinguishing between a true *pattern language* and a collection of antipatterns or non-language (Salingaros, 2000), based on their internal consistency and their connectivity to external patterns (see Figure 11.2). As I discuss later in this Chapter, a true language — be it *pattern language*, *form language*, or spoken language — has a non-trivial internal complexity characterized by a high degree of connectivity.

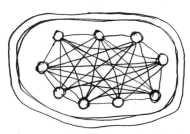

Figure (11.2)
A true language possesses internal connectivity.

TRUE LANGUAGE

My present aim is to be able to discern whether a *pattern language* is genuine, so that it can be connected to a *form language* and thus define an adaptive design method. It is imperative not to be fooled by a collection of antipatterns, otherwise our resulting design process will be non-adaptive, even though this may not be known at the beginning of the process. We will eventually see it in the non-adaptivity of the results, at which time it will be too late to do anything about it (i.e., after an unnatural city such as EUR, Milton Keynes, or la Défense has been built).

NON-LANGUAGE

Pattern languages have evolved, and, as with all evolved systems, they have developed an extraordinary degree of organized complexity. It is not possible to understand all this complexity, let alone replace it by a design method based on deliberately simplified rules. And yet, that has been the basic assumption of twentieth-century architects: that we can simply replace all the evolved architectural solutions of the past with a few rules that someone has made up (and which don't even have the benefit of experimental verification). The organized complexity encoded in a *pattern language* is the end result of an evolutionary development, and cannot simply be achieved all at once. A refusal to apply traditional architectural solutions (patterns) leaves architects only with antipatterns, by default. Really bad mistakes (in architecture, politics, or software development) happen when several things go wrong together. Therefore, sets of related antipatterns tend to recur, each antipattern contributing to the failure of the situation. The fact that they seem to go together is mistaken for the grouping of cooperating patterns in a *pattern language*. Stubbornly reusing these antipatterns merely recycles the same mistakes over and over again.

The analogous non-adaptive failure in a *form language* is more difficult to define. Most of that research is indeed very recent, and relies on mathematical properties (Alexander, 2004). A *form language* that adapts to human beings contains and codifies certain very specific geometrical properties such as fractal structure, connectivity, coherence, and scaling (as discussed in the previous Chapters of this book). Again, a *form language* that does not contain these mathematical properties is not a language at all, because it is too sparse to define a rich language of forms. I will call such a *form language* a "primitive" *form language*, or "non-language" (Figure 11.2). There exists a range of *form languages*, from non-languages, to primitive *form languages*, increasing in complexity of combinatoric expression up to genuine *form languages*.

The linguistic analogy makes it difficult to understand why a primitive *form language* would ever survive. Why maintain a system in use that severely limits one's expression? The reason we do this is that every *form language* has extra-linguistic attributes that help in its proliferation. Once invented, the limited visual vocabulary of a primitive *form language* may be copied unthinkingly by more and more persons. Unlike a true language, which survives through its linguistic utility, a *form language* can survive strictly through its iconic properties (and not its linguistic ones). Indeed, constant repetition through visual copying is the key to its transmission, promotion, and acceptance by an increasing number of architects. Familiarity makes people overlook a *form language's* linguistic deficiencies. (One is reminded of the collapse of literacy in the Middle Ages, when individual letters were copied as "runes" and ascribed with magical meaning by people ignorant of their original linguistic function).

An adaptive design method requires the union of a *pattern language* with a *form language* (Figure 11.1). If either the *pattern language* or the *form language* is flawed, then the design method will fail to create adaptive structures (see Figure 11.3). For example, high-rise towers set in vast open spaces satisfy neither a viable *form language* nor a *pattern language* — they are iconic design failures that get repeated because architects make a lot of money building them. One may claim to employ a *pattern language* together with a primitive *form language* to create structures barely suitable for human habitation and use, such as contemporary buildings that try to use Alexandrine patterns. Those buildings may partially satisfy some functional patterns, but the more they stick exclusively to a minimalist or high-tech *form language*, they more they will feel dead and alienating, so that their users are uncomfortable.

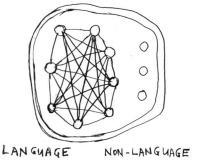

Figure (11.3)
A non-language cannot link to a true language.

LANGUAGE   NON-LANGUAGE

Two instances of partial success come to mind. In the mixed example of central Tel Aviv, an early modernist *form language* is tied to a traditional European urban *pattern language*, as laid out by Sir Patrick Geddes, with successful results. The buildings do not connect so much on an architectural scale, yet they do connect well on the urban scale to create a lively environment. Other illustrative examples with mixed success include dwellings built by alternative "counterculture" architects soon after the *Pattern Language* (Alexander *et. al.*, 1977) appeared. They satisfy all the patterns, but they look somewhat chaotic and unbalanced — far from satisfying Alexander's original intent of ordered geometrical coherence (Alexander, 2004). The reason is that their builders had no *form language* to draw upon. These buildings were built within a culture that did not wish to refer to any tradition, and did not have the capacity to create a new *form language* (the multicolored "psychedelic" art of that culture was never applied to architecture in a way that would help the geometry).

In the opposite instance, one can use antipatterns together with a *form language* to damage both built and natural environments. Twentieth-century buildings were built using a distorted version of the Classical *form language* that are inhuman either because of scale, megalomania, or the desire to intimidate. They may look nice from a distance, but are hostile in actual use. This is a characteristic of Fascist architecture. Some modernist architects were also very fond of employing parts of a *form language* of rich, detailed materials, but to intentionally create alien forms. The surfaces are adaptive in these cases, but the geometry is not (sending a mixed message of attractive materials in a hostile setting). Another failed example is found in recent traditional-looking mansions isolated in American suburbia. They use a *form language* (that happens to be irrelevant to the site) but no urban *pattern language*, so those buildings remain disconnected. They have a great image, but no functionality on the urban scale. It is only the correct pairing of *pattern language* with *form language* that results in an adaptive design.

The architecture of squatter settlements is an interesting case of genuinely adaptive application. Those slum dwellers use a *form language* that is determined by available scrap materials to build their own houses. Residents are preoccupied with basic survival, and have no wish to copy elements of a *form language* that was generated outside their immediate circumstances. There are simply no resources available to make an architectural "statement", although ornament and surface decoration appear on the most modest structures because they are felt to be essential. The human need to make a building adapt through form, surface, and ornament is innate. Everyday people who own and build their own homes definitely apply a *pattern language* (albeit unknowingly) because they want their dwellings to be as comfortable as possible. Here we have an adaptive design method, which, were it not for the miserable conditions of life represented by the overcrowded slums of the world, is an excellent example for architecture schools to study.

As the above examples make clear, an adaptive design method provides the means of creation, but not the product. It gives one the framework and tools for creative expression. It still requires a talented architect or sensitive non-architect to use the language to design a building. Working with a complete, richly-expressive language makes that task immeasurably easier. Great architects can use an existing *form language* in an innovative manner to create new architectural expressions, or they can invent their own *form language*. (A *pattern language*, however, cannot be invented: it has to be discovered). A primitive *form language* severely reduces architectural expression. With a flawed *form language*, new or old, even the greatest architect has trouble making something useful and adaptive.

4. ANALOGIES IN HUMAN COMMUNICATION.

Two complementary languages — *pattern language* and *form language* — are necessary for the process of adaptive architectural design. I can think of a parallel for this in pairing two entirely distinct types of language to enable human communication. Spoken language is used together with nonverbal emotional cues. These independent channels usually interact when one is speaking face-to-face with another person, and even on the telephone. Nonverbal communication gives a message of friendliness, ease of interaction, emotional comfort,·or hostility independently of what the spoken language is communicating. Nonverbal cues are the basis of a host of messages that are often more important than verbal content.

Human beings developed verbal and nonverbal modes of communication, and need both. Nonverbal cues carry through in telephone conversations because one can hear emotional signals encoded in the speaker's tone of voice and inflections. This is obviously not as effective as speaking in front of one-another. A sequence of decreasing information content corresponds to the gradual loss of the nonverbal language, and is represented by regressing from face-to-face meeting, to video-conference, to telephone, to handwritten letter, to e-mail, to typed memorandum. And yet, the actual text could be the same. This loss of expressivity is appreciated by the business world, where the value of serious communication is reflected in the price (in money, time, and inconvenience) that busy executives are willing to pay to arrange face-to-face negotiations.

As both lovers and fighters know very well, one can rely almost entirely on non-verbal language for rapid communication in certain situations. Indeed, in those situations, one can communicate affections or "read" cues without knowing the spoken language of the other party at all. It is also sometimes the case that verbal language is used to decoy the true feelings and intentions of the parties involved. Amateurs cannot disguise their emotional language and so betray their true intentions. Accomplished liars, on the other hand, lie on all informational levels simultaneously: tone of voice, facial expressions, hand gestures, etc. Psychopaths and hardened criminals learn to control their nonverbal cues so that the (contrived) emotional message supports what they communicate through verbal language, and thus succeed in deceiving their victims.

Here we are interested in building things rather than communicating a verbal message. Still, as the linguistic analogy makes clear, a building or urban setting conveys a wealth of information to human beings, and those signals influence the structures' eventual use. The built environment communicates complex messages on many different levels. An architect may naively expect that his or her design communicates a specific message in the most obvious aspects of its form, materials, and surfaces. The built structure may communicate something else altogether: a mixed, much more complex message, or the message could be strongly negative. The architect might offer a verbal explanation of the building's supposed message that totally contradicts what the structure is actually communicating in a sensory, visceral manner. Unfortunately, respected critics believe an architect's misleading words and ignore their own sensory responses to a building, which leads to cognitive dissonance for the public.

It is therefore imperative that we become aware that several different design languages are actively contributing to the overall effect on users. The language of building is necessary to express the building as form, to implement and embody thoughts and needs about space and use. The present model of two languages — a *pattern language* and a *form language* — is a simplification of what is a more complex phenomenon, yet it is a necessary first step to understanding the design process.

In addition to serving as a language for expressing architectural form, a *form language* communicates the state of mind of a society, or at least that of its ruling power elite. Corporate and totalitarian architecture looks and feels aloof; often faceless. The sensitive architectural historian can "read" messages such as power and authority, or, alternatively, compassion and respect for the individual in an architectural *form language*. However, such architectural messages are often disguised by propaganda, also expressed in architectural terms (Chapter 10). We are told by the architectural press that an obviously hostile building whose form deliberately creates alarm is marvelous because it is "innovative", thus deliberately confusing its architectural message.

5. THE INTERNAL STRUCTURE OF FORM LANGUAGES.

All human spoken languages are contained in a general "meta-language", which has a grammatical or syntactical structure common to all known languages (Maynard-Smith & Szathmáry, 1999). Human languages, even in the most technologically primitive cultures known, are not themselves "primitive". Independently of their technological achievements, all groups of human beings have developed a richly complex spoken language. Differences arise in specificities, in the breadth of vocabulary for concepts important to that culture, and in their transition to a written language, but those do not affect the general richness of the language.

This point is easy to explain from the mathematics of communication. In order to describe and communicate complex human activities and interactions, a spoken language itself has to have an extraordinary capacity for encoding complexity. A natural language is an externalization of the complexity of human thought, and has evolved along with the human mind. Even an isolated, technologically primitive tribe has developed complex activities and concepts over millennia, and these are comparable in information content to the complex activities of an urban dweller in the most advanced industrialized nations. For this reason, both sets of people require, and have developed, their own richly complex spoken languages.

An artificial primitive language, on the other hand, would not be sufficient for verbal communication. It would consist of, say, six words such as: yes, no, hot, cold, eat, drink (Figure 11.2). It is a primitive language that an old model of computer would understand, or a person stranded among others who spoke a different language. In this example of a non-speaker amidst people speaking another language, however, he or she will rapidly pick up the host language, facilitated by innate meta-linguistic structures that define that person's own native language.

What we conclude from the study of spoken and written languages is that, whereas each language may appear totally distinct on the surface, its level of complexity is equally high. Every language's internal structure has to obey general principles that are common to all languages. A primitive language or non-language, by contrast, is characterized by the reduction or absence of such internal complexity and structure. The complexity of human thought sets a rather high threshold for the complexity that any language has to be able to express through combinatoric groupings. It has been proposed that the transition from a primitive language to a real language corresponds to the evolutionary transition from the language of apes (and people brought up in linguistic deprivation) to human language (Maynard-Smith & Szathmáry, 1999).

Turning now to architecture, a viable *form language* is also characterized by its high degree of internal complexity. Furthermore, the complexity of different *form languages* has to be comparable, because each *form language* shares a commonality with other *form languages* on a general meta-linguistic level (see Figure 11.4). A primitive *form language* severely limits architectonic expression to crude or inarticulate statements. So, while each *form language* may be distinct in its components, it is not really a complete *form language* unless it possesses a complex internal structure. The exact details of this structure must necessarily parallel the internal structure of any other fully-developed language, and in particular, that of a *pattern language* (Salingaros, 2000). Roughly, these properties can be described as combinatorial, connective, and hierarchical features, which we see in our own written and spoken language.

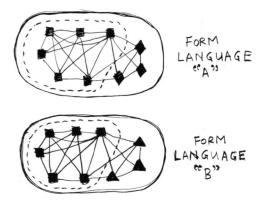

Figure (11.4)
Two viable form languages
share common features.

This argument is borne out by the enormous number of distinct *form languages* developed independently by different peoples around the world. It is reasonable to claim that for each spoken language, there is also a *form language* that those people use to build and to shape their environment. The means of verbal expression and accumulated culture defining a literary tradition has a parallel in an ornamental tradition and material culture, which includes a *form language* that is an expression of inventiveness in geometry and tectonics. A traditional *form language* has generated buildings the same way a spoken language has generated stories and poems, and these express a culture's complexity equally. The *form language* is stored in collective memory and recorded in physical materials, and is older than writing. Each traditional *form language* is distinct, yet possesses a comparably high degree of organized complexity in terms of visual vocabulary and combinatoric possibilities. Erasing a *form language* erases the culture that created it. It is no different than erasing a culture's literature, or its musical heritage.

It is only in recent years that the mathematical sophistication of traditional *form languages* has begun to be documented. Mathematicians and ethnologists are doing this work, while the architectural establishment continues to ignore indigenous building cultures and the human value of what they represent. For example, traditional building and urban geometry in sub-Saharan Africa is now revealed to be essentially fractal, thus revising our customary (and totally erroneous) conception of those cultures as mathematically under-developed — fractals were re-discovered in the West only very recently. Loosely (and deprecatingly) classed together as "vernacular architectures", this vast body of diverse and complex styles, geometries, and ways of understanding space and structure shames the poverty of contemporary architectural styles. Traditional form languages are rich, complete, and technically (not industrially) advanced. In terms of richness and underlying substance, which are crucially important to life, contemporary *form languages* promoted by the Western architectural design magazines would seem to represent an evolutionary regression.

Form languages comprise evolved systems of human geometric expression. Separate from preserving traditional *form languages* for their informational and cultural value, the inevitable evolution of *form languages* makes possible entirely innovative architectural expressions. Such an evolution is possible only if a *form language* retains the high level of its internal complexity. Traditional *form languages* around the world were dismissed as "primitive" by Western colonial and economic powers, and were replaced by variants of Neo-Classical or Beaux-Arts *form languages*. Cultural colonialism in architecture comes about by destroying languages that are thousands of years old, as an affirmation of superiority and power.

Even so, colonial architecture had been complex enough to begin adapting to local *pattern languages*, and thus to evolve adaptively towards the local vernacular. Many older colonial buildings are now treasured, and are included in a country's cultural heritage. When the West turned with vehemence against its own traditional *form languages*, replacing them with an impoverished set of primitive *form languages*, colonial architecture was itself eventually replaced by non-adaptive "International Style" buildings. Worse of all, those people whose *form language* (and culture) had been erased were caught up in the same deception (that this was necessary for economic progress and prosperity), so they embraced the same industrial "look" after political independence.

6. THE TRANSMISSION OF A STYLE.

A *form language* governs the built form in all its expressions: geometry, composition, structure, materials, surfaces, etc. When we reduce all of this to simply an image, we call it an architectural "style". I can now use the model of this Chapter to discuss and explain some significant events in architectural history. To begin with, we are faced with a serious contradiction. Why do some design styles proliferate even though they are poorly adapted to human use and sensibilities? (Such styles or design methods could be deficient because they lack either the *pattern language*, or the *form language*, or both). Even worse, it appears that the most damaging, least adaptive styles actually proliferate with the greatest ease.

The answer is frightening in its implications for our civilization. The most basic, primitive *form languages* spread the fastest in society (see Chapter 10). That is simply because they encode (carry with them) a minimum of information. The "style" as an informational unit that can be transmitted among human minds in a population carries over better when it is simplest. Flat sheer surfaces, transparent glass walls, pilotis, shiny "industrial" materials such as polished steel, etc. define a simplistic visual style, which offers an easily recognizable catchy image. These images are simple because they are the homogeneous products of synthetic materials. Never mind that the components of this primitive *form language* do not define a true *form language*; the public accepts them because of their visual simplicity encouraged by support from respected authorities, i.e., star architects and critics (Chapter 10).

People traditionally developed and preserved adaptive design methods, each containing a *pattern language* and a *form language*. An adaptive design method was conceived as a whole, without splitting it into its two distinct linguistic components. Indeed, it was itself part of culture and religion, which together formed a complex body of inherited knowledge and practices. The theoretical separation of design from culture is useful for analysis, but does not correspond to the practical reality of several millennia of human existence. Actual separation, however, did occur in the post-industrial age. Adaptive design split from culture (which had earlier split from religion), then the *form language* split from the *pattern language*. Architects shed off influence from tried-and-true solutions in order to seek individual expressions.

Detached as it was for the first time from a much larger complex system, a *form language* could evolve and propagate as an independent entity. This released it from traditional constraints, while at the same time giving a *form language* unprecedented channels and mechanisms for transmission. We know of biological entities that split from more complex organisms so as to propagate freely and with enormous success: they are the viruses.

I wish to draw an analogy with the replication of viruses. Extending the notion of image propagation further, we can look to recent events where biological terrorists use viruses. Because of its nature, the virus can exist in an inert, easily-transmittable form such as a powder. This is possible because a virus is a biologically simple structure with very low informational overhead. We know how the spread of a virus can be accelerated, as part of the arsenal of biological terrorists. First, disguise the pathogen in seemingly attractive substances, so as to have the victims consume it voluntarily. This corresponds to the promise that architecture and planning relying on primitive *form languages* solve social problems and liberate oppressed classes (Chapter 10). The people readily accept that. Second, artificially spread samples of the virus in as many places as possible so that the maximum number of persons will become infected. In the propagation of architectural images, the media play a key role, showing and praising carefully selected structures and urban projects (and ignoring everything else) (Chapter 10). Our architectural schools and press have also done a very effective job of promoting primitive *form languages* while unwittingly suppressing true *form languages*.

Someone who has been raised in the twentieth century and has been taught through association that "beautiful" objects have no hierarchical organization will then apply this rule subconsciously to design a building or a city. Even though people might find such environments intellectually acceptable, they can never overcome the negative sensations that such an architecture brings into play. The reason behind this typology can be traced back to artistic and design trends in the 1920s. Design in art and architecture overturned all established rules of treating three-dimensional forms and two-dimensional images. *Form languages* that people had developed as part of their culture and civilization were no longer valued or respected. Concepts such as hierarchical scaling were inadvertently eliminated from design. They had never been written down; they exist encoded in nature and as examples in all traditional art and architecture. The new artificial objects: paintings, sculptures, and buildings influenced the way we think. They served as mental templates for conceptualization.

Why did this occur only at the beginning of the twentieth century and not before? I believe that it had to do with radical social changes spurred by population pressure and political oppression so that for the first time, many people saw a chance of radical social improvement through technology. They were willing to sacrifice adaptive design in exchange for the (false) promise of a better future offered by industrialization (Chapter 10). Prior to that, people on all socioeconomic levels shaped their environment as far as they could to provide physical comfort and emotional well-being.

Another contributing factor was the creation of a new communications network formed by the convergence of telephone, telegraph, newspapers, magazines, and film. The new media tied the world together as never before, yet also made possible the rapid proliferation of advertising and political propaganda. The spread of modernism, combining visually simple images with the promise of a new utopian world, could never have occurred were it not for the new media (Chapter 10). Advertising created the desire for industrial products that we didn't really need. Just as in the case of internet computer viruses, which could not exist before the internet, primitive architectural *form languages* could spread only through the first architectural picture magazines. At the same time, advertising favors the transmission of simplistic messages, slogans, images, and ideas.

As a result of its tremendous power to shape people's minds, advertising quickly transformed from a medium for transmitting commercial information to an instrument of social change and control. Its first target was cultural traditions that blocked the consumption of inferior new industrial products. These inhibitions were overcome by making individuals ashamed of their instinctive preferences, labeling them as "backward", and thereby opening up the public to market influence. Thus, *form languages* that threatened the supremacy of the post-industrial aesthetic of glass, steel, and concrete slabs were stigmatized by the architectural critics. This style based on a specific industrial "look" could not be sold to the world until traditional *form languages* were eliminated. The way the built environment looked anywhere in the world would henceforth be controlled by the advertising media; all traditional *form languages* condemned to extinction in the interest of Western industrial and ideological dominance.

7. MINIMAL COMPLEXITY AND LIFE PROCESSES.

An excursion into biology is helpful here. There is a direct analogy between architecture and living processes. In examining how life arises, the Physicist Freeman Dyson proposes that two distinct processes characterize all living forms: metabolism, and replication (Dyson, 1999). Metabolism involves the physical interaction of an organism with its environment in a way that portions of the environment — i.e., nutrients — enter and are processed chemically by the organism. There is an interpenetration between the organism and the environment which maintains the functions of the organism via a chemical engine.

The other component of life, replication, is the distinguishing characteristic of forms that survive through copies. Although an organism needs pieces of the environment as raw material to build a copy of itself, the replicative process is fundamentally distinct from metabolism. Replication is directly dependent upon coding the organism's structure into a template (DNA), so that replication is theoretically tied to information storage rather than to interaction with the environment around it.

Perhaps the most important distinction between the two components of living structure is their independence. This is better discussed in terms of artificial life, as for example in entities generated by, and residing in a computer. It is possible to create the analogue of a metabolizing entity in the sense that it moves around on the screen and is nourished by devouring other nearby entities. It does not, however, have to reproduce. If one has played with the computer game "Sim City", then one imagines how an internally complex entity can survive indefinitely, and even grow in complexity as long as necessary "nutrients" are inputted. It can carry on an existence independent of other complex entities — it only needs simple supplies.

On the other hand, it is also possible to create a computer virus whose sole function is to replicate. Such an entity does not metabolize — it is simply a minimal piece of code (either computer, or genetic) that uses the internal machinery of a far more complex entity in order to make copies of itself. A pure replicator lacks the ability to metabolize, and thus cannot carry out an independent existence — it is entirely dependent on more complex entities for its continued survival. Without them, it lies dormant as an inanimate, disconnected piece of information (i.e., a crystal). It comes to life — in the sense of getting ready to replicate — only after it enters the living environment of a host's body. This is the reason why biological viruses are considered not to be really "alive", but to somehow occupy the interface between inanimate crystals and living forms.

Therefore, despite architects' concerns about style and adaptation, they missed an essential point that links the two. The high threshold for organized visual complexity in traditional architecture (seen in all evolved cultures) played a decisive role, by helping to maintain adaptation in architecture. When humankind decided to abandon this complexity threshold (under utopian promises of a better future through industrialization), we opened the door to minimalist *form languages* that had unbeatable transmission properties. Humankind had always preserved adaptive design methods — in which the *pattern language* guaranteed a high complexity for the complementary *form language* — as whole (i.e., complete) culturally transmittable systems. By dropping *pattern languages* from the design methods in use, the *form language* could then be simplified as much as anyone wished, which is where we find ourselves today.

8. ARCHITECTURE AS A LIVING PROCESS.

The above concepts from biology and computer science can be applied to architecture to set up metabolic/genetic analogies. This is essential for understanding design as a "living process" that accommodates and coexists with human beings. I identify the metabolic (interactive) aspect of living structure with the *pattern language*. After all, a *pattern language* dictates how built form interacts with human activities, which is the defining characteristic of a useful, adaptive structure. A building is perceived as functionally "alive" when it accommodates human functions in a positive and nurturing manner. The essentials of biological metabolism: interpenetration, nourishment, and repair have their direct analogue in a *pattern language*. Buildings shelter and contain people, who in turn build them and maintain them. Changes affected during repair enhance the adaptivity of the original design.

Forms, spaces, and surfaces can also nourish people psychologically by promoting a sense of well-being. This geometrical/visual aspect is to a large part responsible for supporting human activities, though the effect is much more subtle and is thus all too often ignored. (Architectural theorists have dismissed this component of architecture outright, stubbornly refusing to acknowledge psychological and medical results on the effects of environments). The way something is built and the way it looks (i.e., its *form language*) have a major impact in whether humans feel comfortable or not inside and around such a building. *Form language* affects human response directly. A building that is built in a way that its visual appearance discourages or hinders human activity can be said to be effectively "dead", since no-one wants to use it (see Chapter 4).

Replication of a building style does not depend upon whether it is useful or not, but on its *form language*. The *form language* is therefore its genetic component (see Figure 11.5). A building replicates if for some reason (logical or otherwise) an architect decides to use the same design for another similar building somewhere else. We naively imagine that this copying is due to a building's success in accommodating human beings and their activities, but that is not necessarily the case. A building replicates only because its *form language* is used to build another building, and this decision is independent of the original building's success in terms of its human component. The principal factor behind architectural replication is the ease of copying a particular *form language* (which becomes an unbeatable advantage when dealing with a primitive *form language*). The analogy of a building as a living being is useful in predicting positive and negative effects on its users.

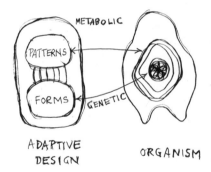

Figure (11.5)
Forms/patterns correspond to
genetic/metabolic structures.

Other factors that influence the success of a particular *form language* include sociopolitical forces that condemn one style while promoting another style; the physical presence of numerous buildings in a particular style around us makes it easy for that style to be copied by everybody; the virtual presence of a particular style promoted in terms of pervasive visual images currently fashionable in the media; etc. Obviously, techniques of advertising and proselytizing can promote a primitive *form language* and spread it in the environment, after which its dominance and familiarity guarantee further spread.

To their credit, early modernist architects criticized the fact that many traditional *form languages* were not used to work with, but were being copied in the most superficial stylistic manner. For example, columns are supposed to be made originally out of tree trunks, but not out of hollow material. Falsifying a stone surface by means of paint looks ridiculous up close and when the paint starts to peel. Formica looks cheap and feels unpleasant to the touch. In recent years, people use plastic or painted metal siding that has the superficial appearance and texture of wooden planks. All of these falsifications are in fact a testament to the persistence of traditional *form languages*, but undermine and devalue the meaning of the original *form language*. Falsified materials falsify the *form language*. Unfortunately, the early discussion on the "honesty" of materials quickly took a wrong turn, and turned into an unquestioning support and promotion of industrial materials.

If the *form language* is too idiosyncratic, then the building, even though it may be perfectly adapted to its uses, will not likely be used as a model for another building. This helps to explain why certain very successful buildings were never used as typological prototypes. For example, Art Nouveau buildings did not take off like modernist buildings did — simply because their *form language* is not as easily copyable. This is in part because their mathematically sophisticated *form language* could not compete with the *form languages* of early modernism (Chapter 10). Of the many competing *form languages* (including several related ones loosely defining modernism) in existence in the early twentieth century, the most simplistic ones had better survival qualities. To use a literary metaphor, if Art Nouveau were a written language, then it is perfectly suited for poetry, but less well-suited for more mundane prose like a shopping list or a computer software manual.

That said, poetry does nourish the human soul, which is the reason why all human societies use their language to compose poems. It is often the presence of emotionally-engaging poetry that helps to make everyday tasks bearable and even pleasant. Such is the effect of Hector Guimard's entrances to the Paris Metro stations (1900-1904), which provide a brief moment of architectural poetry as one enters or exits from the underground subway. For many people, they epitomize the dream of Paris. They were ruthlessly destroyed up to the 1960s (because they didn't conform to the drab minimalist aesthetic designated as orthodox by the architectural establishment). The French government finally realized that, in the eyes of the rest of the world, Paris would be architecturally impoverished without those characteristically Art Nouveau structures.

Other components of human expression are also codified in a traditional *form language*: dark passions, archaic qualities and wildness, ranging all the way to an almost savage intensity. These emotions are latent in the human soul, and thus find their geometrical and ornamental analogues in a particular culture's *form language*. Life itself is written in a passionate language. This is a far cry from the insipid homogenization of post-industrial architectural expression. In recent years, however, violence against architectural form (and human sensibilities) has become fashionable, but this trend must be strongly distinguished from what I am talking about here. Normal individuals never confuse intensity of feeling with actual violence, only psychopaths do so: those are driven to derive sensual pleasure and satisfaction from sadistic acts of destruction. A *form language* expresses optimist and creativity, never nihilism.

A society that is forbidden to express life and sensuality in a visual and tectonic medium turns out of frustration to perverse expressions of negativity, such as death and violence. There is no silencing the human spirit and its creative manifestations in material form; one can only redirect its modes of expression into negative channels. When we cannot express joy and wonder at the universe (because those who control cultural expression have a monopoly on the language), we seek out its opposite. The primitive and increasingly nihilistic *form languages* of contemporary architecture do speak to us directly, even though their message is not what their architects claim it to be. That's the reason for so much empty theorizing in the architectural press: it's an effort to disguise a fundamentally negative message.

Since a *form language* is one-half of the complementary pair *pattern language* + *form language* that comprises an adaptive design method, a *form language* must tie in seamlessly to a *pattern language*. Here is where the crucial distinction is made between effective and ineffective *form languages*, as far as human use is concerned. A primitive *form language* can be enormously successful at replicating, but be totally unsuited for human needs. The reason is that it cannot encode enough complex information to generate structures that actively engage humans in a positive way. *Form languages* that can be used adaptively have to join mathematically with a *pattern language*, and the join is possible only if the two languages share a comparable and compatible internal structure (Figure 11.1).

The process of joining two languages does not appear to have a linguistic parallel. We are used to translating from one language into another, but here I am referring to the creation of an entity (a building) that requires the cooperation of two distinct types of languages. Perhaps the best analogy is found in music. In a Song (say, where a poem is set to music), Opera, Oratorio, or Scripture presented in a musical setting, sung text is married to music, thus combining two linguistic expressions. The most glorious examples succeed in both dimensions: literary as well as musical, and thereby transcend the capabilities of each language alone. If religious text is used, it adds a third, spiritual dimension.

Two abstract languages can interface only if they both share similar structural characteristics (i.e., syntactical and linguistic). Otherwise, they cannot be conceived as complementary. One of these common characteristics is a hierarchical internal structure, while another is an internal combinatorial structure. Just with these two requirements as a criterion, we can exclude some styles as lacking the fundamental basis of a *form language* that can join a *pattern language*. Many modernist buildings are simply too plain in their vocabulary of forms, and therefore lack hierarchical coherence (see Chapter 3). Those that are more complex evidently have a greater range of visual expression, and thus offer a greater chance for adaptivity.

At the other extreme, the deconstructivist style tells you how to take forms apart, not how to put them together. Deconstruction has generated its own primitive (hence easily-copyable) *form language*, consisting of diagonal slashes, jagged lines, shiny high-tech materials, cantilevered shapes, concrete and glass walls, acute angles, etc. This comprises a large vocabulary of forms representing disordered visual complexity, but it all lacks linguistic connectivity. There is no system for synthesizing deconstructivist elements into coherent structures. Deconstruction started out in the field of linguistics, with the stated intention of disrupting the communication process (Salingaros, 2004). Its intent from the very beginning was to sabotage language, thus making it nihilistic. It is no wonder, then, that its architectural *form language* is incapable of generating coherent form. It can only give rise to fragmented structures whose purpose is to deny coherent expression. Architectural deconstruction has commandeered systems and resources (media, government, and academic support; architectural prizes and commissions) in its bid to displace other *form languages*. Its mode of propagation is therefore directly analogous to biological competition, where one organism tries to exterminate another.

It follows that it is hopeless to try to satisfy a *pattern language* using the *form language* of either minimalism, or deconstructivism. Perhaps because of this perceived impossibility, Alexander's *pattern language* (Alexander *et. al.*, 1977) has been all but ignored by the mainstream architectural profession. A major misunderstanding of the value of patterns has led to the neglect of *pattern languages*, because they were (correctly) seen to possess far more complex combinatoric properties than contemporary *form languages* in use. The inability of a primitive *form language* to join a *pattern language* should have alerted architects to the deficiencies of that *form language*. What happened instead is that the primitive *form language* was retained, while the possibility of an adaptive design method (that combines a *form language* with a *pattern language*) was abandoned. This decision, crucial for the evolution of architecture, was influenced by forces embedded very deeply in a culture shaped by advertising and ideology. A society that runs largely on images values an iconic architecture above all else, and is loath to re-attach it to something as abstract as a *pattern language*. Adaptation to human needs is incompatible with an image-driven architecture.

Architects have misinterpreted Alexander's *Pattern Language* as too restrictive. They felt that their creative imagination should not be fettered in trying to satisfy Alexandrine patterns. Perhaps they see that the most innovative part of their design clashes with patterns, and they certainly don't want to sacrifice it. I, on the other hand, propose an architecture that is ruthlessly adaptive to human uses and sensibilities: architecture that connects us to the world. If an architectural "statement" makes people uncomfortable, it should not be built. Review boards should not commission it, and juries should not award it an architectural prize. The *pattern language* provides a "reality check" for an architect's imagination. An architect that can create nurturing environments can adapt an innovative idea to patterns; it takes a secure and courageous one to do so.

9. A NEW ARCHITECTURE.

Form language (actually, fairly primitive versions of a *form language*) is what today's architects focus on, almost to the exclusion of other design constituents. Architects are visually-oriented people, used to thinking in visual terms. I believe that the present discussion can help bring innovation through a new understanding of the complexity of the design process. It is possible to list several insights as points that can be used in practice.

Table 11.1. Seven Points that Guide Architectural Design.

1. Great architecture can, and does result from following a tried-and-true *form language* (in combination with a *pattern language*).

2. The more informationally-rich a *form language* is, the more adapted the architecture could become to the human condition.

3. Innovative architects have also developed their own *form language* (e.g., Louis Sullivan, Antoni Gaudí, Victor Horta, Frank Lloyd Wright, Erich Mendelsohn, etc.).

4. Non-adaptive architecture results from following a primitive *form language*, which does not have enough complexity to allow either richness of architectural expression, or adaptivity to human uses and sensibilities.

5. Genuine architectural and urban adaptivity can follow only from applying a *pattern language* that codifies human movement and practices.

6. An adaptive design method marries *form language* with *pattern language*.

7. If a *form language* is too primitive so that it cannot be married to a *pattern language*, then that *form language* should not be used.

It is possible to begin implementing a program for a new architecture, after we understand architectural forces as explained in this and previous Chapters. These ideas and suggestions should appear as totally practical to present-day architectural students, who have been trained in an architecture of increasing complexity through the use of computer visualization. They have an advantage over the previous generation of architects, who were taught through empty images and forms. Architecture depends on distinct complex languages. The basis for real, adaptive, and sustainable architecture, which was outlined here, is not currently taught in architecture schools, simply because the scientific results are very recent. Education is very easy to change, by replacing the teaching in leading institutions with a curriculum on how to design buildings and cities for human use and having an increased sense of well-being.

A priority for any architectural project today is to formulate or rediscover a viable *form language*, otherwise one is forced to copy the sterile styles around us. No shape or visual vocabulary should be used just because some alleged authority said that it is "honest", "liberating", or "fashionable". An architect who seeks an honest expression in his or her architecture has to employ the nature of materials to help decide on the *form language*. Preference should be given to local indigenous building materials. One can also look to the pre-industrial past for examples of appropriate forms and geometries. The latest industrial materials will be used if they are useful in a particular setting, but not because of ideology. Most of what we build today relies on industrial materials, but these materials don't have to express a modernist *form language*. There is a potential richness to these materials that was not cultivated because of the dominance of the modernist aesthetic.

An ornamental tradition often survives better in small-scale structure and surface design. This can be transferred from other visual expressions such an textiles or pottery back into architecture. Another source of forgotten clues to a lost *form language* may be found in regional historical furniture. This process of discovery should not be misinterpreted as superficial historicizing. The rest of the language must be invented by the architect, who needs to incorporate colors, forms, spaces, and ornaments according to the principles revealed in this book. The new *form language* should be richly expressive, individual, and distinct. Nothing should be complex for complexity's sake, nor should any forced simplicity be imposed.

The new architecture will, not surprisingly, look a lot like traditional architecture (Krier, 1998). If it is successful in connecting to human beings, it will certainly elicit the same feelings of naturalness as those historical built regions still preserved around the world. Yet, as Léon Krier emphasizes, we can build today urban environments that are every bit as comfortable as the greatest examples built in the past. The widely disseminated opinion that we cannot reproduce the best qualities of the past for a multitude of reasons is only propaganda: Christopher Alexander (2004), Léon Krier (1998), and many other humanist architects have built new structures that are innovative, yet timeless in their human adaptation. Those buildings are also more sustainable than buildings that simply try to make an architectural "statement".

These ideas are rapidly coming together with scientific support for a new architectural renaissance. We will see the inevitable turning away from the present architectural system of focusing on idiosyncratic expression, sooner or later, because of its irrelevance to human life. It is time to begin training the young architects who will build the future, and who will be asked to repair the wounds inflicted upon the built environment over the past several decades. In all probability, the demand will come from society itself. When that time comes, graduates of today's institutions who know how to use these principles will thus be more employable. Contemporary schools of architecture should be re-oriented to consider more traditional ideas helping innovation, in the way I have indicated here. This may well propel a re-structuring of architectural pedagogy that allows students to look beyond contemporary expressions for inspiration and knowledge. Young architects can once again be creating a sustainable and rich built environment.

10. CONCLUSION.

This Chapter has presented a theory of design based on the combination of two types of language: a *pattern language*, and a *form language*. The *pattern language* encodes elements of human interaction with buildings, which are to be found throughout traditional architecture and urbanism. The *form language*, on the other hand, corresponds to whatever geometrical style the building or urban region has taken. In principle, there is enormous freedom to choose a *form language* for a new building today. Nevertheless, what is used in place of a *form language* in our times lacks the complexity and connectivity to define a true language. This often results in geometrically and informationally impoverished environments that are unsuitable or unpleasant for human use. Moreover, the adoption of an overly simplistic *form language* precludes the necessary cooperation with a *pattern language*, thus guaranteeing that human needs will never be satisfied via an adaptive architecture.

Once these mechanisms at the basis of design are more widely known, it would appear reasonable that the world could again learn to build its cities in a way to accommodate human beings. Another factor, however, comes into play: a *form language*, once it is split from a complementary *pattern language*, spreads among the population of minds according to how easy it is to copy. The characteristics of a successful *form language* (successful in terms of being used for many buildings) are the opposite of those of a *form language* required for adaptive design. The fast-spreading one is too simplistic for human use, whereas the useful one capable of adaptation spreads too slowly to compete. We are fighting against a scientific phenomenon: adaptive design is complex and thus difficult to spread, whereas pathological design spreads very easily through the visual media. Thus, it is critically important that students and teachers learn to recognize this phenomenon as it is occurring.

Chapter Twelve

ARCHITECTURAL MEMES IN A UNIVERSE OF INFORMATION

1. INTRODUCTION.

Intelligence distinguishes human beings from all other life forms. Much of our intelligence results from (or is manifested in) our ability to construct artifacts. A central component of the human intellect is devoted to establishing connections, such as those between elements in a design that leads to an artistic advance; or those between cause and effect that leads to scientific understanding; or between ideas and applications that leads to a technological advance. This is but a very sophisticated manner of treating information. Human beings are the best information processors among all the animals. Our technology and culture extend our informational abilities artificially, magnifying them by orders of magnitude.

Our desire and ability to connect to the physical world through touch, hearing, smell, taste, vision, and a mental understanding of physical structure extend our conceptual mental apparatus into the external world. Viewed in this way, artifacts are an artificial extension of our memory. Computer memory chips and hard disks are thus merely the latest technological manifestation of a trend that started with bone carvings and progressed through wood, stone, and bronze sculptures, to writing, to printed books, to the media we now have and use.

It is by developing these abilities of connection and memory that humankind has succeeded in dominating other living forms. Recognizing and recording patterns is key to daily survival, and may also be seen as the origin of scientific, philosophical, and artistic developments. A recurring relationship once established among several elements of our world acquires meaning in memory as a pattern. This relationship can then be recorded or codified into a scientific result. It thus becomes part of collective human knowledge, just as our artifacts may be said to codify our collective material culture. The pattern can guide our behavior, or the production of artifacts. The same act of recognizing recurring relations among elements of our world anchors our relations with it, by enabling us to describe, explain, and know it, and thereby act and transform its physical aspects. Certain "patterns" represent informational entities in our minds. These serve to connect

(1)   the world's organization,

(2)   the organization of our knowledge, our artifacts and cultural expressions, and

(3)   the organization of our interactions with the world.

We now live part of our lives in a universe of information, where information storage and its retrieval have increased dramatically. It hardly appears that we are biologically ready to handle this explosion of capacity, which is threatening to change our world in ways that we cannot yet anticipate. Starting with radio commercials and early advertising images in the 1920s, the world of electronic media has grown and enveloped us. Most people naively think of it as a separate universe, but in fact we inhabit it just as much as the tangible, physical world. It is more accurate to say that human beings inhabit a hybrid world formed from the overlap or merging of the physical universe with the universe of information.

Even though it is our own creation, we don't really control it, nor access to it. We naively think that the universe of information has remained the artificial memory bank that was its original intention. Again and again, we find that, once we create a communications network, all sorts of unanticipated entities start to make use of it.

It is necessary to ask then: what entities other than ourselves inhabit this informational universe? Sure enough, we share the physical universe with all biological life forms, but here is a non-biological realm. Which entities compete with our ideas, our knowledge, our thoughts, and our cultural products? The answer is as simple as it is disturbing: pieces of freely propagating clusters of information. These are called "memes". They are informational entities that are greatly simplified versions of patterns, and which gradually replace patterns in organizing our interaction with the world.

Since the beginnings of human communication (that is, several millennia before the advent of new information technologies), memes arose in the informational universe defined by communicating human minds, crossed over to the physical universe as artifacts, then crossed back again as transmittable images and ideas.

A realizable image, movement, or rhythm can be transmitted from one person to another. If the information defining it can assume physical representation as an artifact, this facilitates its transmission. Many artifacts are utilitarian, or have a deep meaning, but a great number of them are not. Nevertheless, they can acquire special communicative properties that aid in their diffusion. By so doing, they add reasons for their existence that are independent of their strict utility, and thus totally distort their intrinsic value (if they had any in the first place). These extra qualities often help to transmit a useless artifact: this is the mechanism whereby patterns are replaced by memes. The cycle closes when an abstract idea's physical representation serves to propagate that idea to other persons.

Sometimes, the connection between an idea and its representation is unexpected and possibly bizarre. An idea can be tied to things that have no relation whatsoever with it, but which nevertheless aid in its transmission. The simplest example is the caption on an image: it can serve either to validate something harmful, or to discredit something beneficial. Once established, however, even an absurd connection survives in our memory. Therefore, an idea, together with its representation and the connection between itself and its representation, form a transmissible unit. This defines a "meme" (Chapter 10 in this book; Dawkins, 1989; 1993; Dyens, 2001).

2. MEMES AND INFORMATIONAL VIRUSES.

In the universe of artifacts, images, and other elements of human culture, some entities act more like viruses than higher organisms (Salingaros, 2004). Just like in the biological case, the virus/organism distinction is based on complexity: the virus has a markedly reduced structural complexity. In the biological case, this is achieved by eschewing large-scale structure and metabolism, retaining only the most rudimentary ability of replication. For this reason, a virus has an organizational advantage for propagating over even the smallest organisms, which have to both replicate and metabolize. (Like airline passengers, those with only carry-on baggage go through check-in faster than those with many heavy suitcases).

A similar thing occurs for computer viruses, which are the simplest pieces of replicating code: they do not perform any useful function as other software does, and so require no complexity overhead. The secret of memes is this: the simpler they are, the faster they can proliferate. Simple slogans, tunes, and images have enormous mnemonic power. In the visual world, this phenomenon has been analyzed in a discussion of comics by Scott McCloud (1993). The progression from a complex, individual image to an abstract, simplified image increases the image's applicability.

This secret was already discovered by early modernist architects of the 1920s. They removed those elements that made architecture individual according to its context, reducing their buildings to simple forms and surfaces. By so doing, they attained the standardization of architecture that was their goal. The "International Style" of cubes and rectangles made out of flat surfaces, and using glass and steel was the result of stripping out all complex elements. This style composed of architectural memes without architectural patterns spread around the world with astonishing rapidity (Chapter 10). Removing any structural information that made buildings adapt to individual human users, local climate, architectural and cultural traditions, and surrounding structures created a generic style that could be erected anywhere. The modernist movement confused the universal with the generic.

3. AN ECOLOGY OF MEMES.

As soon as human beings began to establish a network of storage devices for their acquired knowledge, this network became a vehicle for other, useless entities. These are the "memes", introduced by Richard Dawkins as pieces of information that travel from human mind to human mind (Dawkins, 1989; 1993). Memes are propagated in the collective mind of a society. A meme could be a catchy tune; an advertising jingle; a visual image; a religious or cult symbol; a political slogan; a chant; an idea or opinion (either sensible, or totally unfounded) about some topic; a message tied to an emotionally appealing issue, etc. Memes spread not because of any benefit or advantage to us, but because they have something attractive that makes them stick in one's mind. Memes offer seductive features to people, who then propagate them.

Even though memes are not understood to have intention, we have to consider them as acting for their own benefit. A meme's advantage lies in having more efficient techniques of propagation. The processes that allow a meme to propagate, while advantageous for the meme, are detrimental for human beings. In the case of intentionally harmful memes, such as computer viruses, the meme's intention is coded into its structure. One can largely explain the harmful properties of memes by their propensity to destroy and replace other mental entities. In the informational ecosystem of the human mind, now tremendously extended by new information technologies, memes are simply parasites. They have but one function: to replicate themselves. This normally occurs by displacing other conceptual and informational entities.

The point is a simple one. The evolutionary opening up of human minds so as to extend our consciousness into the outer world also opens them up to invasion by mental viruses. One cannot have one without the other. The price we pay for our vast intelligence is paradoxically our weakness to be influenced by cults, advertising, and political slogans. Product advertising devotes an entire commercial industry to meme production. Political campaigns are inconceivable without advertising. Most advertising memes tend to range from benign to harmful in the long term, whereas certain memes that mix extremist politics with destructive cults have proven deadly.

A meme spreads because it finds "receptor" or "attachment" sites in the receiving organism. Everyone copies from everyone else, regardless of whether a particular meme is harmful or not. Here is where the meme/virus analogy comes in useful — many features of meme propagation are explained by the way biological and computer viruses act. Since memes are entirely dependent on human beings to propagate them, they must offer either a real or imagined benefit. The most successful memes come with a great psychological appeal (Dawkins, 1989). Advertising memes promise to satisfy our desire for sex, attractiveness, and power. Political memes offer superficially plausible answers to deep economic and social problems (or promote a champion who promises to correct all the faults of the political system). Religious memes about justice in the afterlife offer some hope during a bleak existence in an unjust reality. Putting religion aside until the end of this Section, most memes' psychological appeal is a deception. Using a standard ploy from product advertising, biological viruses, and computer viruses, a successful meme presents itself in an attractive package or memetic encapsulation.

As is well known from the world of advertising, memes compete fiercely against each other for our attention. We choose to accept one meme over another on the basis of its psychological appeal. Paradoxically, we tend to misinterpret this competition as a straightforward struggle of beneficial versus harmful informational entities (memes as well as patterns); whereas in most cases the blatantly competing entities are different memes, which are equally harmful to us. Genuinely beneficial memes are rather few in number, and there is as yet no indication that beneficial memes exist in the long term.

As long as people fail to recognize that memes show some of the properties of viruses, they continue to spread. Infectivity depends on the number of copies present in the environment, both as physically-embodied examples, and in pictures shown in magazines, books, and the media. Proliferation is thus exponential, like a biological or computer virus, because the rate of spreading is proportional to the population of viruses at any particular time. The world is alarmed when they see in the media that viral infections are spreading, but people in general ignore the infectious nature of harmful memes. They misinterpret them as benign, or as fashionably desirable, or as a sign of cultural progress and modernity.

In contrast to infection by a biological virus, which produces physical symptoms, the analogous infection by an architectural meme is not easily diagnosed. Thus, those who are infected have no way of knowing this. Since it goes undetected, memetic infection can spread unchecked. Physical symptoms such as fever, or pain and swelling around a wound are a side-effect of our immune system working, yet there is no analogous immune system developed against meme infection. We have no antibodies to tag harmful memes, nor a mechanism to rid us of those memes once they are tagged. The problem arises from a mismatch between biological adaptation and the universe of information.

I have the greatest respect for Dawkins as the originator of the meme idea. Nevertheless, he is, I believe, mistaken to classify religious ideas strictly among the harmful memes. Religion is an organizing system of knowledge (real and imagined) about the universe, which has proven essential for humankind to maintain itself. It is probable that the rise of increasingly complex religious ritual during humankind's earliest days played a significant role in developing our mental capacity. Furthermore, the progressive disappearance of religious practice we witness today, coupled with new information technologies, could have contributed to the unprecedented emergence of destructive memes in our society. I argue that memes, which "develop only for themselves", are vastly different from human patterns, which serve to connect us with our world, and thus to link the physical world to the spiritual world. If people no longer have universal aspirations, and if we are distancing ourselves from the physical conditions of our existence, then mental models begin to develop *strictly for themselves*, and thus end up as memes.

4. CO-EVOLUTION OF MEMES AND HUMAN BEINGS.

Rather than looking at meme creation and propagation as one-sided, Ollivier Dyens describes it as really a two-way process (Dyens, 2001). Humans generate memes, which in turn change human society. The process is one of co-evolution, where it is impossible to say what influences what. That's the whole point of cultural evolution: once a beneficial or harmful meme is adopted by a society, it helps to develop that society for better or for worse. Just as early humans' minds opened up to memes, the memes, in turn, are suspected of forcing the multiplication of the brain's processing power in order to handle the increased input. This created a self-reinforcing loop that could have driven the human brain to quadruple its size during our recent evolution.

Now, the capacity of the human brain is just as easily filled with junk as with useful information, just as a computer hard disk can contain either a million copies of the same image, or a doctoral thesis. This example only underlines my insistence that information should not be assumed to be equally useful. Contrary to the claims of contemporary post-structuralist philosophers, who propose that all information has equal value, and that such information is relative, there exist criteria for judging its utility, pertinence, and quality. The informational universe unfortunately contains and transmits both types of information indiscriminately.

Dyens (2001) elegantly describes how memes require brains (not necessarily human ones) and languages to emerge and spread. "Organic beings and cultures are profoundly entangled in each other ... Media environments — more specifically, the Internet and telecommunication networks, but also such things as the publishing, music, or film industry — enable cultural replicators to free themselves from dependence on organic beings. Cyberspace, for example, is an environment where replicators can reproduce and disseminate independent of organic beings. In addition, from an evolutionary perspective, media environments are more effective, faster, and less brittle than organic ones." (Dyens, 2001; pages 17-18).

Part of this picture has already been adopted by one group of evolutionary biologists, who view evolution as an ecosystem phenomenon, rather than as an isolated process acting on an embedded organismic type. To them, what evolves is the ecosystem and not just the individual organism. Another part of this explanation is tied to realizing that human development is not limited to biological — i.e., genetic — channels, but takes place within a network of artifacts (see the vast literature of paleoanthropology, which says this), neurons, and increasingly, electrical circuits.

One should not confuse memes with patterns. One reads, for example, that bird-calls are a meme for birds. I interpret this otherwise: they are patterns rather than memes. Bird songs are extremely useful for the birds; and they are also very beautiful to us. Furthermore, they serve to connect the birds' lives (i.e. their behavior) to the physical world. If there is indeed a co-evolution between memes and human beings, we should not confuse that with another co-evolution, surely more fundamental, between human beings and their patterns (as I defined in Section 1 of this Chapter). It seems that this confusion exists in the literature on memes, which indiscriminately lumps together all mental entities as "memes". In the same way, all biological organisms are not viruses, and all informational entities are not memes. Even though this Chapter is primarily devoted to memes, one of its goals is to point out that today, memes have proliferated to the detriment of other informational entities.

5. MEMES DISGUISED AS PLAYFUL IMAGES IN AN INFORMATIONAL UNIVERSE.

Architectural memes depend on people and human society for their existence. An informational virus is merely a handy description of actions that persons willingly take to reduce organized complexity in different media. Some individuals strongly believe in propagating a particular type of structure over the earth, and they devote their energies to this task. Architectural movements in the twentieth century were driven by images tied to questionable ideologies (Chapter 10). Alternatively, as in a political movement, persons who do not believe in the ideology might support it nevertheless, because it provides a means of livelihood, income, or career advancement. Such memes propagate because it serves the interest of a group of persons to propagate them. Even if the long-term effects on society are clearly negative, some individuals profit in the short term.

Although we should be careful not to overextend the viral analogy, there is one further insight to be gained from it. Biological viruses have an inert, crystalline form in which they can survive in a hostile environment for a long time. The biological virus becomes active only in an aqueous medium. Once there, it seeks a particular organic entity whose material structure it deconstructs, so as to utilize those pieces to make copies of itself. There is something analogous happening in the architectural world. The archival forms of an architectural meme include a building, its photograph, or a design generated on a computer. The meme's active form, however, inhabits human brains, and commandeers their attached bodies to physically create copies of the image.

Architectural images inhabit both the physical world and the world of information at the same time. This environment comprises the following interlinked components:

Table 12.1. Components of the Universe of Information.

(1) The human sensory system, especially the eye, which inputs information into the brain.

(2) The brain, which processes and stores that information as neural circuits.

(3) Various communications media such as the Internet, newspapers, television, books, and magazines that transmit information to the human eye.

(4) Information encoded in buildings.

(5) Media for information storage such as computer hard discs, the world-wide web, books, magazines, etc. encoding visual and textual information.

In this respect, information and communications technologies are instrumental in spreading architectural memes worldwide.

Computer-Aided Design programs have become an essential component in the universe of information. That is because a virtual building is easier to represent on a computer screen, as compared to actually erecting a physical structure. Instead of utilizing the tremendous creative potential of the electronic medium, however, it has been used to perpetuate images. One might characterize the electronic world of virtual design as a laboratory in which new architectural memes are bred, before being unleashed into the outside world. In an interesting case of co-evolution, popular Computer-Aided Design software has now adapted itself to facilitate the representation of abstract forms, by making it easier to generate them. Because of the initial inability of computers to handle a lot of data and fast processing speeds, representations were made simple, therefore limiting architectural expression. At the same time, this made it more difficult to design traditional structures containing coherent complexity on different scales (which is one characteristic of living structure).

In a virtual laboratory setting, one might have no idea of the destructive power of a particular architectural meme being developed, which becomes evident only after the design acquires physical embodiment as a building. An image very rarely provides the same sensory feedback as the eventual full-scale structure. Virtual design is very much "a game" pursued in the supposed quest of architectural innovation. (I explain in Chapter 10 why this pursuit is, in fact, severely restricted by institutionalized visual memes). Since students and architects see computer-generated images much more than they complete actual buildings, this is a very effective method of transmitting unrealizable structures to their brain.

This way of working has actually turned into a brilliant coup, since those translucent images of unbuilt projects are so ambiguous as to be readable in many different ways. The viewer can inject his or her own conception into the ambiguous image, and so develop a liking for it. Small images on a screen can look seductive or exciting, thus creating a positive emotional attachment with the viewer. Many architectural commissions and prizes are won this way. The same cannot be said of the finished building, however, which does not possess as high a degree of ambiguity — a flaw in conceiving form on the real scale that is often counteracted by using a lot of glass and reflective surfaces. The reality of such buildings born of a digital conception can be disappointing (and even oppressive), but less so if the materials hide or deny the building's materiality.

Architectural memes make an emotional promise: they attract our attention because of their novelty. Forms that depart from our inherited idea of what a building ought to look like offer us surprise. At the same time, the complete separation of forms from real human needs helps to create a new link to a supposed innovation. We are sold the myth that whoever appreciates those memes (or, perhaps, whoever pretends to appreciate them) is a sophisticated, up-to-date individual. If such forms provoke anxiety, all the better. This is a well-known method in advertising: provoke visceral emotions — it doesn't matter which emotions — to better fix an image into our subconscious.

Generating abstract forms on a computer thus becomes an innocent game because it is divorced from the physiological and psychological consequences those full-size built forms will have on human beings. In very much the same way, a teenager can enjoy slaughtering virtual persons in a computer game; whereas real-life combat or terrorism takes a genuinely hardened character. Virtual reality provides a great training-ground for the real thing, not only because it sharpens skills, but especially because it fools the trainee into thinking it is all just a game.

6. IMAGES THAT DEFINE AN ABSTRACT UNIVERSE.

Even a cursory examination of currently popular architectural books and magazines reveals an alien universe of images, radically detached from the real world of life and human beings. Images portrayed in architectural magazines representing buildings that could not possibly accommodate everyday uses become fixed in our memory, so we reproduce them unconsciously. As I outlined earlier in this Chapter, this virtual universe (the universe of information) is merging into the real, physical universe, so that one can no longer distinguish between the two. It is most definitely not a preference between two different types of architectural expression — say, blobs on a computer screen versus traditional buildings drawn on paper — having equivalent aesthetic validity. Rather, I wish to distinguish between architectural patterns that benefit human life, and destructive memes that subjugate the physical world to a virtual one.

In the majority of architecture schools today, memes are realized either as approved models; as design examples offered as good ideas to copy; or as computer-generated designs. All of these combine to define an alternative reality. Any design effort draws upon memes already stored in memory, and this process of recall is subconscious. Academic architects conform to those memes unknowingly in the belief that they are producing original designs. Those architects tend to live in an isolated world of images. They are dependent on images for their architectural experience because actual buildings are much more difficult and costly to experience first-hand. Because of that tenuous relationship, architectural academics tend to promote an architecture that has a striking image but may not be very nice to inhabit. Moreover, their creative output is nowadays judged strictly via a virtual portfolio. Architectural competitions and prizes are awarded on the basis of virtual designs, not necessarily having anything to do with real buildings.

Within this world of images, everything architectural is reduced to visual representations. Architectural training consists in large part of substituting this artificial universe for the real world. From their first days in architecture school, students are asked to put aside their instinctive notions of traditional beauty, natural structure, coherence, and balance. Such notions are classed as outdated, or no longer useful in order to become architects. They instead adopt formal, iconic criteria. Many architects and students have been taught to override their own sensory equipment, and interpret the world according to a contradictory viewpoint. Those conditioned persons can no longer interpret what they see and touch, but function according to an alternative stored world-view. The virtual substitutes for the real inside the mind.

At the same time, this substitution generates an urge to manifest the virtual universe in physical space. Whenever a building is erected according to a set of unnatural images, it is a material realization of the virtual, alien universe. This criticism has nothing to do with computer technology itself, which can be used either way by its human programmers. The same technology, appropriately applied, could help us to generate adaptive, humanistic buildings. Computer-Aided Design programs currently under development incorporate fractal rules and will try to automatically generate an optimal degree of design complexity.

Studies on learning demonstrate that the wiring of the brain changes permanently when exposed repeatedly to the same stimulus. Input uses brain plasticity to create long-term memory. Subconscious thinking processes — such as those we rely on for design — clearly draw upon the schemata stored in the brain. Our mind's output, which most persons naively assume to be totally original, is therefore shaped by what is already there.

Alien buildings impact humankind on many different levels. Firstly, they create unnatural environments for human habitation. Secondly, they conflict with and replace other, more human and traditional forms of architecture. They also make it impossible to build new, innovative buildings that comprise living architectural patterns, forms, and structures. Visible examples do far more damage to civilization than the obvious one inflicted upon the built environment, however. Alien images penetrate into our conscience, and thus profoundly influence our world view. The ideological memes of simplistic, broken forms have acquired physical expression (e.g. buildings; visual and electronic media), which operates as a vehicle that makes possible their transmission to the minds of the population at large. One could make the analogy with the HIV virus, which is suspected of originating in a small group of apes residing deep in the central African forest. By crossing over into the human population with its international travel routes, HIV has successfully spread over the entire globe. It found a vast new population of hosts and more efficient methods of transmission.

Alien buildings embody a physical randomness that is the antithesis of nature's organized complexity. The danger is that such buildings are now registering subconsciously, to be used as mental templates for understanding and creating complex, organized physical order. A person's world-view is stored in their brain's permanent memory, which is being corrupted by images of a sleek, transparent, and broken architecture. It follows that these images will influence everything we design — undoing all our achievements in understanding complex systems and how our world works.

At the same time, all the concepts at the heart of contemporary architectural discourse, such as authenticity, innovation, and creativity, take on a new aspect. We cannot continue to speak of these terms in the traditional manner, as if we were really in control of our permanent memory, since memory now comes in part from external memes.

7. CIRCUMVENTING OUR IMMUNE SYSTEM.

A meme acting as a virus uses packaging or surface configurations. An attractive shell (that appears beneficial to the organism) permits a biological virus to attach to a host and inject its DNA. In the case of an architectural meme, the analogous packaging includes the appearance of aesthetic and social progress and the promise of prestige and career success for the transmitter. A virus has the ability to change its packaging so as to circumvent defenses. Because of a continuous mutation to avoid being eliminated by the natural immune system, viruses are not automatically recognized as damaging intruders. We have evolved our immune system to protect us. A virus cannot make headway unless it also develops sophisticated strategies to fool our immune system. There is no human immune system against informational viruses, though any suspicion or alarm is bypassed through ideologies of expertise and progress.

Apparently, the only defense mechanism we possess against harmful memes is a basic conservatism: we feel uneasy when confronted with memes that contradict what is natural; what has worked in the past generations; what has evolved along with us. This resistance to change works also against any potential innovation, so we have learned to override the signals of alarm. Memes created by people promoting their own agenda convince us to ignore our innate suspicions by promising innovation. The reaction to both innovation and harmful memes is physical, in which our body becomes anxious and alarmed in preparing for a potential threat from the unfamiliar.

For example, the initial attraction of modernist architecture in the 1920s was its claim of "a liberation from the oppressive hegemony of Traditional Architecture" (and, by implication, from all tradition). But then, when people actually moved into modernist apartment houses, they realized that the promised liberation was a myth, and the apartments were cheaply built, unrelentingly dull, difficult to heat or keep cool, low-ceilinged, and had awkwardly placed windows and impossibly cramped kitchens.

The meme's encapsulation was then changed to: "the modern architecture is hygienic and promotes better health". That was enough to last for a while, until people realized that this, too, was untrue. It was then the turn of: "the modern architecture represents the latest engineering results applied to buildings". The industrial materials promoted, however, were more expensive and less durable than traditional materials. But there was a fetish with the new (in the 1920s) industrial materials, while mass production fit ideologically with many social agendas of the time (Chapter 10).

These encapsulations have been extremely successful, and continue to be employed by today's architectural memes. Some more recent meme encapsulations include slogans such as: "free curves liberate us from the restrictive architecture of cubes and right angles"; and "contemporary mathematics of chaos and fractals decrees that we should build broken forms". The latter is, of course, entirely unfounded, but both meme encapsulations help to promote contemporary building styles.

And yet, buildings that do not adapt to their human users; that ignore local traditions; and that refuse to use local materials turn out to be excessively costly, alien to local culture, and often dysfunctional (Salingaros, 2004). *Their only reason for existence is to realize an architectural meme.* Those memes are so deeply imbedded in the emotional portion of our brain that it is extremely difficult to get rid of them. Suggesting to architects that these ideals are actually meme encapsulations representing clever deceptions creates panic; the whole concept of modernity and social progress suddenly appears to be at stake. This emotional reaction is a testament to the effectiveness of the memes' encapsulation.

The situation is artificial, but totally unlike the analogous world of computer viruses, where everyone agrees on the label for a virus. A computer virus damages a computer system, and its creator is punishable by law. The community acts together to identify, tag, and rid infected computers of the virus as rapidly as possible. By contrast, advertising, architectural, and political memes are actively promoted by their respective established industries (although usually created by individuals as those who write computer viruses). We accept those memes because they are intentionally (though deceptively) tagged as "beneficial". In a curious reversal of roles, individuals who question this deception are the ones ostracized by the establishment.

8. SOME ARCHITECTURAL MEMES.

The undeniable success of twentieth-century architectural movements poses difficult explanatory problems. Starting from early modernism, architectural memes have been extraordinarily successful, winning over a determined group of followers. Nowadays, the deconstructivist movement and its ethereal, blob-like successors are in vogue in the architectural world. I have argued elsewhere that modernism and its postmodernist mutations (which include deconstructivism) are opposed to what is naturally preferred by people (Salingaros, 2004). That makes the reasons for those styles' success even more mysterious.

Distinct families of architectural memes began to be created by architects starting at the beginning of the twentieth century. All of these informational viruses share common characteristics, yet by now define a broad range of visually different styles. It would be useful to have a taxonomy of architectural memes available, showing how one strain evolved from another, and also noting which meme crossed over from another discipline such as philosophy or politics into architecture (analogous to biological viruses transferring from animals to humans). It is not the aim of this Chapter, however, to systematically classify the known architectural memes. Some obvious examples can be described as follows:

Table 12.2. Some Common Architectural Memes.

(1) *Dominance of the large scale.* When the largest scale is dominant, there are no visible differentiations on any lower scale. This meme generates smooth, "pure" forms, with either plane or curved surfaces. This meme is also called "hierarchy reversal".

(2) *Empty modules.* When these are joined together, the whole shows no substructure. This is the ancestral meme for plate-glass walls, reflective metal sheets, and flat, smooth, prefabricated concrete panels.

(3) *No thick boundaries.* Walls just end in a sharp edge, without a proper boundary. No wide differentiation frames a structural element. Columns end abruptly instead of having a differentiating capital and base.

(4) *Severe geometry.* This meme contradicts the often very relaxed rectangular forms of traditional architecture, but also its rounded forms, whose curvature arises out of the geometry. Normally, tectonic needs are expressed in terms of arches and vaults, by a curvature that is tied to symmetry and to the rectangularity of the rest of the building. In traditional architecture, we find curved scales that facilitate human actions and sensibilities superimposed on forms that may be rectangular on another scale. Many borders are frequently curved. Two very different methods oppose this natural geometry: strict rectangular edges and corners with an unnecessary precision eliminate all curvature; or, abandoning a rectangular geometry altogether, edges and corners are made as sharp and obtrusive as possible, using acute angles.

(5) *Warped geometry.* Going further and abandoning linearity, rounded edges and corners avoid any straight lines, with an overall building form made to look like a free-flowing sculpture for no structural reason.

Obviously, these five methods of opposing the geometry attached to traditional architecture also contradict each other, but what they have in common, which is their goal, is to force the natural geometry that arises out of tectonic needs. Sometimes, all the methods are used together, applied to different sections of a contemporary building. Some of these architectural memes are illustrated here (see Figure 12.1).

These are just a few of the very powerful visual memes that have been evolving since the early 1920s. The point I wish to make is that there is absolutely no practical or even aesthetic reason to adopt any one of them, and many reasoning architects have argued that they degrade the life, utility, and structural qualities of a building.

The memes described here come from political ideology, and have nothing whatsoever to do with satisfying people's architectural needs. For example, the meme for curtain walls is linked to freedom. Modernist texts of the 1920s talk about how to liberate the human spirit by using glass as a construction material. A manifestly false idea "transparency = liberation" has nevertheless very attractive iconic and ideological properties. It became almost a fetish. Considering the times in which it was born (revolutionary movements; crumbling traditional power elites), this meme relied on very strong social forces for a boost. After it was adopted by society, it became a central credo of contemporary architecture, even as its initial (fabricated) justification was forgotten.

Another meme is responsible for eliminating all ornament from architecture. It is also deeply-rooted in modernist ideology. Dating from 1908, this meme propagates the identification "empty surfaces = intellectual progress". Its roots are to be found in a confused jumble of ideas about industrial production and the role of artisan handcrafts in an ideally egalitarian society. Supposedly, architectural ornament wastes money and can be afforded only by the rich elite, so we should ban it altogether and thus bring all architecture down to the level affordable by the common factory worker. This meme has acquired an enormous dominance because of the negative but catchy slogan: "ornament = crime". Today, nobody thinks that this statement has any truth in it, but it is too late, since the meme has long ago been incorporated into the collective architectural subconscious.

It is easy to see how these architectural memes have found an ideal new ecosystem in the universe of information. For example, digital models of buildings on a computer screen show only the largest scales. The software itself works by filling within fixed edges as smoothly as possible, and so naturally generates smooth surfaces. Columns and walls are mathematically simplest to extend linearly until they come up against another structure. The simplest drawing algorithms, therefore, support the first three architectural memes listed above (Table 12.2). Memes (4) and (5), also in the above list, compete with each other in the universe of information, representing extreme departures in opposite directions away from normal tectonic forms that arise from using traditional building materials.

Figure (12.1)
Some architectural memes, principally
from the modernist style. No attempt is
made to classify them, nor to show their
evolution.

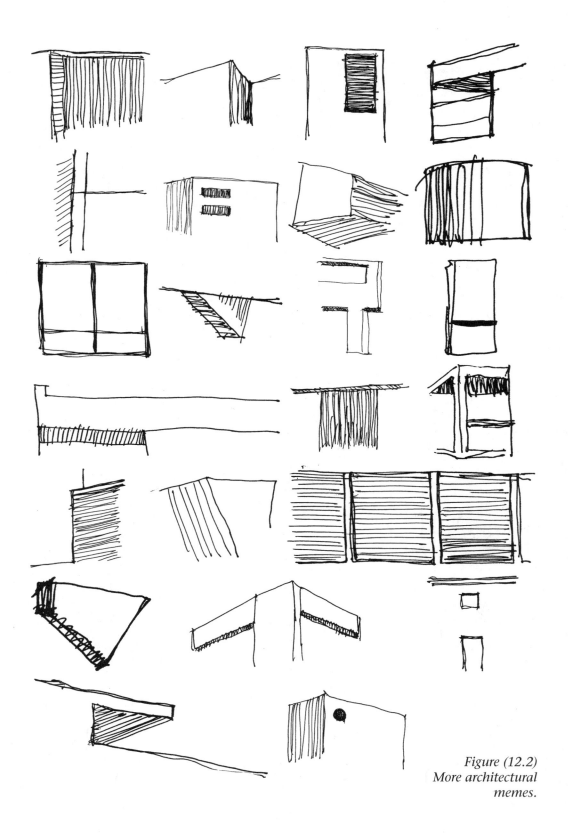

Figure (12.2)
More architectural
memes.

As long as one builds with natural materials, which are ultimately fragile or available in modules of small size, one is forced to adopt a particular geometry so that the building doesn't fall down. The structure is, in part, a solution to the problems of erecting a building against the gravitational force and physical stresses. This naturally imposes a restricted vocabulary of forms. The nature of the materials defines a *form language*, which generates a spectrum of possible structures: walls of a roughly rectangular geometry; vaults; columns; arches, etc. (see Chapter 11). A column's capital and base are necessary for tectonic reasons when one builds with traditional materials. A few non-traditional *form languages* were developed that extend and enrich traditional *form languages*, using industrial materials.

Modernist and postmodernist architecture is a reaction against the geometrical restrictions of traditional buildings. At the same time, many contemporary buildings in a traditional style are in fact memes — because they are expressed with industrial materials that do not define the vocabulary of traditional forms. They are images that are entirely independent of tectonic forces and thus falsify the *form language* they are superficially expressing. What interests me in this Chapter, however, is the expression of images that have no reason for being other than their opposition to traditional forms: visual memes motivated by an anti-traditionalist ideology.

9. MONSTERS AND ROBOTS.

In a few science-fiction films, an extraterrestrial alien or virus invades a human's memory, replacing it with copies of itself, or with instructions to produce copies of the alien. This is precisely the action of certain biological parasites that invade a host's brain, then direct the organism to self-destruction in a way that completes the parasite's reproductive cycle. In contemporary society, our own technologies are playing the same invasive role of replacing our neural memory banks within our brains. As Dyens states: "Machines control our memories, they own the fundamental materials that shape us, and they manage the structures that generate human meaning and perspective." (Dyens, 2001; page 38).

Ironically, humankind has feared the possibility of intelligent, emotionless robots running amok. The danger is instead realized from within our own species, from humans merging with the universe of information. It is not mechanical robots that we have to fear, but human beings conditioned to act in an unfeeling manner, like intelligent robots (the opposite to the dumb, mobile robots we are now building). Throughout history, human beings have been indoctrinated through psychological conditioning so as to block their primary sensory brain circuits, leaving only the higher-level circuits operational. Those persons are only partially connected to their environment. By intentionally blocking their lower-level circuits in the intelligence hierarchy, we have created unemotional "human machines" operating with the intellectual capacity that can easily be turned to destruction.

Individuals whose memory has been replaced by memes can be effective in unpleasant or dangerous tasks. They are indeed examples of the ideological "modern man", produced for industrial purposes. Such persons can be directed to erect and inhabit discomforting structures: something any human being with keenly-developed feelings finds emotionally and physiologically difficult. They can also be directed to destroy. Programmed individuals have no qualms about destroying living structure in nature, and the living structure present in what other human beings have painstakingly produced before them.

Normally, objects, creations, and built environments embodying organized complexity are emotionally nourishing to our senses; so much so that it is painful to eliminate them. Cultural memory encompasses those artifacts that harbor an organized complexity which is very close to both biological and inanimate natural structures. Persons who are not otherwise programmed by visual memes feel an intimate rapport with such artifacts and with nature. Victims of this programming promoted by the media — human beings conditioned to follow industrial and postindustrial fashions without reflection — are largely detached from this complexity, however, and have also been detached in a fundamental way from their surroundings. They are ideal occupants for towers of apartments or offices that are the twisted skyscrapers in the latest architectural style.

The ungrounded "modern man" continues to play an active role in transforming our world. He is in part the product of a co-evolution between human beings and memes of the postindustrial culture. For those of us who might not like what humankind is evolving towards, we need to understand this process before attempting to influence it.

10. KNOWLEDGE VERSUS INFORMATION.

Human intelligence is dependent upon evolutionary development of the brain/sensory system. The brain and sensory systems co-evolved in a hierarchy of layers. The older (lower) layers act to give an instantaneous response to stimuli in the environment (Chapter 4). Input and output get more and more sophisticated with additional layers, with more computing power being expended to interpret stimuli, and more processing before output. Finally, we acquired the conscious processing and analysis of thoughts that distinguish human beings from other animals. This layering corresponds pretty well to what we know as the anatomical layers of the evolved brain. The higher levels are either missing in the lower animals, or they are present in significantly lesser quantities, showing a remarkable growth and development in humans.

The complexity of modern life produces huge amounts of information that we must somehow deal with. Actual mastery of the material relevant to building becomes very difficult. Immediate availability through computer networks of everything anyone's ever said or done, on any topic whatever, exacerbates the problem. We have a plethora of information, and so have become ever more dependent on "experts" who select which of this information we should be exposed to; because it is physically impossible for us to wade through all of it. The situation, therefore, is ultimately no different than in ages when information was not freely available, and an authority controlled the information to be released. The only difference now is that, once individuals locate the right sort of information, the situation can be reversed almost overnight, and the control of the "experts" thrown out.

Central to my thesis is the recognition that culture evolves in a positive direction by organizing complex information that connects us to the real world. Increasing the number of connections among informational entities leads to greater complexity, and thus it becomes necessary to organize that complexity into a comprehensible (hierarchical) system. The opposite process, usually leading to retrogression, consists of losing both complexity and organization — losing information that has been painstakingly gathered and organized as human knowledge, or losing the connective structure that makes it accessible.

The majority of memes are harmful because they replace the complexity of the universe and the relations we establish with our world, with a false, disconnected reality. Memes carry very few connections, and those they do have are meaningless, which moreover prevents the creation of true connections necessary to our understanding of the world. While it is true that memes always coexist with knowledge, they represent a useless wiring of the network forming our knowledge base.

This fundamental problem was already addressed by the architect Christopher Alexander. He tried to identify true architectural knowledge in recognizing patterns that recur throughout the history of humanity and all over the planet (Alexander et. al., 1977). These patterns organize our treatment of built space and our relationship to it. Alexander decided to make explicit knowledge that up to that time had been only implicit, and to do this in a way that would suspend the propagation of non-adaptive or idiosyncratic notions about architecture. Since the beginning of the twentieth century, unfounded ideas have governed the construction of buildings and cities (which I have described in this Chapter as an invasion by harmful memes). In explaining this stock of architectural knowledge, Alexander chose to also describe the specific manner in which information is organized: a "pattern language" is a hierarchical informational structure (Salingaros, 2000) composed of relatively autonomous patterns connected as follows: (1) to each other on different hierarchical levels; (2) to the physical and biological world as well as to patterns of living appropriate to distinct human civilizations; and (3) to the totality of human knowledge, empirical, scientific, and metaphysical.

Each pattern is presented as a process of resolving a recurring architectural problem: the relationship between a certain context, the forces that recur in this context, and a spatial configuration that permits these forces to resolve themselves (Alexander, 1979). This allows designers, builders, and inhabitants to discuss collectively what can serve as architectural patterns and models. Altogether, this method gives rise to results that constitute genuine architectural knowledge.

The tool of pattern languages has been enthusiastically adopted by the Computer Science community to handle the structure and production of increasingly complex software (Gabriel, 1996). These practitioners define, in addition to patterns, the concept of an "antipattern", which is a false solution that is nevertheless reutilized (see Chapter 11). An antipattern possesses formal characteristics that trick whoever adopts it into thinking that it is the result of a logical development. There is in fact no difference between an antipattern and a meme.

Knowledge is fragile and much less prolific than raw information, depending as it does on discovery and confirmation. By contrast, informational junk can be generated in any context, and in any quantity. Traditional stores of knowledge represent customary wisdom. I am referring, in particular, to knowledge and beliefs that are not scientifically verifiable, yet are in fact necessary for the proper working of human society, and even to maintain scientific knowledge. Belief systems cannot be justified in the way science can be justified; they rely on informal connections, practices, and understandings.

There is a value and meaning in the highest of human creations as opposed to their raw information content. Bach's *Saint Matthew Passion* is worth far more to civilization than two-and-one-half hours of television soap operas interspersed with commercials. I know that post-structuralist philosophers have tried to argue the opposite, but I believe they are terribly mistaken. Ultimately, we will have to appeal to the value of information so as to distinguish between memes (beneficial and harmful) and true knowledge.

11. CONCLUSION.

Human beings can recognize intuitively elements of their world and the connections that unite them to it. Sensory and mental connections occur almost instantly. This innate ability enabled us to survive and evolve. More advanced problem solving, however, entails a stepwise process that establishes a sequence of transformations from the problem to its solution. The alternative to intelligent design is unreasoned matching to some given visual or mnemonic prototype — a meme.

In that case, there is no transformation nor adaptation to the criteria of the problem. A generic solution is given by visual memes, which are thereby imposed on the situation. The method is now one of substitution instead of resolution. Memes replace the constraints of the problem by visual images. This requires no intellectual effort; only the acceptance of an image provided by somebody for whatever reason. By replacing the sequence of adaptive design steps, one is in fact suppressing in part the mechanisms for intelligent thought in general. This can lead people to live in a false reality; such as is accomplished by psychological conditioning.

One's internal world-view can be replaced entirely by a set of memes. These will then define an alternative, abstract universe for that particular individual. As our society is living more and more in the universe of information, the dangers of altering one's internal reality multiply with the number of memes around us. Whereas in the past, one would normally worry only about particularly virulent cults, advertising, and political campaigns, today we are immersed in a virtual universe of memes that can very easily substitute for the physical universe. It's like an alternative religion. In this final Chapter, I tried to point out some features of this interdependence, and to focus on the dangers posed by architectural memes freely propagating in the universe of information.

CREDITS

Chapter 1
THE LAWS OF ARCHITECTURE FROM A PHYSICIST'S PERSPECTIVE
Original version published in *Physics Essays*, volume 8, number 4 (1995), pages 638-643. Reprinted by permission of Physics Essays Publications. Spanish version published in *El Hombre y la Máquina*, number 16 (April 2001), pages 12-23.

Chapter 2
A SCIENTIFIC BASIS FOR CREATING ARCHITECTURAL FORMS
Original version published in *Journal of Architectural and Planning Research*, volume 15, number 4 (1998), pages 283-293. Copyright, Locke Science Publishing Company, Inc. Reproduced with permission.

Chapter 3
HIERARCHICAL COOPERATION IN ARCHITECTURE:
THE MATHEMATICAL NECESSITY FOR ORNAMENT
Original version published in *Journal of Architectural and Planning Research,* volume 17, number 3 (2000), pages 221-235. Copyright, Locke Science Publishing Company, Inc. Reproduced with permission. French version published in *Revue BénéFique (Lyon)*, volume 2 (2002), pages 151-174.

Chapter 4
THE SENSORY VALUE OF ORNAMENT
Originally published in *Communication & Cognition*, volume 36, number 3/4 (2003), pages 331-351. Reprinted by permission.

Chapter 5
LIFE AND COMPLEXITY IN ARCHITECTURE
FROM A THERMODYNAMIC ANALOGY
Original version published in *Physics Essays*, volume 10 (1997), pages 165-173. Reprinted in: Uta Wolf, *Chasing Butterflies: The Patterns of Chaos Theory and the Built Environment*, University of Westminster, London, 2002, pages 63-74. Reprinted here by permission of Physics Essays Publications. Results of this Chapter are reproduced in Appendix 6 of Christopher Alexander's *The Nature of Order, Book 1*, pages 469-472 (Alexander, 2004).

Chapter 6
ARCHITECTURE, PATTERNS, AND MATHEMATICS
Original version published in *Nexus Network Journal*, volume 1 (1999), pages 75-85. Reprinted in *Any Architect* (March 2004). Reprinted here by permission of Kim Williams Books.

Chapter 7
PAVEMENTS AS EMBODIMENTS OF MEANING FOR A FRACTAL MIND.
By Terry M. Mikiten, Nikos A. Salingaros, and Hing-Sing Yu
Originally published in *Nexus Network Journal*, volume 2 (2000), pages 63-74. Reprinted by permission of Kim Williams Books.

Chapter 8
MODULARITY AND THE NUMBER OF DESIGN CHOICES.
By Nikos A. Salingaros and Débora M. Tejada
Originally published in *Nexus Network Journal*, volume 3, number 1 (2001), pages 99-109. Reprinted by permission of Kim Williams Books.

Chapter 9
GEOMETRICAL FUNDAMENTALISM.
By Michael W. Mehaffy and Nikos A. Salingaros
Originally published in *Plan Net Online Architectural Resources* (January 2002). Italian version published in *L'Inventario della Fierucola* (Florence), number 24-25-26 (August 2003), pages 24-38.

Chapter 10
DARWINIAN PROCESSES AND MEMES IN ARCHITECTURE:
A MEMETIC THEORY OF MODERNISM.
By Nikos A. Salingaros and Terry M. Mikiten
Originally published in *Journal of Memetics — Evolutionary Models of Information Transmission*, volume 6 (2002). Reprinted in *DATUTOP Journal of Architectural Theory*, volume 23 (2002), pages 117-139. Reprinted here by permission.

Chapter 11
TWO LANGUAGES FOR ARCHITECTURE
Original version published in *Plan Net Online Architectural Resources* (February 2003). Reprinted in: A. Giangrande & E. Mortola, Editors, *Architettura, Comunità e Partecipazione: Quale Linguaggio?*, Università Degli Studi Roma Tre — Facoltà di Architettura (Aracne Editrice, Rome, Italy, 2003), pages 41-45.

Chapter 12
ARCHITECTURAL MEMES IN A UNIVERSE OF INFORMATION
Original version published in both English and French in *Mondes Francophones* (February 2006).

GLOSSARY

Abelian Group Z_2. The simplest collection of elements, consisting of a single 0 and a single 1. Mathematical Groups in general have many more elements, and much more complex relations among those elements.

achromatopsia. Color blindness.

adaptive design method. A method that uses feedback to satisfy human physical and emotional well-being.

agnosia. Pathology of the brain that prevents visual understanding, even though the image is perceived.

Alexandrine pattern. A recurring architectural solution that combines geometry with social practices. For example: "a comfortable room needs light from two sides".

algorithm. A mathematical rule that computes something.

algorithmic continuity. A mathematical rule that can compute many different things. This is the opposite of needing many different rules for different parts of the same computation.

antipattern. A mistaken architectural solution that nevertheless gets repeated from ingrained custom.

architectural complexity. Term defined here to denote the degree of disorganized complexity in a building or structure. A high degree of architectural complexity comes from having many different components that interact randomly, and cannot be organized.

architectural entropy. A measure of the degree of visual disorder. Entropy measures disorder in physical systems.

architectural harmony. Term defined here to denote the degree of cooperation among components of a larger whole. It is achieved by having visual connections and symmetries.

architectural life. Term defined here to denote the degree of organized complexity in a building or structure. A high degree of architectural life comes from having many smaller components that interact and are highly organized.

architectural meme. A very simple visual component, such as a flat square panel or shiny metal tube, that sticks in memory and turns up in one's designs unconsciously.

architectural temperature. Term defined here to denote the visual intensity. Increases with increasing detail, color contrast, and curvature.

Art Deco. Architectural style popular from 1925, marked by ornament combined with surface richness. The term was actually coined by Le Corbusier, who used it pejoratively.

Art Nouveau. Curved and richly-colored architectural style practiced at the end of the 19th century and beginning of the 20th century by Victor Horta, Louis Sullivan, Hector Guimard, Antoni Gaudí, and others.

associative memory. When one event triggers the recall of another event.

Beaux-Arts. Nineteenth-Century European architectural style.

bilateral symmetry. Reflectional or mirror symmetry.

bulk function. Quantity that characterizes an entire volume.

Cantor pattern. A fractal pattern that looks like a dotted line.

Cartesian grid. Rectangular orthogonal grid.

cerebral cortex. The main upper part of the brain.

Classical. Architectural style that relies upon the Greek and Roman typologies.

classical physics. Physical knowledge up to the beginning of the twentieth century.

co-evolution. Two entities evolving together, each influencing the other's development.

cognitive binding. Occurs when our senses produce a resonant state in our perception.

cognitive rules. How human beings perceive their world and make sense of that information.

coherence. Observable state where all components come together in balance, and support one-another.

coincident scales. Two different sets of design elements that happen to have the same size.

color constancy. The ability of the human eye to adjust perceived color despite to-tally different illumination; i.e., a tomato appears red in widely varying light conditions.

combinatorial, combinatoric. Process whereby pieces can be put together in many different ways.

complexity overhead. (See **informational overhead**).

complexity theory. What we understand about the structure of systems that have many interacting components.

compression. Term used in this book to denote squeezing together information so that it takes up less volume.

constraint. Mathematical condition that must be satisfied.

crystal lattice. The atoms of crystals lie in an ordered, regular pattern, which gives the crystal its visible symmetries.

Darwinian process. A technique that generates alternatives, then selects from among them.

dendritic. Branching into smaller and smaller channels, just like a tree.

derivative. Mathematical term denoting the change in a quantity.

differential equations. Class of mathematical problems describing changing quantities.

discrete. Comes in different sizes, as opposed to a continuous distribution.

DNA. Organic molecule containing the genetic information in all organisms.

doped. Term used to denote a crystal containing intentional impurities.

ecosystem. Collection of organisms that live together, compete with each other, and rely upon one-another for food.

electron. Elementary particle that circles around the nucleus to create an atom.

emergence. A process by which many pieces put together interact to endow a com-plex system with new and sometimes unexpected properties.

emergent properties. Observable properties of a complex system that result from its complexity, and which are not present in the individual parts.

encapsulation. Packaging. Used here to denote an idea that envelops another idea.

end-stopped neuron. Brain cell that responds when we see lines up to a given length, but not longer.

entasis. Subtle curvature in Classical Greek architecture that corrects for optical illusions, making a building appear straight.

enthalpy. Physical term measuring heat energy.

entropy. Physical term denoting the degree of disorder and randomness in an ensemble.

Expressionism. Architectural style characterized by flowing curves, practiced by Erich Mendelsohn and others.

factorial. Product of all integers up to that number, e.g. 5! = 120.

Fallacy of Misplaced Concreteness. Effect proposed by the philosopher Alfred North Whitehead, in which an imagined concept replaces the real world in one's mind.

fermion. Class of elementary subatomic particles that includes the electron and proton. Fermions can only be paired if they have opposite properties, otherwise they repel each other.

Fibonacci sequence. 1, 1, 2, 3, 5, 8, 13, 21, 34, 55, ... in which the next term is the sum of the two previous terms.

form language. A collection of forms, designs, surfaces, and a way of putting them together to make a building. The components of a design style.

fractal. Design or physical structure that shows detail at every magnification. A self-similar fractal is similar at every magnification, whereas a statistically self-similar fractal need not be. Because of their substructure on all scales, fractals are not smooth, and so appear as broken or jagged.

fractal approximation. Combining smaller and smaller copies of the same unit to represent a complex object.

fractal dimension. A straight line has dimension one. A fractal line has dimension slightly greater than one, since it fills in a little area next to it.

fractal encoding. Representing a complex pattern using a fractal, which relies on a simple rule to generate its different components.

Fractal Image Compression (FIC). Data compression scheme used in computing, which uses similarity of a picture at different scales to reduce the size of the electronic file.

fractal simplicity. Complex-looking fractal patterns are actually very simple, because they can be generated by a simple rule.

fractal structure. Observed structure that has either of the two fractal properties: not smooth anywhere; and recursion at different magnifications.

fractal tuning. Acceptance of a complex signal by a receiver that depends upon it having a particular fractal structure.

genetic. Information that an organism uses to build itself.

geometrical fundamentalism. The overly narrow and excessive reliance on pure geometric solids such as cubes, cylinders, and rectangular slabs for design

geometrical meme. A very simple image of a structural component, such as a corner, edge, or surface, which is easy to remember.

geometric self-similarity. Things that look the same when scaled up or down.

Gestalt Laws. Laws on how we perceive forms, derived in psychology.

glide symmetry. When a design repeats after being moved in one direction, then reflected in an orthogonal (perpendicular) direction.

Golden Mean. 1.618...

Graphics Interchange Format (GIF). Computer encoding of images, widely used for the World-Wide Web.

hardwired. Circuit fixed in advance by our biology, and thus not modifiable.

hierarchical coherence. Property of a system with many different scales that are all connected to form a coherent whole.

hierarchical cooperation. Visual state resulting when the different scales in a structure or pattern link to each other to create a unified whole.

hierarchical linking. Mechanism that relates two or more different scales.

hierarchical organization. Property where several different scales are connected.

hierarchical scaling. Obvious similarity for forms on different scales.

hierarchical system. A collection of interacting components that have different sizes.

hierarchy. An ordering of elements according to their size: either large to small, or small to large.

hierarchy reversal. Design trick where things that ought to be small are made large, thus reversing the natural hierarchy.

homogeneous. Lacking internal differentiations.

homogenization. Process of making something homogeneous.

ideal number of scales. Formula that computes a number for how many distinct scales (well-defined sizes of components) there should be in a building.

informational overhead. Structure other than the minimum genetic information that any organism needs to survive and reproduce.

integration. Mathematical term denoting the combining of information to get a result.

International Style. Rectangular modernist buildings in concrete, glass, and steel.

isospin. Quantity related to the electric charge that distinguishes the proton from the neutron.

iteration, iterative. An operation applied repeatedly to get better and better results.

Koch pattern. A fractal pattern that looks like a snowflake.

living environments. Metaphorical term used to denote building or urban spaces which feel "alive", and which make a user feel "alive".

macroscopic. Visible size, as opposed to microscopic.

macula. Central and most sensitive region of the eye's retina.

Mandelbrot set. A particular fractal pattern.

meaning structure. Related thoughts and memories that allow us to understand a concept.

meme. A snippet of information: visual, musical, written, or spoken. It could be an advertising image, an advertising jingle, or a recurring architectural image.

meme attachment. Process by which a meme attaches itself to human memory.

meme encapsulation. A shell surrounding a meme that endows it with different properties. An attractive shell can encapsulate a harmful meme, just as a noxious shell can be made to encapsulate a beneficial meme, making it unattractive.

meme propagation. The spread of a meme among people's minds.

meme propagation factor. Condition that helps in transmitting a meme among different human minds.

memetic transmission. The process by which memes (ideas, images, fragments of tunes) cross from one human mind to another.

metabolic, metabolism. The process by which an organism ingests food, converts it to useful components, and gets energy from it as well.

meta-language. The general linguistic structure that is ancestral to all spoken languages.

metaphor. Use of a word to describe something totally different, but which suggests a resemblance.

microscopic. Too small to be visible.

modernism, modernist. Broad architectural style defined by the Bauhaus, and practiced by Le Corbusier, Ludwig Mies van der Rohe, Walter Gropius, and others.

modern physics. Knowledge of matter, such as quantum mechanics and relativity, developed after the beginning of the twentieth century.

modular design. System of design which uses the same repeating unit.

modularity. Property of system that can be decomposed into modules, or, conversely, can be built up from modules.

module. In systems theory, a module is a semi-independent unit that contains a certain amount of complexity. In architecture, a module is understood as a building component that comes in a standard size.

monumentality. Architectural expression of grandeur, requiring large buildings and spaces.

motor system. Biological term for the parts of the brain and nerves that control muscles and movement.

multiplicity rule. A rule for the distribution of sizes found throughout nature and artificial complex systems, requiring a system to have only very few components of large size, several components of intermediate size, and very many in a spectrum of smaller sizes.

natural scaling hierarchy. Visual system where component sizes increase or decrease by a factor of approximately 2.7.

neuron. Nerve cell in the brain responsible for thinking, memory, visualization, etc. Neurons throughout the body outside the brain transmit information to the brain's neurons.

neutron. Elementary subatomic particle that forms part of each atomic nucleus.

nucleon. General term for the two elementary subatomic particles that form the atomic nucleus. The two nucleons, the proton and the neutron, look almost the same except for having a different electrical charge.

organized complexity. A state where a complex system is linked internally to a very large degree.

ornament. Mathematical expression of design, usually encoding lots of visible information.

paradigm. Conceptual and logical basis for understanding a topic.

parallel architecture, parallel computer. Many smaller computers linked together to work simultaneously on one problem.

pattern. This could be a visual pattern, or an Alexandrine pattern, which is a recurring architectural solution that combines some geometrical guidelines with social practices.

pattern language. A set of Alexandrine patterns that allows their combination to help design human environments.

pattern recognition. Cognitive process whereby the human brain recognizes a mathematical pattern.

Peano pattern. A fractal pattern in mathematics that looks like a lattice.

perceptual binding. (See **cognitive binding**).

percolation. Passing slowly through a filter.

pion. An elementary subatomic particle that intermediates the force which binds the atomic nucleus together.

Platonic solids. Sphere, cylinder, cube, etc.

point function. Quantity that varies from point to point.

polynomial. Mathematical function with a curved graph.

problem space. All possible variant solutions to a problem, or different ways the problem can be posed, viewed as points belonging to some abstract space.

proton. Elementary subatomic particle that forms part of each atomic nucleus.

quantized, quantum. Term from physics denoting quantities that come only in discrete sizes or values.

quantum electrodynamics, quantum mechanics. A branch of physics that studies fundamental interactions on the subatomic scale, which lie at the basis of electricity and atomic structure.

recursion, recursive. A process that can occur over and over, each time building upon what it did the previous time.

reductionist, reductive. Overly simplistic approach that loses the essential qualities of a complex phenomenon.

reflectional symmetry. When half a design is the same as the other half: it could look like its reflection in a mirror.

replication, reproduction. The process whereby one object or organism makes many copies of itself.

rotational symmetry. When a design repeats or is the same if it is rotated by a given angle.

scale. A measurement that is defined by physical elements all of that size.

scaling coherence. Property of a design in which all its different scales are tied together visually.

scaling hierarchy. A sequence of different scales in a building or structure, arranged from small to large, or large to small.

scaling ratio. In two designs that are similar but of different scale, this is the magnification factor.

scaling rule. Rule proposed here saying that consecutive scales in a design should be related by the same ratio.

scaling similarity, scaling symmetry. Property of two designs where one is a scaled-up copy of the other.

selection. The process of choosing among options by using a set of criteria.

self-organization. Process by which a system achieves spontaneous order.

self-similar fractal. Fractal structure that shows exactly the same design at each magnification.

self-similarity. Property of a design that looks the same at each magnification.

short-range force. A force that holds two elements when they are very close together, but has no effect if they are separated by a large distance.

similarity ratio. Specific ratio needed to magnify a picture so that the pattern looks the same.

similarity transformation. Scaling up a design.

solution space. All possible solutions to a design problem imagined as dots in some abstract space.

spatial coherence. Property of a structure or environment that makes it appear coherent.

Spinor group in n dimensions. A mathematical set of elements that obey complex interrelations among themselves. Used in this book as an example of a complex system.

statistical. Quantity that is measured by means of averaging different information rather than by a single measurement.

structural order. The result of many different mechanisms that make a structure internally coherent, not in an abstract sense, but as perceived by a human being.

supercooled. Liquid that is hard, like common glass, but has not crystallized.

surface design. Visual information on surface.

symbiosis. Biological term denoting the mutually-beneficial coexistence of two different organisms.

symmetries. Any recurrence of a portion of a design, such as through reflection, rotation, translation, etc.

syntactical rules. Rules for grammatical ordering in a language.

system. A combination of components that interact to work together.

systems theory. What we know about the structure and workings of complex systems.

Taylor series. Mathematical approximation that sums smaller and smaller corrections.

tectonic structure. The components that make a building stand as a solid structure.

thermodynamic model. Introduced in this book to measure the degree of organized complexity in a building by using an analogy with thermodynamics.

thermodynamic potential. Quantity that characterizes a physical system.

thermodynamics. A branch of physics that studies heat, energy, disorder, crystallization, etc.

transfinite numbers. Branch of mathematics that studies different sizes of infinities.

transitive relation. If A connects to B, and B connects to C, then A connects to C.

translational symmetry. When a design repeats in one direction after a given distance.

travertine. Textured crystalline limestone that is close to marble.

triangle classification. Introduced here to plot all architectural styles in history together.

vacuum. In the physics of elementary particles, a vacuum is not empty, but consists of mutually annihilating virtual electron-positron pairs (which we never see).
visual coherence. Property of a design or structure that makes it appear unified.
visual cortex. Part of the brain that is devoted to visual processing.

REFERENCES

Alexander, C. (1959) "Perception and Modular Co-ordination", *Journal of the Royal Institute of British Architects,* **66**, pp. 425-429.

Alexander, C. (1964) *Notes on the Synthesis of Form* (Harvard University Press, Cambridge, Massachusetts).

Alexander, C. (1979) *The Timeless Way of Building* (Oxford University Press, New York).

Alexander, C. (1984) "Sketches of a New Architecture", in: *Architecture in an Age of Scepticism,* edited by D. Lasdun (Oxford University Press, New York), pp. 8-27.

Alexander, C. (1993) *A Foreshadowing of 21st Century Art* (Oxford University Press, New York).

Alexander, C. (2004) *The Nature of Order* (Center for Environmental Structure, Berkeley, California).

Alexander, C., Anninou, A., Black, G. & Rheinfrank, J. (1987) "Towards a Personal Workplace", *Architectural Record Interiors,* **Mid-September**, pp. 131-141.

Alexander, C., Fisher, T. & Freiman, Z. (1991) "The Real Meaning of Architecture" *Progressive Architecture,* **7.91**, (July), pp. 100-112.

Alexander, C., Ishikawa, S., Silverstein, M., Jacobson, M., Fiksdahl-King, I. & Angel, S. (1977) *A Pattern Language* (Oxford University Press, New York).

Alexander, D. M. & Globus, G. G. (1996) "Edge-of-Chaos Dynamics in Recursively Organized Neural Systems", in: *Fractals of Brain, Fractals of Mind*, edited by E. MacCormac & M. I. Stamenov (John Benjamins, Amsterdam), pp. 31-73.

Allen, T. F. H. & Starr, T. B. (1982) *Hierarchy: Perspectives for Ecological Complexity* (University of Chicago Press, Chicago).

Archer, L. B. (1970) "An Overview of the Structure of the Design Process", in: *Emerging Methods in Environmental Design and Planning*, edited by G. T. Moore (MIT Press Cambridge, Massachusetts), pp. 285-305. Earlier version appeared in: *Design Methods in Architecture*, edited by G. Broadbent & A. Ward (Lund Humphries, London, 1969).

Ball, P. (1999) *The Self-Made Tapestry* (Oxford University Press, Oxford).

Barnsley, M. F. & Hurd, L. P. (1993) *Fractal Image Compression.* (A. K. Peters, Boston).

Batty, M. & Longley, P. (1994) *Fractal Cities* (Academic Press, London).

Bauman, Z. (2000) *Modernity and the Holocaust* (Cornell University Press, Ithaca, New York).

Benedikt, M. (1999) "Less for Less Yet", *Harvard Design Magazine,* **Winter/Spring 99**, pp. 10-14.

Blair, S. S. & Bloom, J. M. (1994) *The Art and Architecture of Islam 1250-1800* (Yale University Press, New Haven, Connecticut).

Blake, P. (1974) *Form Follows Fiasco* (Little, Brown and Co., Boston).

Bloomer, K. (2000) *The Nature of Ornament* (W. W. Norton, New York).

Bonta, J. P. (1979) *Architecture and Its Interpretation* (Rizzoli, New York).

Booch, G. (1991) *Object Oriented Design* (Benjamin/Cummings, Redwood City, California).

Bovill, C. (1996) *Fractal Geometry in Architecture and Design* (Birkhäuser, Boston).

Broadbent, G. (1973) *Design in Architecture* (John Wiley, London).

Broadbent, G. (1990) *Emerging Concepts in Urban Space Design* (Van Nostrand Reinhold, London).

Brodie, R. (1996) *Virus of the Mind* (Integral Press, Seattle, Washington).

Calvin, W. H. (1987) "The Brain as a Darwin Machine", *Nature*, **330**, pp. 33-34.

Calvin, W. H. (1990) *The Cerebral Symphony* (Bantam Books, New York).

Calvin, W. H. (1997) "The Six Essentials? Minimal Requirements for the Darwinian Bootstrapping of Quality", *Journal of Memetics: Evolutionary Models of Information Transmission*, **1**, approximately 7 pages.

Charles, Prince of Wales (1988) "Speeches on Architecture", in: *The Prince, the Architects, and New Wave Monarchy*, edited by C. Jencks (Rizzoli, New York).

Charles, Prince of Wales (1989) *A Vision of Britain: A Personal View of Architecture* (Doubleday, London).

Colomina, B. (1994) *Privacy and Publicity: Modern Architecture as Mass Media* (MIT Press, Cambridge, Massachusetts).

Conrads, U. (1964) *Programs and Manifestoes on 20th-century Architecture* (MIT Press, Cambridge, Massachusetts).

Crompton, A. (2002) "Fractals and Picturesque Composition", *Environment and Planning B*, **29**, pp. 451-459.

Cross, N. (1989) *Engineering Design Methods* (John Wiley, Chichester).

Darton, E. (2000) *Divided We Stand: A Biography of New York's World Trade Center* (Basic Books, New York).

Dawkins, R. (1989) *The Selfish Gene*, New Edition (Oxford University Press, Oxford), Chapter 11.

Dawkins, R. (1993) "Viruses of the Mind", in: *Dennett and His Critics*, edited by B. Dahlbom (Blackwell, Oxford), pp. 13-27.

Day, C. (1990) *Places of the Soul* (Aquarian Press, Wellingborough, England).

de Jong, M. (1999) "Survival of the Institutionally Fittest Concepts", *Journal of Memetics: Evolutionary Models of Information Transmission*, **3**, approximately 12 pages.

Dennett, D. C. (1995) *Darwin's Dangerous Idea* (Simon & Schuster, New York).

Dyens, O. (2001) *Metal and Flesh* (MIT Press, Cambridge, Massachusetts).

Dyson, F. (1999) *Origins of Life*, Revised Edition (Cambridge University Press, Cambridge).

Edelman, G. M. & Tononi, G. (2000) *A Universe of Consciousness* (Basic Books, New York).

Eilenberger, G. (1985) "Freedom, Science, and Aesthetics", in: *Frontiers of Chaos*, edited by H. O. Peitgen & P. H. Richter (MAPART, Forschungsgruppe Komplexe Dynamik der Universität Bremen, Germany), pp. 29-36.

Fiksdahl-King, I. (1993) "Christopher Alexander and Contemporary Architecture", *A+U — Architecture and Urbanism*, **Special Issue** (August).

Fischler, M. A. & Firschein, O. (1987) *Intelligence: The Eye, the Brain, and the Computer* (Addison-Wesley, Reading, Massachusetts).

Fisher, Y. (1995) *Fractal Image Compression* (Springer Verlag, New York).

Fletcher, Sir B. (1987) *A History of Architecture*, 19th Edition, edited by John Musgrove (Butterworths, London).

Frazier, N. (1991) *Louis Sullivan and the Chicago School* (Crescent Books, Avenel, New Jersey).

Frei, H. (1992) *Louis Henry Sullivan* (Artemis Verlag, Zurich).

Gabriel, R. (1996) *Patterns of Software* (Oxford University Press, New York).

Gehl, J. (1987) *Life Between Buildings* (Van Nostrand Reinhold, New York).

Gibson, J. J. (1979) *The Ecological Approach to Visual Perception* (Houghton Mifflin, Boston).

Goldberger, A. L. (1996) "Fractals and the Birth of Gothic: Reflections on the Biologic Basis of Creativity", *Molecular Psychiatry*, **1**, pp. 99-104.

Greenberg, M. (1995a) "Architecture: Can Laws Rule Beauty?", *San Antonio Express-News*, Sunday, October 15, page 1G.

Greenberg, M. (1995b) "Fixed Laws of Beauty Invite Debate", *San Antonio Express-News*, Sunday, October 22, page 1G.

Grünbaum, B. & Shephard, G. C. (1987) *Tilings and Patterns* (Freeman, New York).

Halliwell, J. (1995) "Arcadia, Anarchy, and Archetypes", *New Scientist*, **12** (August), pp. 34-38.

Haselberger, L. (1985) "The Construction Plans for the Temple of Apollo at Didyma", *Scientific American*, **253**, No. 6, pp. 126-132.

Heylighen, F. (1993) "Selection Criteria for the Evolution of Knowledge", in: *Proceedings of the 13th International Congress on Cybernetics* (Association International de Cybernétique, Namur, Belgium), pp. 524-528.

Heylighen, F. (1997) "Objective, Subjective and Intersubjective Selectors of Knowledge", *Evolution and Cognition*, **3**, pp. 63-67.

Hillier, B. (1996) *Space is the Machine* (Cambridge University Press, Cambridge).

Hillier, W. R. G. & Hanson, J. (1984) *The Social Logic of Space* (Cambridge University Press, Cambridge).

Hubel, D. H. (1988) *Eye, Brain, and Vision* (Scientific American Library, New York).

Hutchinson, G. E. (1959) "Homage to Santa Rosalia", *The American Naturalist*, **93**, pp. 145-159.

Jefimenko, O. D. (1989) *Electricity and Magnetism*, 2nd. Edition (Electret Scientific Co, Star City, W. Virginia), p. 493.

Johnson, S. (2004) *Mind Wide Open* (Scribner, New York); pp. 56-57.

Jones, J. C. (1970) *Design Methods* (John Wiley, Chichester, England).

Jordy, W. H. (1986) "The Tall Buildings", in: *Louis Sullivan: the Function of Ornament*, edited by W. de Wit (W. W. Norton & Co., New York).

Kauffman, S. (1995) *At Home in the Universe* (Oxford University Press, New York).

Klinger, A. & Salingaros, N. A. (2000) "A Pattern Measure", *Environment and Planning B: Planning and Design*, **27**, pp. 537-547.

Krier, L. (1998) *Architecture: Choice or Fate* (Andreas Papadakis, Windsor, Berkshire, England).

Kroll, L. (1987) *An Architecture of Complexity* (MIT Press, Cambridge, Massachusetts).

Küller, R. (1980) "Architecture and Emotions", in: *Architecture for People*, edited by B. Mikellides (Holt, Rinehart and Winston, New York), pp. 87-100.

Kunstler, J. H. (1993) *The Geography of Nowhere* (Touchstone, New York).

Lakoff, G. & Johnson, M. (1999) *Philosophy in the Flesh* (Basic Books, New York).

Lauwerier, H. (1991) *Fractals* (Princeton University Press, Princeton, New Jersey).

Le Corbusier (1927) *Towards a New Architecture* (Architectural Press, London). Original title: *Vers Une Architecture* (Editions Crès, Paris, 1923).

Le Corbusier (1987) *The City of Tomorrow and its Planning* (Dover, New York). Original title: *Urbanisme* (Editions Crés, Paris, 1924).

Levine, A. J. (1992) *Viruses* (Scientific American Library, New York).

Licklider, H. (1966) *Architectural Scale* (The Architectural Press, New York).

Llinás, R. (2002) *I of the Vortex* (MIT Press, Cambridge, Massachusetts).

Loos, A. (1971) "Ornament and Crime", in: *Programs and Manifestoes on Twentieth-Century Architecture*, edited by U. Conrads (MIT Press, Cambridge, Massachusetts), pp. 19-24.

Mainstone, R. J. (1988) *Hagia Sophia* (Thames and Hudson, New York).

Mandelbrot, B. B. (1983) *The Fractal Geometry of Nature* (Freeman, New York).

Marr, D. (1982) *Vision* (W. H. Freeman, San Francisco).

May, R. M. (1973) *Stability and Complexity in Model Ecosystems* (Princeton University Press, Princeton, New Jersey).

Maynard-Smith, J. & Szathmáry, E. (1999) *The Origins of Life* (Oxford University Press, Oxford).

McCloud, S. (1993) *Understanding Comics: The Invisible Art* (Harper Perennial, New York).

Mehrabian, A. (1976) *Public Places and Private Spaces* (Basic Books, New York).

Mesarovic, M. D., Macko, D. & Takahara, Y. (1970) *Theory of Hierarchical Multilevel Systems* (Academic Press, New York).

Michaels, C. F. & Carello, C. (1981) *Direct Perception* (Prentice-Hall, Englewood Cliffs, New Jersey).

Mikiten, T. M. (1995) "Intuition-based Computing: A New Kind of 'Virtual Reality'", *Mathematics and Computers in Simulation*, **40**, pp. 141-147.

Miller, J. G. (1978) *Living Systems* (McGraw-Hill, New York).

Moughtin, C., Oc, T. & Tiesdell, S. (1995) *Urban Design: Ornament and Decoration* (Butterworth, Oxford, England).

Nasar, J. L. (1989) "Perception, Cognition, and Evaluation of Urban Places", in: *Public Places and Spaces*, edited by I. Altman & E. H. Zube (Plenum Press, New York), pp. 31-56.

Nicolis, J. S. (1991) *Chaos and Information Processing* (World Scientific, Singapore).

Noton, D. & Stark, L. (1971) "Eye Movements and Visual Perception", *Scientific American*, **224**, No. 6 (June), pages 35-43. Reprinted in: *Image, Object and Illusion*, edited by R. Held (Scientific American, Freeman, San Francisco, 1974), pp. 113-122.

Norwich, J. J., Editor (1978) *Great Architecture of the World* (Bonanza Books, New York).

Padrón V. & Salingaros, N. A. (2000) "Ecology and the Fractal Mind in the New Architecture", *RUDI — Resource for Urban Design Information* <www.rudi.net>, approximately 12 pages.

Passioura, J. B. (1979) "Accountability, Philosophy, and Plant Physiology", *Search (Australian Journal of Science)*, **10**, No. 10, pp. 347-350.

Rittel, H. W. J. (1992) *Planen, Entwerfen, Design* (Kohlhammer Verlag, Stuttgart).

Rolls, E. T. & Treves, A. (1998) *Neural Networks and Brain Function* (Oxford University Press, Oxford).

Rudofsky, B. (1964) *Architecture Without Architects* (Doubleday, Garden City, New York).

Rudofsky, B. (1977) *The Prodigious Builders* (Harcourt Brace Jovanovich, New York).

Russell, F. (1979) *Art Nouveau Architecture* (Arch Cape Press, New York).

Salingaros, N. A. (1998) "Theory of the Urban Web", *Journal of Urban Design*, **3**, pp. 53-71. Reprinted as Chapter 1 of *Principles of Urban Structure* (Techne Press, Amsterdam, Holland, 2005).

Salingaros, N. A. (1999a) "The 'Life' of a Carpet: an Application of the Alexander Rules", in: *Oriental Carpet and Textile Studies V*, edited by M. Eiland Jr. & R. Pinner (International Conference on Oriental Carpets, Danville, California), pp. 189-196.

Salingaros, N. A. (1999b) "Urban Space and its Information Field", *Journal of Urban Design*, **4**, pp. 29-49. Reprinted as Chapter 2 of *Principles of Urban Structure* (Techne Press, Amsterdam, Holland, 2005).

Salingaros, N. A. (2000) "The Structure of Pattern Languages", *Architectural Research Quarterly*, **4**, pp. 149-161. Reprinted as Chapter 8 of *Principles of Urban Structure* (Techne Press, Amsterdam, Holland, 2005).

Salingaros, N. A. (2004) *Anti-architecture and Deconstruction* (Umbau-Verlag, Solingen, Germany). French edition: *Anti-architecture et Deconstruction* (Umbau-Verlag, Solingen, Germany, 2005).

Salingaros, N. A. (2005) *Principles of Urban Structure* (Techne Press, Amsterdam, Holland).

Salingaros, N. A. & West, B. J. (1999) "A Universal Rule for the Distribution of Sizes", *Environment and Planning B: Planning and Design*, **26**, pp. 909-923. Reprinted as Chapter 3 of *Principles of Urban Structure* (Techne Press, Amsterdam, Holland, 2005).

Salthe, S. N. (1985) *Evolving Hierarchical Systems* (Columbia University Press, New York).

Simon, H. A. (1962) "The Architecture of Complexity", *Proceedings of the American Philosophical Society*, **106**, pp. 467-482. Reprinted in: Herbert A. Simon, *The Sciences of the Artificial* (M.I.T Press, Cambridge, Massachusetts, 1969), pp. 84-118.

Smith, C. S. (1969) "Structural Hierarchy in Inorganic Systems", in: *Hierarchical Structures*, edited by L. L. Whyte, A. G. Wilson & D. Wilson (American Elsevier, New York), pp. 61-85.

Sommer, R. (1974) *Tight Spaces* (Prentice-Hall, Englewood Cliffs, New Jersey).

Steen, L. A. (1988) "The Science of Patterns", *Science*, **240**, pp. 611-616.

Stern, R. A. M. (1988) *Modern Classicism* (Rizzoli, New York).

Thompson, D. A. W. (1952) *On Growth and Form*, 2nd Edition (Cambridge University Press, Cambridge).

VanRullen, R. & Thorpe, S. J. (2004) "Perception, decision, attention visuelles: ce que les potentiels evoques nous apprennent sur le fonctionnement du systeme visuel", in: *L'Imagerie Fonctionnelle Electrique et Magnetique: Ses Applications en Sciences Cognitives*, edited by B. Renault (Hermes, Paris), pp. 95-121.

Venturi, R. (1977) *Complexity and Contradiction in Architecture*, Second Edition (Museum of Modern Art, New York).

Venturi, R., Scott-Brown, D. & Izenour, S. (1977) *Learning From Las Vegas* (MIT Press, Cambridge, Massachusetts).

von Meiss, P. (1991) *Elements of Architecture* (E&FN Spon, London).

Washburn, D. K. & Crowe, D. W. (1988) *Symmetries of Culture* (University of Washington Press, Seattle).

Watkin, D. (2001) *Morality and Architecture Revisited* (University of Chicago Press, Chicago).

Weibel, E. R. (1994) "Design of Biological Organisms and Fractal Geometry", in: *Fractals in Biology and Medicine*, edited by T. F. Nonnenmacher, G. A. Losa & E. R. Weibel (Birkhäuser Verlag, Basel), pp. 68-85.

Weingarden, L. S. (1987) *Louis H. Sullivan: The Banks* (MIT Press, Cambridge, Massachusetts).

West, B. J. (1997) "Chaos and Related Things: A Tutorial", *The Journal of Mind and Behavior*, **18**, pp. 103-126.

West, B. J. & Deering, B. (1995) *The Lure of Modern Science* (World Scientific, Singapore).

West, B. J. & Goldberger, A. L. (1987) "Physiology in Fractal Dimensions", *American Scientist*, **75**, pp. 354-365.

Williams, K. (1998) *Italian Pavements: Patterns in Space* (Anchorage Press, Houston, Texas).

Williams, K. (2000) "Environmental Patterns: Paving Designs by Tess Jaray", *Nexus Network Journal*, **2**, No. 1 (January), approximately 5 pages.

Wolfe, T. (1981) *From Bauhaus to Our House* (Farrar Straus Giroux, New York).

Yarbus, A. L. (1967) *Eye Movements and Vision* (Plenum Press, New York).

Yu, H.-S. (1996) "Effects of environmental factors on the endocrine system", in: *Handbook of Endocrinology*, edited by G. L. Gass & H. M. Kaplan (CRC Press, Boca Raton, Florida), pp. 43-68.

Zeeman, Sir E. C. (1962) "The Topology of the Brain and Visual Perception", in: *Topology of 3-Manifolds*, edited by M. K. Fort (Prentice-Hall, Englewood Cliffs, New Jersey), pp. 240-256.

Zeki, S. (1993) *A Vision of the Brain* (Blackwell Scientific Publications, Oxford).

Zerbst, R. (1993) *Antoni Gaudí* (Benedikt Taschen Verlag, Köln).

Zigmond, M. J., Bloom, F. E., Landis, S. C., Roberts, J. L. & Squire, L. R. (1999) *Fundamental Neuroscience* (Academic Press, San Diego, California), Chapter 52: "Object and Face Recognition", by M. Farah, G. W. Humphreys & H. R. Rodman.